Praise for

The **Politically Incorrect** Guide to

the British Empire

"As someone who grew up in India, I often hear people ask, 'What have the British done for us?' Until I read this book, I didn't have the full answer. And here is Crocker's answer: 'Apart from roads, railways, ports, schools, a parliamentary system of government, rights, separation of powers, checks and balances, the rule of law, and the English language...nothing!'"

> —**Dinesh D'Souza**, President of the King's College and bestselling author of *The Roots of Obama's Rage*

"*The Politically Incorrect Guide to the British Empire*™ offers a cautionary tale for Americans who don't believe the sun could ever set on our great land. Even the grandest nations collapse when a people no longer believes in itself or its mission. Harry Crocker's book is a jolly good read for Anglophiles and history buffs in general."

> —**Brett M. Decker**, Editorial Page Editor of *The Washington Times* and former Governor of the Hong Kong Foreign Correspondents' Club

"H. W. Crocker's *Politically Incorrect Guide*™ *to the British Empire* is a vivid, wide-ranging and persuasive defence of an empire that spread freedom, democracy and the rule of law to all the corners of the earth. As Crocker shows, the British people supported the Empire because they believed in the superiority of their civilisation. This belief was neither false nor hypocritical, and Crocker adroitly assembles the proof that the Empire was both a liberating force in a dangerous world, and a testimony to those old virtues—grit, leadership and the stiff upper lip—which were taught to British children of my generation, and which are being air-brushed from history by the cult of political correctness. This brave and persuasive book deserves to be read in all courses of school history: it tells an inspiring story in an inspiring way."

> —**Professor Roger Scruton**, philosopher, founding editor of *The Salisbury Review,* and author of more than two dozen books, including *Art and Imagination* and *A Political Philosophy: Arguments for Conservatism*

The Politically Incorrect Guide™ to

the British Empire

The **Politically Incorrect Guide**™ to

the British Empire

H. W. Crocker III

Since 1947
REGNERY
PUBLISHING, INC.
An Eagle Publishing Company • Washington, DC

Cataloging-in-Publication data on file with the Library of Congress

ISBN 978-1-59698-629-9

Published in the United States by
Regnery Publishing, Inc.
One Massachusetts Avenue, NW
Washington, DC 20001
www.regnery.com

Manufactured in the United States of America

10 9 8 7 6 5 4 3 2 1

Books are available in quantity for promotional or premium use. Write to Director of Special Sales, Regnery Publishing, Inc., One Massachusetts Avenue NW, Washington, DC 20001, for information on discounts and terms or call (202) 216-0600.

Distributed to the trade by

Perseus Distribution
387 Park Avenue South
New York, NY 10016

For Fiona, Regis, Rafferty, Garnet, Auberon, and Trajan

CONTENTS

"The British Empire was a great and wonderful social, economic and even spiritual experiment, and all the parlour pinks and eager, ill-informed intellectuals cannot convince me to the contrary."

—*Noël Coward, diary entry, 3 February 1957*

Part I

RULE BRITANNIA

Chapter 1

THE ENDURING EMPIRE

Τhe British Empire still exists, thank goodness, with its outposts in the Falkland Islands, Bermuda, Gibraltar, the British Antarctic Territory, Pitcairn Island, and a peppering of other British Overseas Territories (including Anguilla, the British Virgin Islands, and St. Helena) and Crown Dependencies (closer to home, the Isle of Man and the Channel Islands). Together they ensure that the sun still does not set on the British Empire. At its height, though, Britain's empire was the largest ever, covering a quarter of the globe—or half of it, if you count Britain's control of the seas—and governing a quarter of the world's population.

The empire was incontestably a good thing. The fact that it is controversial to say so is why this book had to be written. In the groves of academe, colonialism and imperialism are dirty words, the *fons et origo* of Western expansion with all its alleged sins of racism, capitalism, and ignorant, judgmental, hypocritical Christian moralism. But if the Left hates imperialism, so do many so-called paleoconservatives or paleolibertarians who blame the British Empire for dragging the United States into two unnecessary—in their minds—World Wars.

Still, most Americans are sympathetic to Britain. They think of her as our oldest and most reliable ally, even if they might be ambivalent at best about the British Empire, or harbor a knee-jerk disapproval of it: "Isn't the empire what we fought against in 1776?" In fact, no. "Aren't Americans anti-imperialists by birth?" John Adams didn't think so when he foresaw in 1755, with prescience and pleasure, the transfer "of the great seat of empire to America."[1] Thomas Jefferson didn't think so when he referred to America as an "empire of liberty"[2] or urged the annexation of Canada. And President James K. Polk didn't think so when he proudly claimed, after the Mexican War, to have "added to the United States an immense empire."[3] For Irish-Americans, of course, the ancient animosity against England, inherited from the old sod and lovingly nurtured, makes them dubious, or worse,[4] about the British Empire—though, as we'll see, much of this animosity is based on Shamrock-shaded myths.

To hate the British Empire is to hate ourselves, for the United States would not exist if not for the British Empire. It was that Empire that created the North American colonies, giving them their charters, their people, their language, their culture, their governments, and their ideas of liberty. The inherited "rights of Englishmen" going back at least to the Magna Carta of 1215, were planted on American soil by English people in an overt act of profit-making imperialism. Moreover, the American War of Independence was not a war against the idea of empire. It was a war guided by men like Washington, Franklin, Adams, Hamilton, and Jefferson, who wanted an American Empire of their own—and who were in fact partly motivated by the British Empire not being imperialist enough.

After the War of Independence, Britain's trade with the United States surpassed what its trade had been with the Thirteen Colonies. Even with the interruption of the War of 1812, Britain was not only a trading partner, it was a tremendous source of new Americans. From the end of that war (1815) through the presidency of Zachary Taylor (1850), roughly 80 percent of British emigrants came to the United States;[5] we can presume they saw America as a second Britain, but one with more opportunity. Despite occasional diplomatic kerfuffles, there was an ineluctable bond between Britain and the United States, a bond that encompassed everything from the influence British literature had over American writers to the quietly conducted power politics of the Royal Navy helping enforce the Monroe Doctrine. In 1899, when Rudyard Kipling published his famous poem about picking up the white man's burden, his purpose was not to urge his fellow Britons to greater sacrifices but to congratulate the United States for accepting an imperial mission in the Philippines, joining Britain not as a global rival but as a partner in extending the blessings of Christian civilization.

At the time, Theodore Roosevelt thought Kipling's poem was bad verse but good politics. Today, at least in English literature courses, if it is taught at all it is merely another exhibit in a long litany of Western condescension to, and exploitation of, native peoples. But Kipling frames the white man's burden rather differently. It means binding your best men to serve another people, to take up what he says will be a thankless task, yet one that a mature and Christian people must do—to banish famine and sickness, to provide peace and order, to build roads and ports, to seek the profit of another rather than oneself.

Kipling knew the British Empire as well as any man—and he saw it clear-eyed, with all the blood and sacrifice and repression, of self and others, it entailed. He was a patriot for his own country, but India was his country too, the country where he was born and where his imagination was ignited. The British Empire of the twenty-first-century academic lecture hall, however, is something utterly different. The idea that the British Empire was a white man's burden is treated with scorn, contempt, and ridicule. The Empire was not a responsibility borne by self-sacrificing Britons—on the contrary, the Empire was a vehicle of rapacious, self-serving capitalists responsible for racism, slavery, and oppression on a global scale. But which was it really?

True, the British Empire was responsible for a portion of the slave trade. But it was also responsible for ending it. Indeed, the British Empire's war against slavery was actually a major factor driving imperial expansion, as the Royal Navy patrolled the coasts of Africa, the Persian Gulf, and the East Indies, and sent troops inland, especially in Africa, to put slavers out of business. British taxpayers also paid off the former slave owners in the British West Indies—spending twenty million pounds (about 37 percent of the British government's revenues in 1831)[6]—to ensure that slaves were liberated or made apprentices.

True, the British Empire was animated by the belief that a public school-educated Englishman was capable of governing any number of native peoples. But the Empire also relied to an extraordinary extent on the cooperation of the native peoples; their governing structures were often left largely intact; their aristocracies were generally treated as legitimate elites; and it was the native peoples themselves who provided many or most of the foot soldiers who enforced the imperial Pax Britannica.

True, the British conquered other peoples, drew lines on maps, and declared large portions of the globe part of the Empire. But it is also true that in doing so the British introduced their ideas about the rule of law, liberty, and parliamentary self-government, not to mention their games of cricket, soccer, rugby, tennis, and golf; their literature; their ideas about what constituted fair play; and—to use an imperial word, a Hindi word—their ideas of what was *pukka* and what was not.

No Plan but Profits, Progress, and Pole-Axing the French

"We seem, as it were, to have conquered and peopled half the world in a fit of absence of mind."

Sir John Robert Seeley, *The Expansion of England: Two Courses of Lectures* (Macmillan & Co., 1891), p. 8

The British Empire was driven in large part by commercial interests, but these were joined by other interests as well. There were missionary and military interests, of course, but there was also the sheer adventurous, or prideful, desire to paint the map red, something that caught the imagination of many an empire-builder, from the colossal capitalist Cecil Rhodes to the founder of Singapore, Stamford Raffles. If profit was a motive, it is also true that it was the British themselves who often created the infrastructure (the roads, the ports, the railways), developed the products (rubber, tobacco, gold), and provided the markets that brought these far-flung areas into the world economy to a far greater extent than they had been before.

And if we are to talk about oppression on a global scale it might be well to remember which country sacrificed a generation to preserve liberal ideals against the militarism and aggression of the kaiser's Germany; which country stood alone against Hitler after the fall of France in 1940; and which country, though riven by Bolshie labor unions and Cambridge spies and traitors, was the most stalwart European opponent of Bolshevism and Communism. As the British historian Christopher Dawson wrote in 1932, the Bolsheviks regarded the British Empire, "not without reason as the chief element of cohesion in the divided ranks of their enemies."[7]

In World War I and World War II, and to a certain degree in the Cold War, when one speaks of Britain one speaks of the Empire. In both World Wars, Britain was joined by the self-governing dominions of Canada, Australia, New Zealand, and South Africa; units came from every nation within the Empire; and the all-volunteer Indian Army served on battlefronts in Europe, Africa, the Middle East, and the Far East—the Indians providing more than three million men all told. When the Cold War turned hot, Britons, Canadians, South Africans, and ANZACs (Australians and New Zealanders) fought in Korea; Rhodesians, Fijians, and ANZACs served with the British in Malaya; and the ANZACs were in Vietnam.

When Britain could no longer maintain the Pax Britannica, it became the Pax Americana. The transition was sometimes less successful than it should have been because of American ambivalence about empire. In World War II the Americans were often suspicious of Britain's postwar imperial designs, and President Franklin Roosevelt was obsessed with getting the British out of Hong Kong and India (he compared the Indians to the North American colonists of 1776). Rather than empire, Roosevelt believed in a sort of liberal idealism and internationalism, much of it channeled through his plan for a United Nations—an alternative institution and vision, and one that has proven far more prone to bureaucracy, corruption, officiousness, and incompetence than the British Empire.

Today, it is the British Empire rather than the United Nations that still provides the unacknowledged, unspoken standard by which most observers measure a country's success. If we say that Canada, Australia, and the United States are generally successful countries, we say so because they have followed the British model of liberty and free commerce. If we judge a country like Zimbabwe a failure we do so *not* because it is governed contrary to the majority of countries in the United Nations and *not* because it is governed contrary to African traditions but because it is governed contrary to British laws and traditions—even as it maintains a pretense of following them. Zimbabwean judges wear wigs and go through the motions of upholding the legal model inherited from Britain. Zimbabwe holds parliamentary elections even if the outcome is preordained and ensured by intimidation and violence. The very fact that the Zimbabwean government maintains a semblance of British institutions is testimony that the British legal and political model has legitimacy in public opinion.

There is another point to be made—and that is simply that the British Empire, for all its occasional missteps and outrages, was a global, Shakespearean stage on which Britons could take part in a glorious adventure, playing Hotspur to headhunters and Henry V to Hottentots. If that sounds boyish, it is meant to, because the Empire was boyish; it trained boys to its tasks in schools of self-denial, cold dirty baths, bad food, long runs, stiff upper lips, the imperial languages of Greek and Latin, "playing the game," and embracing the ideal of service. It was an advanced form of commercial, military, and political outdoor recreation for Boy Scouts (themselves a creation of the British Empire). Young men, straight out of school, could find themselves in distant lands acting as lawgivers to primitive tribes and dangerous brigands; they were men of conservative sentiments, liberal ideals, and boyish pluck. In the famous observation of George Santayana,

> Instinctively the Englishman is no missionary, no conqueror...he travels and conquers without a settled design, because he has the instinct of exploration. His adventures are all external; they change him so little that he is not afraid of them. He carries his English weather in his heart wherever he goes, and it becomes a cool spot in the desert, and a steady and sane oracle amongst all the deliriums of mankind. Never since the heroic days of Greece has the world had such a sweet, just, boyish master. It will be a black day for the human race when scientific blackguards, conspirators, churls, and fanatics manage to supplant him.[8]

Alas that day is here, ushered in by United Nations bureaucrats, liberal internationalists, native kleptocrats, liberated Islamists, and Third World Communists and National Socialists, all of whom emerged as Europe's empires retreated. The retreat of the British Empire was not progress—either for Western Civilization or in many cases for the countries achieving independence. In the case of Africa, certainly, independence has meant a dramatic, chartable economic regression relative to the rest of the world—not to mention savage wars and famines that imperial powers could have prevented or contained. There have been some independence success

A 7-Step Timeline of British Imperialism

1. **Twelfth Century:** Henry II, armed with the authority of the pope (an Englishman as it turns out) and armed in traditional fashion as well, attempts to bring English civilization to Ireland, a process still underway nearly a millennium later.

2. **Fifteenth Century:** First English voyages of exploration to reach North America led by that redoubtable Englishman John Cabot, better known as Giovanni Caboto of Genoa (though he did sail from Bristol under the royal authority of Henry VII of England).

3. **Sixteenth Century:** English ships begin trading on the coast of Africa, and enter the slave trade. Sir Francis Drake attempts to impress the benefits of free trade upon Spain's colonies in the New World by plundering them. Sir Walter Raleigh fails to establish a lasting colony in North America.

4. **Seventeenth Century:** Spain's education continues at the hands of the likes of Morgan the pirate. English planters move into the Caribbean. England grants charters for colonists in North America. The East India Company sets up shop in India.

5. **Eighteenth Century:** Britain acquires New France (Quebec) in the French and Indian War, removing a great threat from the American colonists. Britain asks the colonists to help pay for the war—which of course amounts to tyranny—and rather than pay taxes, the Americans drive the red-coated tax collectors from their shores, and then pay higher taxes to their own government. Canada is willing to pay taxes to Britain and stays in the Empire. The British East India Company proves so efficient that it ends up ruling large swaths of India.

6. **Nineteenth Century:** Britain bans slavery and the slave trade and sets the Royal Navy to war against the slavers. Britain establishes anti-slavery bases in Africa and the Gulf States. The empire expands into the Far East through enterprising young Englishmen of the likes of Stamford Raffles and James Brooke. Britain takes

continued

responsibility for India from the East India Company. Britain becomes responsible for the government of Egypt and the operation of the Suez Canal (built by the French). South Africa becomes a major British interest and mining magnate Cecil Rhodes dreams, and helps to achieve, a British Empire in Africa that stretches from Cape to Cairo.

7. Twentieth Century: Britain wins two World Wars, helps create the modern Middle East out of the wreck of the Ottoman Empire, and after 1945 beats a relatively hasty retreat from India. In 1956, the United States, out of anti-imperialist prejudice, backs the anti-Western Egyptian dictator Gamal Abdel Nasser against wartime allies Britain and France during the Suez Crisis, encouraging further European retreat and further aggression by Nasserite pan-Arabist radicals who topple the pro-Western government of formerly British Iraq. Britain shows how to defeat Communist insurgents through a campaign of "hearts and minds" (and anti-terrorist patrols by Gurkhas, native headhunters, and British troops) in Malaya. Britain defeats the murderous Mau-Mau cult before granting independence to Kenya. In 1982, Britain shows that imperial retreat has its limits by defeating Argentine aggression in the Falkland Islands.

stories—not just the United States, Canada, New Zealand, and Australia, but Singapore, Hong Kong, and, it appears, India, South Africa, and Malaysia, and perhaps a few other locales where the vision of Britain's empire-builders might yet be fulfilled. Many a Briton thought it his duty, in the words of the scholars Lewis H. Gann and Peter Duignan, "to carry civilization, humanity, peace, good government, and Christianity to the ends of the earth."[9] That duty still exists for those who want it, and perhaps it would repay our study to see how Britain's imperialists actually did it.

But before we do that, let's imagine what life would be like today if the Empire were still largely intact; let's think of the way things could have been.

Chapter 2

MR. POTTER'S EMPIRE

*T*ransport yourself to the flat of Algernon Braithwaite-Burke Potter in Knightsbridge SW3 London. Still dressed in his pajamas (another Hindi word), he has enjoyed a rather long night on the town. He has put the kettle on for tea and is stooping to pick up the post and the papers scattered on the floor just beneath the mail slot.

At his home in the country he has help, but here in his London flat he is the consummate self-sufficient bachelor. He is used to making sacrifices and saying to himself: "There's a war on, after all." He isn't quite sure where, but there is always a small war on somewhere—the price one pays for the benefits of the greater Pax Anglicana.

Mr. Potter tosses the post aside on the breakfast table and unfolds the papers—*The Times* and *The Telegraph*, and out of noblesse oblige, to know what the lower orders are thinking or, more accurately, to know what page three girl they're ogling, *The Sun* (which he does not receive in the country; he doesn't want to scandalize the servants). He prefers his papers ironed to crisp folds in the morning, but without help he has to make do.

The Telegraph holds pride of place. Let's see: on the front page, British Palestine. How tiresome. It must have seemed awfully clever, no doubt, in 1945, when Winston came up with the wheeze of offering guaranteed jobs and free housing allotments for skilled laborers in uniform—who were promised early release from the service—if they agreed to emigrate to "the New Jerusalem," Palestine, which Churchill reorganized as a self-governing dominion. The offer was extended to coal miners in Wales, longshoremen in Liverpool, and low-wage workers in Scotland who were promised settlements on the sunny Mediterranean coast of Palestine ("live in the Holy Land while holidaying at the seaside"). In short order, there was an amazing exodus of some three million likely Labour voters—demobbed soldiers, colliery workers, and Glaswegian slum dwellers—who came off the voting rolls in Britain and put a Labour government in power in Jerusalem, a government pledged to nationalizing industries that Palestine did not yet have.

By that bit of electoral legerdemain, wily Winston ensured a skin-of-the-teeth Conservative victory in 1945, foiled Labour's plans to grant India independence, and stifled the development of socialism at home. But oh at what a cost! An endless parade of newspaper stories about Palestine grinding to a halt, with national strikes by Arab taxi drivers; or about skinheads refusing to attend the World Cup (to be played in Jerusalem) unless the authorities lifted the ban on alcohol and pork pies ("Let them eat falafel," said Mordecai Gizzo, the chairman of the Palestinian Football Association); or about Zionists trying to annex the Gaza Strip out of the hands of admittedly frightful retirees from Birmingham, Manchester, and Leeds. Who was it that said the British Empire was a vast system of outdoor relief for the upper classes? He certainly got that wrong! Dreadful.

Oh dear, what else is going on? Let's see, in Iraq, the Anglo-American authorities had arrested one Saddam Hussein, mob boss of the Baathist syndicate involved in narcotics, prostitution, and pornography. Fed up with his recidivism, they had turned him over to a local tribal council...and apparently the less said about that the better.

In Anglo-American Iran, the shah was hosting the latest French fashion designers (well, since we had the oil, we had to allow the French something) for "Catwalk Tehran." The shah was promoting Tehran as something like a

Paris *sur la* Caspian (Tehran, of course, was not actually *on* the Caspian, but one had to make allowances). The theme of Catwalk Tehran, at which famous British models were appearing, was "Lifting the Veil of Eastern Mystery." It appeared from *The Telegraph*'s photographs that veils were not all they were lifting. My goodness....

Turn the page. Ah Rhodesia, the farmland of Africa, bursting with produce, sponsoring an Imperial Agricultural Exhibition, with farmers, ranchers, and tea planters from all over British Africa and the world...which reminded Mr. Potter that he needed to pop over to Harrods for some Kenyan beef that he planned to wash down with that new Cape Pinotage he had bought. Always something new out of Africa.

Oh well done! The Australians were whacking holy hell out of India in the test match—and served them right too. He didn't like the behavior of some of these new Indian cricketers; lying down on the pitch, Gandhi-style, to protest decisions from the umpires. Disgraceful. If they can't behave like gentlemen, well then....

Let's see, Asian news: Hong Kong's borders had expanded yet again; having annexed all of Guangdong, Guangxi, Fujian, Jiangxi, Hunan, and Hainan, it had now grabbed Zhejiang and Jiangsu, the provinces bordering Shanghai. The Dalai Lama in British Tibet was hosting a rock concert, of all things—trendy vicars apparently weren't just an Anglican phenomenon. And the governor of British Singapore, in a friendly bit of rivalry, pledged that Singapore would displace Hong Kong as the chief entrepôt of the Far East. Well, it looked as though he had his work cut out for him.

In the Americas, Britain and the United States were conducting joint naval operations in the Caribbean and South Atlantic. Jamaica was debating whether its police force should be armed given the slight uptick in crime, caused largely it seemed by a small group of drug-addled ghetto dwellers who worshipped as a divinity an obscure American radio show host named Rusty Humphries—these of course were the Rustyfarians, and they had gone on sprees of burglary to buy radios with which to tune in to their god, who kept them abreast of American political news. The Falkland Islanders, meanwhile, were hosting an International Southern Hemisphere Highland Games competition, which included the rarely performed event of speed-castrating sheep—a competition dominated by the Australians, who weren't called "diggers" for nothing.

And then, of course, there was Ireland. Ireland, it had to be confessed, remained in the Empire largely by force. It was essentially self-governing, but foreign policy belonged to Westminster, which retained an inveterate suspicion of the Emerald Isle (too many Irish politicians had taken a shine to the kaiser in 1914, Hitler in 1939, and later the egregious Yasser Arafat of the Palestinian Republican Army—who had worn a green-checked keffiyeh "in solidarity with the oppressed masses of Ireland"). Britain's role was to restrain Irish excesses (save for those related to drink) and encourage the sport of hurling (mandatory in all Irish schools) so that running around the green fields of Ireland bashing each other's brains out would be the favored recreation of most Irishmen, keeping them well out of trouble. Ireland remained a wonderful recruiting ground for the Army. In fact, the latest news from Ireland was that the Army was expanding to create a new Irish Regiment, Prince Charles's Own Tipperary Armored Cavalry (or Tipplers in Tanks).

And speaking of tipplers, he had tickets to tonight's NFL Europe game at Wembley: the London Monarchs versus the Amsterdam Admirals. The game was sponsored by Morgan's Rum, and every adult patron was entitled to one shot of rum, which to Mr. Potter's mildly hungover taste buds sounded like just the ticket. He had done a stint of his own in the Royal Navy and was absolutely certain that every Briton had a bit of the pirate in him. Well-intentioned pirates, needless to say, like Gilbert and Sullivan's pirate king: loyal to the Crown and the house of peers, and ever ready to liberate wealth, territory, and the occasional future page three girl from the unworthy. It had been mostly Spaniards in the old days, though it could just as easily be Frogs, or lesser breeds without the law. That was how it all began, after all, with a nation of sea dogs taking to their ships to pillage and plunder—and yes, plant, patrol, and persevere—for King and Country, God and glory, gold and gammon.

Part II

NORTH AMERICA

Chapter 3

CALLING THE NEW WORLD INTO EXISTENCE TO REDRESS THE BALANCE OF THE OLD[1]

They were in Mexican waters, the harbor of San Juan Ulúa, when they spotted a dangerous Spanish flotilla—thirteen ships laden with guns and men. The Englishmen, led by John Hawkins and Francis Drake, were trapped; and they had reason to expect trouble. Hawkins had captured slaves in West Africa and sold them and other goods to Spanish colonists in the New World, enforcing free trade in the Spanish Caribbean at the barrel of a gun, burning and pillaging when local Spanish officials tried to follow Spanish law and not trade with foreigners. Now it looked as though the Spaniards might seek vengeance.

The Englishmen were repairing their ships when the flotilla came into view. Aboard the Spanish flagship was the new viceroy of Mexico, Don Martin Enriquez. The viceroy agreed to let the Englishmen finish their repairs and buy what supplies they needed. The Spanish ships laid anchor alongside them. It was, of course, a ruse, one that Hawkins sniffed out—but in the blazing battle, Spanish cannons, arquebuses, pistols, knives, and cutlasses cut down three hundred Englishmen. Five English ships were sunk or captured. Only two ships remained, the *Judith*, under Francis Drake, which made a quick skedaddle for England, and the *Minion*, overloaded with survivors, one of whom was Hawkins. Doomed with so many men and so few provisions aboard, he dropped a hundred men on the shores of Texas,

Did you know?

- ♔ Protestant Pirates founded the British Empire in the New World

- ♔ The American colonists were not anti-imperialists; they rebelled because they wanted an empire of their own

- ♔ The British Empire still exists in the Americas

where most all of them died or were captured. One sailor made it back to England sixteen years later after adventures worthy of an Errol Flynn hero.

An Empire of Liberty

Drake later used the Battle of San Juan de Ulúa (1568), part of England's running war of piracy against Spain, to justify his every outrage against the perfidious papists. The Spaniards, however, had good reason to feel put out. They followed the rules, more or less. They established their colonies in the New World and used them to enrich themselves and the treasury of their country. They kept to the true faith, and though not Biblical literalists like the Protestants, they did not see how piracy could be squared with the commandment: "Thou shalt not steal."

The Englishmen, though pirates, knew right was on their side. The Protestantism of England was a unique thing. It was a state church that tried, even if it failed, to accommodate everyone. It was Calvinist enough to justify an Englishman in thinking that he was one of the elect—certainly over any papist. It was broadminded enough that, whatever persecutions were leveled against Catholics and Dissenters (and against the former in particular, the sanctions were severe), it allowed, up to a point, a man to fill in the details of his creed as he saw fit (every man his own priest). It required on the one hand that one not take religion very seriously—or how could one square the idea that kings made better religious authorities than popes—while on the other hand it imbued the people with an enormous sense of self-righteousness, which however annoying to outsiders is a great strength to a nation: no man is more certain of being on the side of liberalism, reason, and tolerance than the man who has invented his own creed against the presumed bigotry, repression, and superstition of an old one.

The English church had doctrines, but chief among them were (a) not to be a papist and (b) to follow as gospel whatever was approved by the Crown. Anglicanism was really patriotism with a prayer book—and England's pirates were nothing if not patriotic. They disparaged or destroyed representations of the Virgin Mary, but venerated Elizabeth, the Virgin Queen. They would pray in regular, required meetings aboard ship before they plundered and pillaged for profit, for the defense of the realm, and to punish the deluded followers of the Whore of Babylon. Drake and Hawkins and Walter Raleigh and Martin Frobisher were private commercial adventurers and explorers, yes, but they were all present and commanding ships as naval officers of the Crown against the Spanish Armada in 1588 too. They were men of Queen and Country who believed that by serving themselves and serving England they were serving Heaven's Command—self-interest, patriotism, and Providence were one.

One of the chief ideological architects of an English empire[2] in the New World was the geographer and Protestant divine Richard Hakluyt the younger. In his *Discourse Concerning Western Planting* (1584), he urged on Walter Raleigh's adventures in the New World, writing that "No greater glory can be handed down than to conquer the barbarian, to recall the savage and the pagan to civility, to draw the ignorant within the realm of reason."[3] He laid out the commercial, political, and military benefits of such an empire. Among these were trade and the production of new crops, finding useful employment for unemployed soldiers and beggars, but also bringing liberty to lands now dominated by Spanish "pride and tyranny," where the enslaved "all yell and cry with one voice, *Liberta, liberta*," and where English valor and naval prowess could provide freedom.

From the beginning, then, the British Empire thought of itself as an empire of liberty.

Plunder and Plantations

English sea dogs played Robin Hood in the Caribbean only after England was firmly in the Protestant camp under Queen Elizabeth I, who reigned from 1558 to 1603. As queen of England and Wales and parts of always turbulent Ireland, with a potentially hostile Scotland north of the border, and hostile France and Spain across the Channel, Elizabeth was perpetually looking for ways to keep her enemies off balance. Her most dangerous enemy was Spain. Spain had become a vast overseas empire. By 1521, Mexico had become New Spain; twenty-one years later, the Incan empire had become the Spanish Viceroyalty of Peru. Spain was also a continental power. It was trying to crush a Protestant revolt (which England supported) in the Spanish Netherlands and was fighting Muslims in the Mediterranean.

Queen Elizabeth had little interest in bankrolling rival colonies of her own—she couldn't afford it—but she had a great deal of interest in raiding Spain's. Her support went to her daring, patriotic, profitable pirates, some of whom doubled as explorers. Martin Frobisher was one such. In his voyages of 1576 through 1578, he set off to find the Northwest Passage, the presumed nautical shortcut to the riches of the East. While finding neither China nor India nor riches, he leant his name to Frobisher Bay and navigated part of Hudson Bay.

The sea dog Francis Drake, who like Frobisher earned himself a knighthood, not only sailed around the world (1577–80), fighting the Spanish wherever they could be found, but also relieved the Spanish of their gold and silver in Panama and Peru, laid stake to Nova Albion (California, setting the western boundary of what became the "manifest destiny" of America's continental empire), commanded ships against the Spanish Armada, and eventually met his death of dysentery in 1596 off the Spanish Main, with Spanish ships in his sight.

Sir Walter Raleigh, another worthy pirate, tried to establish settlements that would provide England with gold and silver mines to rival Spain's. He tried twice (1585 and 1587) to found a colony at Roanoke Island, North Carolina, but failed. The second failure left the mystery of "the lost colony"—Roanoke abandoned, the only clue being the word CROATAN carved into a tree.

The Roanoke Mystery

No one knows what happened to the Roanoke colonists, though they might have fled to Hatteras Island and joined the friendly Croatan tribe. According to some accounts, the English settlers and Croatans intermarried, giving birth to a tribe of light-skinned, fair-haired, grey-eyed, English-speaking Indians. Some have tried to link the Croatans (now extinct) to the Lumbee, a tribe that claims as one of its descendants Heather Locklear, which, if true, speaks well of the English bloodlines of Raleigh's settlers. It also leads to an interesting and only rarely made argument for the British Empire. Without it we would not have had *T. J. Hooker.*

North Carolina's shores don't seem so forbidding to us, but in the sixteenth century they seemed rather more so. When Raleigh next attempted to found a colony, it was on the far wilder shores of Guiana, where he expected to find the lost golden city of El Dorado. His adventures met with ridicule back home and no permanent settlement in the jungle.

The colonies came when enterprising men like Raleigh gave way to enterprising companies, like the Virginia Company, which bankrolled the first lasting English settlement in the New World at Jamestown, Virginia, in 1607. It was followed by the establishment of the Plymouth Bay Colony in 1620, in what is now Massachusetts. The settlers' motives were various: some were religious dissenters; most, however, were fortune-seekers. What they found, or developed, was humbler fare than the gold and silver raided from New Spain, but it made for a hard-working people. They cultivated tobacco and sugar. They trapped and traded for furs. They fished the rich coastlines or brought timber from the forests. Unlike the Spanish conquistadors, priests, and hidalgos, or the French Jesuits and voyageurs, the English settled the land with their families, staking out farms or establishing towns and shops.

The landowners who dominated trade in the sugar islands became very wealthy indeed, and there was an American aristocratic class that held enormous landed estates along the Atlantic seaboard, but the vast majority of British immigrants to the New World came as indentured servants. In some cases their condition was not much different from that of a slave, though with freedom promised after four to ten years of service. They were a varied lot: farmers attracted by cheap land, tradesmen looking for better prospects, the poor and idle swept off Britain's streets, felons and rebels sentenced to labor in the colonies, and, especially after 1700, the Scotch[4] and the Irish, who soon made up the majority of indentured servants.

Until the eighteenth century, most British immigrants came to the British Caribbean. It had a far higher mortality rate for Britons than the North American mainland, but also offered a greater prospect for riches—sugar plantations were the gold mines of the English colonies. The British colonized St. Kitts (1623), Barbados (1627), Nevis (1628), Antigua and Montserrat (1632), and the Bahamas (1646) and seized Jamaica from Spain (1655). Britain's empire continued to spread, including attempts to establish mainland plantations in Surinam (which eventually went to the Dutch), British Guiana (Guyana), and British Honduras (Belize). Britain's Caribbean possessions were pirate's lairs, sugar plantations, and rum distilleries; they were also battlegrounds, contested territory well into the eighteenth century; and in due course, they became the employers of slaves.

We Want *You* for the New World

Slavery was not an original part of Britain's colonial system, but the colonists needed workers. The native Indians (those who survived European diseases) were considered unsuitable: shiftless, untrustworthy, and lacking the Protestant work ethic. European indentured servants died in astonishing numbers, victims of malaria, yellow fever, and other calamities. So the colonists adopted the Spanish Caribbean custom of importing slaves from Africa.

Spain accepted slavery in its colonies even though the Catholic Church had abolished slavery in Europe during the Middle Ages;[5] the colonists pleaded necessity, though the Church was dubious. Outside of Christendom, the situation was different. Slavery had never disappeared in the Islamic world—indeed, between 1530 and 1780, roughly concurrent with the Atlantic slave trade, the Muslim Barbary pirates enslaved more than a million white Christian Europeans.[6] In Africa, slavery was a long-standing domestic industry, and European slavers tapped into it. The black slaves crossing the Atlantic were usually taken by African warriors and traded by native chiefs for a variety of goods. The slaves were then packed aboard ships where one in ten might die (more in the early years of the trade), eating into the profits, if not the consciences, of the slave traders. It was a dangerous and ugly business. The slave traders' crews suffered even higher mortality rates than the slaves, mostly from fevers contracted on the West Africa coast: *"Beware, beware, the Bight of Benin, for few come out though many go in,"* went the famous rhyme.

What a Maroon

Unlike his son, the founder of Pennsylvania, Admiral William Penn was no Quaker. When he ripped Jamaica from Spanish hands in 1655, he discovered the island was bedeviled by a band of polygamous brigands made up entirely of escaped slaves: the Maroons. The British fought them with redcoats and levies of Miskito Indians (imported from Honduras) until the Maroons were brought to heel by treaty in 1739. In a typical imperial compromise the Maroons were granted their own territory, enlisted as allies to put down future slave rebellions, and became slave owners themselves.

The African slaves might have been judged hardier and better workers than the native Indians and European indentured servants (the Irish, needless to say, were regarded as particularly incorrigible), but in the Caribbean they too died young, and were often worked to death. Caribbean masters found they could not breed slaves fast enough to replace the loss, so the slave trade grew. Perhaps three million black slaves were brought to British possessions in the New World, and in some of them, especially in the Caribbean, they became the majority.

The British Empire banned the slave trade in 1807 (enforcing the ban with the Royal Navy's West Africa Squadron) and prohibited slavery in nearly every part of the empire with the Slavery Abolition Act of 1833, which established a process of gradual emancipation that liberated all slaves by 1840 and compensated their owners with cash payments that amounted to twenty million pounds. Nothing in Britain's involvement in slavery and the slave trade so became the Empire as its leaving of it.

"Setting the World on Fire"

The Caribbean dominated British strategic thinking, but it was in the Ohio Territory that, in the famous words of Horace Walpole, a "volley fired by a young Virginian in the backwoods...set the world on fire."[7]

The Seven Years' War extended from the Caribbean to Africa, from the North American continent (as the French and Indian War) to the Indian subcontinent, from the Mediterranean to the Pacific. Winston Churchill in his *A History of the English-Speaking Peoples* calls it "The First World War," and it all began with the action of a twenty-three-year-old lieutenant-colonel named George Washington.[8]

Washington was leading his troops to solidify Virginia's claim to the Ohio Valley against the French. The result was a short, sharp engagement on 28 May 1754 that killed ten Frenchmen (another twenty were captured) and that inspired Washington to write, "I heard the bullets whistle, and, believe me there is something charming in the sound"[9]—a sentiment that many a British imperial officer might have seconded. Less charming was the allied Indian chief who smashed a tomahawk through the skull of a French officer, Ensign Joseph Coulon de Villiers de Jumonville, whom Washington was trying to interrogate. The Indian washed his hands in the Frenchman's brains.

To the French, Washington's ambush was an act of murder: Jumonville, they cried, had been on a diplomatic rather than a military mission. His brother, Louis Coulon de Villiers, moved swiftly to surround and capture Washington and his men at their hastily constructed Fort Necessity. As part of his surrender, Washington, ignorant of French, signed a document convicting himself of murder.

In 1755, General Edward Braddock arrived from England. He took Washington as his aide and vowed to avenge the Virginian's defeat, clear the Ohio Valley of Frenchmen, and even march into Canada. It was an epic march (among his wagon drivers were Daniel Boone and future American general Daniel Morgan), but as it turned out, the sixty-year-old Braddock—a stout, choleric veteran who had been in the army since he was fifteen—never made it to Canada. In fact, he never made it out of the Ohio Valley. His men were massacred in a well-placed French and Indian ambush that left more than 60 British and American officers—and all but 459 of his 1,400 other ranks—killed or wounded. Washington heard plenty more zinging bullets that day: four pierced his clothes and two shot horses from beneath him. Among the dead was General Braddock. Washington had him buried in an unmarked grave on their retreat to prevent the Indians from desecrating the corpse. Washington's gallant leadership in extracting what was left of Braddock's army made him something of a popular hero—a fame that would later make him a general, though not in the king's service. The greater hero of the war, however, was an Englishman named James Wolfe.

Imperial Summit: Wolfe at Quebec

When Winston Churchill appointed R. A. "Rab" Butler president of the Board of Education in 1941, he told him, "I should not object if you could introduce a note of patriotism into the schools. Tell the children that Wolfe won Quebec."[10] If Braddock's defeat at the Battle of the Monongahela represented the military disaster that so often began British imperial wars, James Wolfe's winning of Quebec represented the stunning victory by a memorable commander that so frequently ended them.

Ginger-haired, skinny, with a pointed nose, weak chin, and a history of bad health, Wolfe hardly looked the hero. He was eccentric and so emotionally volatile that some doubted his sanity. But for all that, he was extremely capable, ambitious, intelligent, and dedicated to self-improvement of body (through martial exercises) and mind (he taught himself Latin and mathematics and read deeply in both literature and military strategy). He was an experienced soldier—commissioned at thirteen and seeing his first combat at sixteen—and chivalrous. In a famous incident, he refused to kill a captured and wounded Highlander after the Battle of Culloden, though ordered to do so. He was truly an officer and a gentleman. But most of all he had the patriotic faith that was the lifeblood of the empire: "For my part, I am determined never to give myself a moment's concern about the nature of the duty which His Majesty is pleased to order us upon. It will be a sufficient comfort…to reflect that the Power which has hitherto preserved me may, if it be his pleasure, continue to do so; if not, that is but a few days more or less, and that those who perish in their duty and in the service of their country die admirably."[11]

At the Battle of Quebec (1759) Wolfe, a thirty-two-year-old brigadier general, found his apotheosis. The night before his surprise assault behind Quebec City, he recited Thomas Gray's "Elegy in a County Churchyard," which ends with the line "The paths of glory lead but to the grave." To his assembled brigadiers, he said, "Gentlemen, I would rather have written those lines than taken Quebec."[12]

But take Quebec he did. He snuck his troops past French sentries by night, lined his red-coats up on the Plains of Abraham to the skirl of bagpipes, and then waited as the French marched out to meet him. When they were only forty yards distant, the redcoats fired, in what the British military historian Sir John Fortescue wrote was "the most perfect [volley]

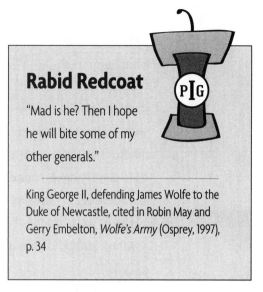

Rabid Redcoat

"Mad is he? Then I hope he will bite some of my other generals."

King George II, defending James Wolfe to the Duke of Newcastle, cited in Robin May and Gerry Embelton, *Wolfe's Army* (Osprey, 1997), p. 34

ever fired on any battlefield, which burst forth as if from a single monstrous weapon, from end to end of the British line."[13] A second volley tore through the French. The Britons advanced and fired, advanced and fired, until they were ordered to charge. Wolfe, shot first through the wrist, then in the groin, and finally in the chest, was led away, mortally wounded. An officer told him, "The enemy, sir. Egad, they give way everywhere!" Wolfe gave his final orders and said: "Now God be praised, I will die in peace!"[14] He died the conqueror of New France. With the Treaty of Paris ending the Seven Years' War in 1763, the entirety of Canada was ceded to Britain.

An Empire of Their Own

One Frenchman, at least, recognized that Wolfe's victory would be troublesome for the British Empire. Charles Gravier, the Comte de Vergennes, noted that "Delivered from a neighbor they have always feared [the French], your other colonies [the Americans] will soon discover that they stand no longer in need of your protection. You will call them to con-tribute toward supporting the burden which they have helped to bring on you, they will answer by shirking off all dependence."[15] That was exactly what happened.

The Americans of the Thirteen Colonies saw a vast imperial domain stretching before them; the only thing standing in their way was the reluctant Mother Country that was more interested in appeasing the Indians of the frontier than fighting them. In 1769, *The American Whig* editorialized, "Courage, then Americans! The finger of God points out a mighty empire to your sons.... The day dawns, in which this mighty empire is to be laid by the establishment of a regular American Constitution...."[16]

John Adams, like many of the founding fathers, saw this future clearly:

> Soon after the Reformation, a few people came over to the new world for conscience sake. Perhaps this apparently trivial incident may transfer the great seat of empire to America.
>
> It looks likely to me: for if we can remove the turbulent Gallicks, our people, according to the exactest computations, will in another century become more numerous than England itself. Should this be the case, since we have, I may say, all the naval stores of the nation in our hands, it will be easy to obtain mastery of the sea; and then the united force of all Europe will not subdue us. The only way to keep us from setting up for ourselves is to disunite us. *Divide et impera.*[17]

Alexander Hamilton (in *The Federalist*), Thomas Jefferson, and many of the founders later referred to the United States they had created as a great "empire." Benjamin Franklin foresaw, in 1767, that "America, an immense territory, favored by nature with all the advantages of climate, soil, great navigable rivers and lakes, must become a great country, populous and mighty; and will, in a less time than is generally conceived, be able to shake off shackles that may be imposed on her and perhaps place them on the imposers."[18]

But of course there were no shackles on the Americans. They were the freest people in the world under the protection of the most liberal power of its time. The colonies had been treated with the most lenient supervision, often described as "benign neglect," and the colonials enjoyed a higher standard of living (they were taller, healthier, and better fed than their English counterparts) and minuscule taxation compared to the average Englishman. The Americans had a long tradition of self-government given them by the British; and the British had, in the past, rarely interfered with colonial assemblies.

When Britain did intervene it was to fight Frenchmen or Indians or to temper populist passions and act as a force of disinterested moderation. There were only two fetters on the Americans. One was the Proclamation Act of 1763, which to the dismay of the colonists designated all lands west of the Appalachian Mountains as Indian Territory. The Indians were under the protection of the Crown, and redcoats were stationed on the frontier to keep the peace. Trade, which had been a source of friction between the Indians and the colonists, was to be regulated by the British. Britain wanted to mollify the Indians; instead she enraged the colonials, who saw their manifest destiny blocked by Indian-loving redcoats.

The second fetter was the long-standing Navigation Acts, which confined American trade within Britain's mercantile system. But this was no new innovation, it was hardly burdensome, and the British authorities had largely ignored the Americans' rampant smuggling: what piracy was to the Caribbean, smuggling was to the Thirteen Colonies.

An Imperial Family Quarrel

It is wrong to think of the American War of Independence as a popular struggle on either side of the Atlantic. In Britain, many were the voices in and out of Parliament (even in the army and the navy) who had no enthusiasm for a cousins' war and who sympathized with the colonists for standing

Kipling on the American War of Ingratitude—er, Independence

"Our American colonies, having no French to fear any longer, wanted to be free from our control altogether. They utterly refused to pay a penny of the two hundred million pounds the war had cost us; and they equally refused to maintain a garrison of British soldiers.... When our Parliament proposed in 1764 to make them pay a small fraction of the cost of the late war, they called it 'oppression,' and prepared to rebel."

Rudyard Kipling and C. R. L. Fletcher, *Kipling's Pocket History of England* (Greenwich House, 1983), p. 240

up for the traditional rights of Englishmen, even if these were being taken to a somewhat libertarian extreme. In America, John Adams estimated that at the war's outset, one-third of the population were Patriots, one-third were Loyalists, and one-third were uncommitted, which leads to the rather sobering conclusion that in 1776 perhaps two-thirds of Americans thought the war for independence was either unnecessary or wrong. At the war's end (1783), the statistics are equally sobering. As the historian J. M. Roberts has pointed out, "A much larger proportion of Americans felt too intimidated or disgusted with their Revolution to live in the United States after independence than the proportion of Frenchmen who could not live in France after the Terror."[19]

During the War of 1812, the second cousins' war, the United States, in good imperial fashion, even hoped to conquer Canada (where many loyalists had fled). Thomas Jefferson—who was never much good at things naval and military—predicted that "The acquisition of Canada this year as far as the neighborhood of Quebec will be a mere matter of marching."[20] As it turned out, Jefferson's "empire of liberty" had a northern border.

The Politics of Prudence

What was important for the British Empire, in the aftermath of the War for American Independence, was that British imperialists learnt the wisdom of the great parliamentarian Edmund Burke that "Magnanimity in politics is not seldom the truest wisdom; and a great empire and little minds go ill together."[21] The British might have been right in principle in the American War for Independence—as Dr. Samuel Johnson put it, "taxation is no tyranny"[22]—but wrong in terms of prudence. Better to sacrifice the principle than to lose the colonies.

Britain put the wisdom of magnanimity to good use in Canada: granting French Canadian Catholics freedom of religion in the Quebec Act of 1774 (to the outrage of Calvinist pastors in New England); devolving most governing authority to the Canadians themselves with the 1840 Act of Union; and creating the Northwest Mounted Police (later the Royal Canadian Mounted

King George III Had It Right

"The rebellious war now levied is become more general, and is manifestly carried on for the purpose of establishing an independent empire. I need not dwell upon the fatal effects of the success of such a plan. The object is too important, the spirit of the British nation is too high, the resources with which God hath blessed her too numerous to give up so many colonies which she has planted with great industry, nursed with great tenderness, encouraged with many commercial advantages, and protected at much expense of blood and treasure."

King George III's Address to Parliament, 27 October 1775

Police), the Mounties, whose charming scarlet tunics, Smokey the Bear hats, and operatic talents made them less threatening than the lobster-back troopers who so affrighted the Americans.

Retaining Canada for the Empire was no mere consolation prize. The Canadians fought side by side with the British in both World Wars, more than 625,000-strong in the Great War and more than 1.1 million-strong in the Second World War. At the end of World War II Canada had the world's fourth largest air force and third largest navy—and we can only wish it had such military predominance today.

The Empire Strikes Back

Canada became an independent dominion in 1931, and achieved complete independence, while remaining a constitutional monarchy within the British Commonwealth, in 1982. But the British Empire still retains a few outposts in the Americas: Anguilla, Bermuda, the British Virgin Islands, the Cayman Islands, Montserrat, the Turks and Caicos Islands, the Falkland Islands, and South Georgia and the South Sandwich Islands. In 1982, Argentina invaded the Falklands and South Georgia, and perhaps to the Argentines' surprise, Britain roused herself to defend her territories, even if they lay at the other side of the world. On 19 April 1982, *Newsweek*'s cover story featured a picture of the aircraft carrier HMS *Hermes* and the headline "The Empire Strikes Back."

The Argentines had jealously eyed the Falklands before. In 1833, they had actually snuck a garrison on the islands that the Royal Navy had to forcibly remove. In 1977, the British thought it prudent to park a nuclear submarine nearby. The islanders themselves were staunchly, resolutely British.

The Argentines gambled that the British lion was toothless, its incisors worn away by the sugary dispensations of the battening welfare state. It turned out they were wrong.

Argentine forces made their assault on the islands on 2 April 1982. The few Royal Marines were disarmed. The question now was: what was Britain going to do about it?

By all appearances, the Royal Navy was in no state to mount a campaign to retake islands 8,000 miles away. But within three days, a convoy had set sail. It took a month for the British fleet to cross to the South Atlantic, but it arrived on the scene with a bang. The Royal Marines, part of the South Georgia Force, struck first, retaking the island on 25 April: "Be pleased to inform Her Majesty that the White Ensign [of the Royal Navy] flies alongside the Union Jack in South Georgia. God Save the Queen."[23] The arrival of the main fleet was punctuated by the sinking of the Argentine cruiser the *General Belgrano* on 2 May.

The Falklands War was no bloodless affair, the Royal Navy lost two destroyers, two frigates, and a cargo ship to Argentine air assaults. Britain's air support was limited to 34 carrier-based Harrier jump jets that had to neutralize 220 Argentine jet fighters. By the time the British forces had brought about the Argentines' surrender on the Falklands on 14 June (the British recaptured the South Sandwich Islands without incident on 20 June), 250 British soldiers, sailors, airmen, and Marines had been killed, along with three Falklands civilians. To some that might seem a high price to pay for the retention of distant islands inhabited by 3,000 fishermen and shepherds. But if their freedom was dearly bought, they know as well as anyone that British liberty is beyond price.

Chapter 4

SIR FRANCIS DRAKE
(1540–1596)

"I have brought you to the treasure house of the world."

—Sir Francis Drake to his men[1]

 n Buckland Abbey, the manor house of Sir Francis Drake, there lies a snare drum. According to Henry Newbolt—whose poem "Drake's Drum" (1895) was memorized by generations of British schoolboys—it was left with these instructions:

> Take my drum to England, hang et by the shore,
> Strike et when your powder's runnin' low;
> If the Dons sight Devon, I'll quit the port o' Heaven,
> An' drum them up the Channel as we drummed them long ago.

The drum has allegedly sounded at various dramatic moments: during the Falklands War, the Battle of Britain, even during the launch of the *Mayflower* to the New World, making Drake a sort of patron saint of England—except that as a Protestant he disdained patron saints.

Did you know?

- Drake was the first Englishman to see the Pacific

- King Philip II of Spain put a price of 20,000 ducats (about $10 million) on Drake's head

- Drake's drum allegedly sounds whenever England is in danger

Francis Drake: Preacher's Kid Turned Pirate

Drake's father, Edmund Drake, was a farmer and lay Protestant preacher. According to pious legend Edmund was chased into exile after a Catholic uprising in Devon. In fact, it appears he skipped town because he was a thief, though he was later pardoned so he could continue his holy work.

Francis, meanwhile, grew up in Plymouth, raised by his kinsman William Hawkins, and apprenticed to the sea. His guardian made his fortune on trading expeditions to Africa and Brazil, later becoming a king's pirate against the French. Drake imbibed from the Hawkins family its spirit of enterprise and the idea that piracy could be profitable and patriotic.

If he lacked formal education, Drake knew his trade, was a dedicated student of practical manuals like *The Art of Navigation*, and was a leader. As was common in his time, he ran a puritanical ship. Sailors were rough-hewn men, but they were forbidden swearing, gambling, and shirking communal prayers. His favorite aid for communal prayer was John Foxe's *Book of Martyrs*, which kept his men at a fiery pitch of self-righteousness against the papist French and Spanish.

Drake accompanied William Hawkins's son John on several slave-trading voyages. On one of them, finding the slave pickings sparse, they joined two tribal chieftains in an attack on the barricaded village of an enemy tribe. The combined assault—the Africans attacking by land, the English deployed as a riverine force—was successful. Hawkins, however, was disappointed that the Africans retained most of the captured enemy for themselves— some as slaves, others to be roasted alive for a cannibal feast. The slaves given to the English were the lucky ones.

These slaves were not bound for English colonies, which did not yet exist, but for the colonies of hated Spain, which put Hawkins and Drake in a rather ironical position, though the irony seemed to have escaped them. They burned with patriotic, religious hatred against the Spanish and yet were insistent on trading with them—and trading with them at the point of a gun, because the Spanish colonials were required to trade only with Spanish (or Spanish-licensed) ships. But the English sea dog method was to set off a few cannon and threats until the Spaniards agreed to trade; customs duties were of course ignored; and the English matched trading with raiding. It was an economic-moral system we might call "Whatever I Do Is Right." The English did not lack self-esteem.

Raider of the Spanish Main

As a captain, Drake dabbled briefly in slavery, but his real interest was robbing Spaniards; and in this role Drake convinced himself that self-defense by the Spanish was not only perfidious but robbed him of spoils that were rightfully his. After a little practice in the West Indies, working with Huguenot pirates, he targeted the port city of Nombre de Dios in Panama. It was here that Spain exported the silver and gold that fed the treasury of the Escorial and kept its armies paid.

The port had few citizens and was poorly defended, but Drake's attack was inept: the treasure ships had already sailed away. His assault earned him a musket ball in the leg; and his only booty was a wine ship—enjoyable spoils certainly, but not gold or silver. Its capture was unlikely to strike fear into the hearts of his enemies.

Drake, however, was not done. He formed an alliance with the Cimarrones, black slaves who had escaped their Spanish masters and lived as highwaymen. The Cimarrones had no use for loot (so they buried it); they simply wanted to harass the Spaniards. Drake was canny enough to see the potential for a nice bit of double billing. With the help of the Cimarrones he might unearth some buried treasure and lay an ambush on a Spanish gold train. First he had to wait through the rainy season. During that time one of his brothers died attacking a Spanish ship and another died of what was likely yellow fever.

The Protestant-Pirate Work Ethic

"Eager of action, and acquainted with men's nature, he never suffered idleness to infect his followers with cowardice, but kept them from sinking under any disappointment by diverting their attention to some new enterprise."

from Dr. Samuel Johnson's *The Life of Sir Francis Drake*, in Arthur Murray, ed., *The Works of Samuel Johnson, LL.D.* (Alexander V. Blake, 1838), vol. II, p. 325

After a botched attempt at raiding a gold-laden mule train, Drake found another ally: a Huguenot pirate named Guillaume Le Testu. Together, they seized more bars of gold and silver than they could possibly carry—and in good pirate fashion, they left some as buried treasure to dig up later. They never got it. The Spaniards launched a ferocious pursuit, recovered the buried treasure (its site betrayed by a captured Huguenot pirate), and executed Le Testu. But lucky Drake and his men escaped, and decided that after a year of suffering and fighting, it was time to head for England and a hero's welcome, for England surely did love her pirates.

For all Drake's cleverness, determination, and courage—which were duly celebrated—he rather spoiled the effect by laying claim to his late brother John's estate, despite the fact that John had left behind a young widow (whose later suit against Drake was upheld). Drake was a self-made man—and he took every advantage he could to advance that self-making.

The Terror of All the Seas

During his adventures and sufferings in Panama, Drake had seen the Pacific Ocean (the first Englishman to do so). He was determined to see it again. After helping the Earl of Essex in a campaign in Ireland, with the usual attendant slaughter, Drake accepted the queen's commission to sail down the east coast of South America, through the Straits of Magellan, and up the west coast of South America—ostensibly on a mission of trade, but trade in Elizabethan parlance, when it involved the New World, meant robbing Spanish ships and ports. The mission was to be led by three equal partners, Drake, John Wynter, and Thomas Doughty, though Drake was given command, and the partnership would soon unravel.

Drake's expedition set sail on 15 November 1577—and again, after storms drove it back to Plymouth, on 13 December. His flagship was the the *Pelican*, and even his own men were kept largely ignorant of the flotilla's destination. Drake did not want his piratical plans exposed, though they became apparent soon enough when the English pirates captured Spanish and Portuguese ships off the coast of Africa, taking from them what they wanted (including a Portuguese pilot) and then setting them free.

By the summer, the voyage became contentious, with Doughty accusing Drake's brother Thomas of theft and implying that Drake himself was Doughty's rightful inferior, given Doughty's superior birth and influence in Queen Elizabeth's court. In a squalid little trial, Drake found Doughty guilty of mutiny and treason, and then inveigled the crew to sentence him to death. Doughty asked that he be left onshore; but no, said Drake, he could not be left to the mercies of the Spanish. He could be kept prisoner aboard another ship, but then that ship would have to return to England and miss out on the spoils of the voyage. This too, proved unpopular; and so Doughty was ordered executed. He took it in good gentlemanly fashion, dining with Drake and sharing communion with him beforehand—all of which adds to the rather sickly pallor of the episode, which ended with Doughty's head lopped off and Drake holding it up and invoking the lesson: "This is the end of traitors."[2]

Whenever misfortune struck, in storm or strife, the crew blamed Doughty's ill-omened execution. Drake had the chaplain, who gave voice to the crew's sense of guilt, clapped in chains, thrust below deck, and slapped with an armband that read, "Francis Fletcher, the falsest knave that liveth."[3] Drake also declared him excommunicated. While many Protestants held that every man was his own priest, Drake apparently believed that every captain was his own pope.

After Doughty's execution, Drake rechristened the *Pelican* as the *Golden Hind*. It was certainly his ambition to fill it with gold. Drake had left England with five ships. He entered the Straits of Magellan with three, and entered the Pacific with only the *Golden Hind*; brutal storms crushed the *Marigold* in the Straits and buffeted the *Elizabeth* so badly that her captain John Wynter had to beat a retreat to England.

For both ships and ports, the coast of Chile was prime raiding territory, and Drake hit them, and dodged his pursuers (though an initial landing among the Indians had left him with arrow wounds, one just below his right eye). His big haul came near Lima, Peru, where he seized, in separate actions, two treasure ships full of gold, silver, and jewels; the second ship, *Nuestra Señora de la Concepcion,* was so laden with treasure that it took Drake's men six days to strip it and store the valuables on the *Golden Hind*.

On 26 September 1580, after circumnavigating the globe, Drake presented his glittering treasure to the queen. Drake's share made him one of the wealthiest men in England. The queen, entitled to half the expedition's plunder, was quite pleased and ennobled Drake in 1581, the same year that he, in short order, became a member of Parliament, mayor of Plymouth, and thus a man of the establishment.

Still, he remained a man of action. In 1585, Drake mounted another great raid on the Spanish. With him was Martin Frobisher—an explorer and pirate like himself—whom he made vice admiral, and more than twenty ships. They began by raiding the coast of Spain itself, then headed west, burning their way through the Cape Verde Islands (where, alas, they picked up a deadly fever that killed hundreds of Drake's men), and then to the West Indies where they sacked Santo Domingo in January 1586, even rounding up the city's women to drop their jewels into the pirates' collection plates. It is a tribute to Drake's mastery of tactics that his plan of attack was used by Admiral William Penn and General Robert Venables in 1655—with disastrous results. Not everyone had Drake's touch. Even so, his expedition—which included attacks on Cartagena, Colombia, and Saint Augustine, Florida, as well as an evacuation of the colonists of Roanoke Island—failed to turn a profit, and only about half of Drake's men returned alive. It was a tribute to Drake's own stamina that he was one of them.

Armada!

On 15 March 1587, Drake received the queen's commission to raid Spain, especially its ports where it was preparing for an invasion of England. Drake struck Cadiz on Spain's southwest coast, pillaging merchant ships (more than twenty), fighting boldly "for our gracious Queen and country against Antichrist and his members,"[4] blasting everything in sight in Cadiz harbor, and then burning and looting along the Portuguese coast and the Azores. In Drake's famous phrase, he was "singeing the beard of the King of Spain."

In Spain they called Drake "el Draque," the Dragon, and King Philip II offered a reward of 20,000 ducats (about $10 million today) for anyone who could douse his flames. But if Drake was a dragon, it was part of the patriotic

---

The Lord Helps Those Who Help Themselves

"But if God will bless us with some little comfortable dew from heaven, some crowns or some reasonable boo[ty] for our soldiers and mariners, all will take good heart again, although they were half dead."

Sir Francis Drake, quoted in Harry Kelsey, *Sir Francis Drake: The Queen's Pirate* (Yale University Press, 1988), p. 298

---

myth that he was a phlegmatic English one. On 19 July 1588, news reached Drake at Plymouth that the Spanish Armada had been spotted off the coast of Cornwall. Drake, the popular story goes, was playing bowls with his colleagues.

> The game was stopped, all eyes were turned towards the Channel. Yes, there at last, far out to sea, the proud Spanish vessels were to be seen. They were distant yet, but a sailor's eye could see they were mighty and great ships, and the number of them was very large. But the brave English captains were not afraid.
>
> "Come," said Drake, after a few minutes, "there is time to finish the game and to beat the Spaniards too."[5]

Drake had actually advocated a strike on the Spanish before they embarked for England. It was obviously too late for that now. Drake was vice admiral of Elizabeth's fleet under Lord Howard of Effingham. In a splendid show of ceremony and respect, Drake lowered his admiral's flag when Howard's ship first came into view, and Howard raised his as Drake's was lowered. A series of fires over England—lighted beacons—alerted England's captains to the invasion, and in the weeks that followed, the English sea dogs darted between the Spanish ships, utterly routing them, leaving a storm to finish them off. When the fight was over, Philip II's ships looked like they'd been through a nautical bonfire of the vanities, galleons shattered and sunk or wrecked along the shores of Ireland; as many as 20,000 Spaniards lost; and amidst the carnage and catastrophe stood Drake on

Drake on Tactics

"The advantage of time and place in all martial actions is half the victory."

Quoted in Stephen Coote, *Drake: The Life and Legend of an Elizabethan Hero* (Thomas Dunne Books/St. Martin's Press, 2003), p. 250

his quarterdeck. In true entrepreneurial fashion he had managed not only to fight the Spaniards, but to grab captives to be ransomed and a treasure chest of gold to be divided with the Crown.

Such enterprise did not endear Drake to some of his captains—Martin Frobisher, for one, loathed Drake's swashbuckling greed (though Elizabeth's depleted treasury relied on it)—and the great glory of victory was marred somewhat by the exchequer's inability to promptly pay the men who had saved England, and by an outburst of disease that ravaged the sailors, with thousands dying of dysentery or typhus. Worse, at least for Drake, was that when the queen assigned him the task of finishing off the remnants of the Spanish fleet the following year, he failed utterly—indeed he was distracted with a hapless siege of Corunna, and an equally hapless attempt to liberate Portugal from Spain—and lost royal favor.

It was not until 1595 that Drake—now well over fifty, and feeling it—was able to outfit another expedition against Panama with royal approval and investment. It started badly, with Drake quarreling with John Hawkins, and it got worse, with Hawkins succumbing to a mortal illness, the campaign proving a bloody failure, and Drake himself dying of dysentery—or as one of his officers, Sir Thomas Baskerville said, "as I think through grief." Drake's last wish was to be buckled into his armor "that he might die like a soldier."[6] He was buried at sea off the Panamanian coast in a lead-lined coffin that, to the delight of thrill-seeking divers, has never been found.

The English do love their rogues, and in Drake they had a brilliant one. Spain, with the approval of the pope, had claimed the New World as its own. Drake put paid to that pretension, and in the process opened up the New World to English imperialism. In the popular mind he was a patriot, a hero, and a godly Protestant—and of course, a pirate, which only added to his charm. He stood for freedom (or for looting), against a Spain that was

"Fast-bound in misery and iron, with chains / Of Priest and King and feudal servitude." Drake was the

> seaman who late had scourged
> The Spanish Main; he whose piratic neck
> Scarcely the Queen's most wily statecraft saved
> From Spain's revenge: he, privateer to the eyes
> Of Spain, but England to all English hearts,
> Gathered together in all good jollity.

It was Drake who had led "a force of nigh three thousand men wherewith to singe / The beard o' the King of Spain"[7]—and what could be better than that?

Chapter 5

SIR HENRY MORGAN
(1635–1684)

"Got a little Captain in you?"

—*the slogan for Captain Morgan's Rum*

enry Morgan—now known more for his rum than anything else—was a Welshman whose uncles fought on opposite sides of the English Civil War (1641–1652). Uncle Edward served with the gallant, high Anglican Royalists, the Cavaliers; Uncle Thomas served with the puritanical Protestant Parliamentarians, the Roundheads. The latter won, unfortunately, and under Oliver Cromwell (Lord Protector of England, Scotland, and Ireland, 1653–58) they proved to be extremely aggressive in foreign policy. Under the guidance of an apostate Catholic priest turned Protestant chaplain, Thomas Gage, Cromwell endorsed a strategy to bedevil Spain in the New World, of which Gage had some knowledge. The strategy was "the Western Design." It was, in essence, a plan to revive the glorious days of Sir Francis Drake of more than half a century before; the goal of "the Western Design," however, was not just to raid the Spanish Main, but to seize it and the Spanish West Indies.

Launched in 1654, the Western Design was, on the whole, a miserable failure (and landed Admiral William Penn and General Robert Venables some months in the Tower of London; for, like a James Bond villain,

Did you know?

- After being arrested and sent to London as a pirate, Morgan was knighted and returned to Jamaica as its deputy governor

- Morgan was equally vigorous in exterminating pirates—his former colleagues—as he had been in terrorizing the Spanish Main

- Morgan did not, ahem, "drink responsibly"

Cromwell did not take failure lightly), but it provided action for a young soldier named Henry "Harry" Morgan. It also brought the English Jamaica (in 1655), which might have seemed but a wee speck in the Caribbean, but was actually a crucial island base. It put the wind behind the backs of English pirates and privateers who preyed on Spain's ships and colonies.

"More Used to the Pike Than the Book"

We have little account of Morgan's early years in Wales, England, and Jamaica. Of his early life, Morgan said only that he "left school too young" to be an expert in law (though he tried, as a respectable buccaneer, to stay reasonably within it), and was "more used to the pike than the book."[1] We also know that Morgan later sued and won a judgment against a man who claimed Morgan had been an indentured servant.

He was not a sailor either (though Jamaica's governor would give him the rank of admiral). He was a soldier, and it seems certain that after the conquest of Jamaica he was kept busy fighting Spanish guerrillas in the mountains. His public life began with the restoration of the monarchy to England under Charles II. Under the new royalist governor in Jamaica, Lord Windsor, the army was converted into militia units and in 1662 Henry Morgan appears as a captain in the Port Royal Regiment. Its first mission: attack Cuba.

Charles II, being a Catholic-leaning Anglican, did not have Cromwell's burning desire to pillage Spanish churches, smash their images of the Virgin Mary, take axes to their altars, desecrate their Eucharists, and steal their golden chalices and crucifixes. But as king, he gained a quick appreciation of the value of England's New World holdings (or "foreign plantations," as they were called), and demanded "free commerce" between the English plantations and the "territories belonging to the King of Spain"—by force if necessary.[2]

As in the day of Drake, so in the day of Morgan, the Spanish refused to acknowledge that anyone else had a right to be in the New World, and trade had to be run through Spain's strict bureaucratic channels. Nevertheless, many Spanish outposts in the New World, however much they feared the English Vikings, engaged in sometimes elaborately concealed trade with the English, French, and Dutch.

But because Spain did not concede Jamaica to England—insisting that it, like all other New World territories, belonged to Spain[3]—Cuba remained a serious threat to Jamaica's security. Jamaica's Spanish rebels had been supplied from Cuba, and it was decided that giving Cuba the old Francis Drake treatment would prove England's seriousness about insisting on free trade with Spain's colonies. The attack was to be made by Commodore Sir Christopher Myngs. Myngs was popular in Jamaica because he was a friend of the buccaneers (though a professional navy man, the Spaniards considered him an out and out pirate). He was skilled and brave, as were the soldiers, like Captain Morgan, he brought with him—and their raid on Santiago de Cuba in October 1662 was a roaring success. At the cost of only six men killed they captured six ships and enormous quantities of loot, and blew Santiago's fortress to smithereens.

Myngs returned to action in January 1663, sailing for an attack on the Mexican port of Campeche. It too was successful, though at a much higher cost. Myngs himself was badly wounded while leading the landward attack, and thirty of his men were killed.

In 1664, Jamaica's new governor, Sir Thomas Modyford, declared peace with Spain. Morgan was not of a mind to listen—even if his uncle Edward was now lieutenant governor.[4] Morgan was apparently ignorant of the order—at any rate while he was at sea—clutching the paper that made him a fully commissioned privateer, and thus free to raid the Spanish Main. While Uncle Edward, a colonel, was commissioned to attack the Dutch Caribbean islands (as part of the Second Anglo-Dutch War of 1665 to 1667),

Morgan raided Mexico with four of his fellow captains. With fewer than two hundred men, Morgan's raiders roamed the coast of Central America, sacked inland towns, and came home bearing immense spoils of war and incredible stories of profitable adventure—stories that established Morgan as a true leader of men. While Morgan's exploits were diplomatic embarrassments, such embarrassments were easily ignored when they were so popular and so useful for Jamaica's treasury. Morgan and his men were heroes, reminders of the glory of Good Queen Bess and Sir Francis Drake. He was promoted a colonel in 1666, charged with Jamaica's defense, and had by this time married Uncle Edward's daughter and used his wealth to become a planter. He was a respected man.

Vice Admiral of Buccaneers

In 1667, Governor Modyford suspected the nefarious Spaniards might invade Jamaica—though Spain was at that moment at war with France, not England. Still, it seemed like a good excuse to commission Morgan to seize a few Cuban Spaniards for questioning. It is a tribute to Morgan's reputation that he soon had seven hundred men ready to sail—not just Englishmen, but a polyglot crew of buccaneers and pirates. Together they stormed the town of Puerto Principe, where Morgan's men outfought regular Spanish soldiers and sacked the town with all due diligence; it yielded, however, paltry rewards.

Morgan, undaunted, decided that an attack on Panama would be a nice way to round out his voyage. His associated French pirates demurred and retired to their lairs at Tortuga or elsewhere. Morgan pressed on, raiding Portobello, an inland town that was caught utterly unaware, his buccaneers again proving doughtier fighters than the Spanish regulars. Having reduced the town and robbed it of all that was worth robbing, Morgan demanded its ransom from the president of Panama. The *presidente* notified Morgan that

The Best Economic Stimulus Package: Privateering

"It furnishes the island with many commodities at easy rates. It replenishes the island with coin, bullion, cocoa…. It helps the poorer planters by selling provisions to the men-of-war. It hath and will enable many to buy slaves and settle plantations…." It keeps the pirates of the Caribbean friends rather than foes, provides spies for the Jamaican governor against the designs of the Spanish, "and bring[s] no small benefit to his Majesty and his Royal Highness" in prize money. The pirates, privateers, and buccaneers, "keep many able artificers at work in Port Royal and elsewhere at extraordinary wages…. They are of great reputation to this island and of terror to the Spaniards…."

from the Minutes of the Council of Jamaica, 22 February 1666, reproduced in David F. Marley, *Pirates of the Americas* (ABC-CLIO, 2010), pp. 425–26

he did not negotiate with corsairs and that he was on the march to defeat him. To this Morgan replied,

> We are waiting for you with great pleasure and we have powder
> and ball with which to receive you. If you do not come very soon,
> we will, with the favor of God and our arms, come and visit you
> in Panama. Now it is our intention to garrison the castles and
> keep them for the King of England, my master, who since he had
> a mind to seize them, has also a mind to keep them. And since I
> do not believe that you have sufficient men to fight with me
> tomorrow, I will order all the poor prisoners to be freed so that
> they may go to help you.[5]

This was a nobly stated bit of effrontery because of course "the King of England, my master," had no idea Morgan had annexed the town on his behalf (indeed His Majesty had signed a treaty of peace with Spain). But Morgan was as good as his word. The Spaniards, finding they could not relieve Portobello, ransomed it.

Morgan returned to Port Royal and organized his largest expedition yet—a thousand freebooters to attack Cartagena. With them was a thirty-four-gun frigate, HMS *Oxford*, sent by the Duke of York (the future King James II) for Jamaica's defense. It was to be the flagship for Morgan's new expedition. Unfortunately, during the rollicking New Year's revels to welcome the year 1669 and celebrate their plan of attack, its powder magazine exploded killing virtually everyone on board, more than two hundred men, leaving only ten survivors—among them, Morgan.

Morgan's "We Few, We Happy Few"

"If our numbers are small, our hearts are great, and the fewer we are, the better share we shall have in the spoils!"

Morgan before the attack on Portobello 1668, quoted in Stephan Talty, *Empire of the Blue Water: Captain Morgan's Great Pirate Army, the Epic Battle for the Americas, and the Catastrophe that Ended the Outlaws' Bloody Reign* (Crown, 2007), p. 104

Such an accident was bound to dampen even Captain Morgan's undaunted spirit; desertions followed. With his reduced force, Cartagena was out of the question, but an assault on Maracaibo, Venezuela, was not. Warned of his approach, the Spaniards abandoned—but booby-trapped—the fort that guarded the inlet that led to the town. Morgan's men found the slow-burning fuse that was meant to send them and the fort to destruction. The town of Maracaibo was also abandoned, but Morgan's men scoured the area, rounded up captives, and tortured them to find where their valuables were hidden. If Morgan's experience is anything to go by, torture works; his men meted out the same treatment to the citizens of the nearby town of Gibraltar. But as Morgan prepared to lead his men back into the Caribbean a note arrived from a Spanish admiral. He had three Spanish warships blocking the inlet, and the fort guarding the inlet had been regarrisoned—its guns would be leveled directly at Morgan's ships. The admiral had come "with orders to destroy you utterly and put every man to the sword" unless Morgan and his men were prepared to surrender and give up their loot.

Morgan read the letter to his men—and as buccaneers are wont to do, they scoffed. If they had risked their lives to gain treasure, why would they not risk their lives to keep it? Morgan then dictated his official reply: "Sir, I have your summons, and since I understand you are so near, I shall save you the labor with your nimble frigates to come here, being resolved to visit you with all expedition, and there we will put to hazard of battle in whose power it shall be to use clemency (yours we are acquainted with; nor do we expect any)." It closed with a final insult, dating the letter "from his Majesty of England's city of Maracaibo...."[6]

That was the spirit—and it was backed by force, as Morgan, with the skill of a trained soldier and the cleverness of an entrepreneurial English sea dog, was about to outwit the Spaniards once again. He sent a captured Cuban ship—crewed by only a dozen men, and wooden dummies dressed in sailors' gear—to the Spanish flagship. When the ships were grappled together, the Spaniards discovered the ruse—but too late. The freebooters, plunging over the side, had set the ship ablaze, and the fire ship soon engulfed the flagship. The other two Spanish ships ran aground by the fort. One was scuttled by fire; the other captured by the buccaneers.

There was a temporary stalemate. Morgan didn't think he could run his ships past the fort's guns, so he mounted an overland attack, but it was repelled. A few days later Morgan made a show of landing a large raiding party for another landward attack—but it was merely a decoy to get the

Spaniards to move their guns to face inland. After they did, and night fell, Morgan sailed his flotilla safely away.

The overarching irony was that while England was trying to get Jamaica to cooperate with its policy of peaceful coexistence with Spain, the Spanish in their frustration had decided that the only rational course was to enlist their own privateers to attack the English, which they duly did. In retaliation, Governor Modyford, ignoring London (as was popular in Jamaica) named Morgan admiral and commander in chief with a commission to attack every Spanish ship that crossed his path.

Morgan embraced his roving commission and throughout the summer and fall of 1670 he raided the Spanish. The highlight came in December, by which time Morgan had gathered together a seaborne army of two thousand buccaneers—the largest ever assembled: Englishmen, Frenchmen, Dutchmen, united by a hatred of Spain and a willingness to risk life for loot. On Christmas Day they recaptured Providence Island (a colony originally established by English Puritans). It was the first step on Morgan's path to sack Panama. In January 1671, he captured the fort guarding the entrance to the Chagres River at the narrow waist of central Panama. Morgan's plan was to lead his men across the Isthmus to the Pacific side where they would find the famously wealthy Panama City.

Morgan garrisoned the captured river fort with several hundred freebooters and then led fifteen hundred buccaneers on a seven-day trek through the Panamanian jungle. When they emerged outside Panama City, they found a Spanish army drawn up to meet them. But the buccaneers proved better soldiers, with steadier discipline. The Spanish militia, cavalry and infantry, charged impetuously—and then fled with equal dispatch when met by blasts from buccaneer guns. The buccaneers suffered fifteen casualties—the Spanish, four hundred to five hundred. Morgan's privateers stormed the city, only to find that most of its treasure had been moved offshore, to ships Morgan couldn't reach. Morgan's expedition had been a military coup, but his men were in it for profit and there was very little of that to be had—certainly nothing large enough, in the minds of many of them, for the hazards they had endured and the long march back up to the Chagres that had to follow.

The Governor's Deputy

In Spring 1671, Jamaica received a new governor from England, Sir Thomas Lynch. Lynch bore orders to arrest his predecessor Sir Thomas Modyford, but assured him that his arrest was largely to impress Spain with England's good faith in trying to maintain the peace between their two countries (though Modyford was imprisoned in the Tower of London for two years and Lynch would soon be hanging pirates who failed to heed his warnings that Jamaica was no longer a haven for "the Brethren of the Coast," the self-governing Protestant pirates who had so long been its protectors). Also, in due course, came orders that he was to arrest Morgan for his unauthorized (by London) raid on Panama.

Morgan, however, was unwell—a dangerous fever kept him bedridden, wrapped in sweat-sodden blankets—and Lynch did not want to alienate the affections of the people of Jamaica by mistreating their hero. It was not until April 1672 that Morgan was judged well enough to travel, and when he did so, he was borne away not as a convict but as a very important person who needed to return for consultations with the government in London. There too, the government seemed uninterested in pressing charges against him (he was not imprisoned, but left at liberty) and by the summer of 1673 the mood in London had reversed: Morgan seemed just the man to secure Jamaica's future. In 1674, he was knighted and returned to Jamaica as deputy governor to the newly appointed governor, Lord Vaughn.

Among other duties, Morgan was charged with ending piracy in the Caribbean, and this he did with all the mocking gusto he had brought to ravaging the Spanish Main. At times, his new career could make him appear cruel and hypocritical. But he was no crueler to his former friends the pirates than they had been to the Spanish.

As a private citizen Morgan increased his landholdings. In his social life, old habits died hard. He caroused in true pirate style, with a well-earned reputation for heavy drinking in a place and time when the standards for "moderate" drinking were rather capacious—and his waistline began to show signs of his regular debauches. The raffish privateer was fast becoming a supersized fatty. In 1683, he found himself bounced from the island council as no longer sober-minded enough to represent the new respectable face of Jamaica—a face that was being powdered by the return of Sir Thomas Lynch as governor. Before he died in 1688, Morgan was, by the king's consent, allowed to rejoin the council— but Morgan's last years were those of a cantankerous physical wreck.

Morgan the (Reformed) Pirate

"I have put to death, imprisoned and transported to the Spanish for execution all English and Spanish pirates that I could get."

Letter from Sir Henry Morgan, deputy governor of Jamaica, 9 April 1678, quoted in Stephan Talty, *Empire of the Blue Water: Captain Morgan's Great Pirate Army, the Epic Battle for the Americas, and the Catastrophe that Ended the Outlaws' Bloody Reign* (Crown, 2007), p. 273

Nevertheless, Morgan, like Drake, had always been driven by ambition—ambition for money, glory, and respect. Drake had bought his manor house to have the appurtenances, if not the bloodlines, of a gentleman. Morgan had become a planter, and he left his wife with holdings that, in today's terms, likely made her a modest millionairess. Both men were patriots, and like all patriots they no doubt wanted to be remembered by history.[7]

If you want to pay your respects to Morgan, it's impossible. His grave fell into the ocean when an earthquake collapsed Port Royal. Still, a burial at sea was obviously suitable, and it would no doubt amuse the old rogue to learn that he is today best known as the grinning, bearded, red-coated, high-booted, sword-resting, caped, pistol-belted, and tricorned captain that is the label trademark of a well-known brand of rum. It is, after all, a fitting tribute.

Chapter 6

CHARLES CORNWALLIS, 1ST MARQUESS CORNWALLIS (1738–1805)

"The reasonable object of ambition to a man is to have his name transmitted to posterity for eminent services rendered to his country and to mankind."

—*Cornwallis in a letter to his son Lord Brome, 28 December 1786*[1]

ornwallis was a proto-Victorian. If he lacked the breed's eccentricity, he fully embodied its devotion to duty and high moral character. He was responsible, temperate, and industrious; domestic and countrified in his preferences, he nevertheless seemed to chafe when not employed by his country—which employed him quite a lot, across three continents.

Typical of his class, he was sent to a hard school—Eton, where pupils learned Latin declensions and Spartan habits. Also typical of his class—and a tribute to its education—he was undaunted by hardship, unimpressed by threats, indifferent to danger, sure in command, practical in his assessments, and high-minded in his duty. He was, his father noted, a "very military"[2] young man; Cornwallis always thought of himself foremost as a soldier.

Cornwallis's military career began at seventeen, when he became an ensign in the fashionable 1st Grenadier Guards. Unlike many young officers, he took his military vocation seriously. He went to the continent to see action, and even finagled himself a staff appointment in Germany during the Seven Years' War. In 1763 he took up his political duties in the House

Did you know?

♔ Cornwallis supported the protests of the American colonists— until they turned to rebellion

♔ Cornwallis was an innovator in using elephants to transport artillery

♔ Cornwallis resigned as Lord-Lieutenant of Ireland when King George III refused to grant toleration to Catholics

of Lords, where he joined the Rockingham Whigs and established himself as a liberal in favor of conciliating rather than taxing the American colonies. In 1768, he married Jemima Tullekin Jones, the daughter of a regimental colonel. The couple was ardently devoted; it was alleged she died (in 1779) because his long absences fighting the American colonists broke her heart. Her death, Cornwallis wrote, "effectually destroyed all my hopes of happiness in this world. I will not dwell on this wretched subject, the thoughts of which harrow up my soul."[3]

The Reluctant General

When he was sent to America to suppress the rebellion in 1776, he was promoted to lieutenant-general of Britain's North American Army, which still left him third in command, subordinate to generals Sir Henry Clinton and Sir William Howe. All three generals had supported the colonists before the war, and it showed. Howe was pessimistic about Britain's ability to suppress the rebellion, especially after the Battle of Bunker (or actually Breed's) Hill where the Americans proved a stubborn foe. Howe fought with a caution born of half-heartedness and even let Washington's army escape New York when he could possibly have crushed it. Cornwallis was cautious too, but the British succeeded in driving the Americans before them, even if the king's forces suffered stinging rebukes at Trenton and Princeton.

In October 1777, Howe resigned and Sir Henry Clinton was appointed his successor. Clinton preferred the safety of New York, its charming social life, and the comforting arms of his mistress to campaigning; and Cornwallis, though he remained a dutiful subordinate, tried to resign his commission. He yearned for home and believed the government was undercutting the army in North America in order to fight the French in the Caribbean. The king refused his resignation, but Cornwallis was finally granted leave and returned to England in December 1779 to find his wife, Lady Cornwallis, desperately ill. He stayed with her through the winter until she died in February. It was her death that compelled Cornwallis to forgo thoughts of home and the company of his two young children and to return to the grim and unsatisfactory war in America; the reserved Englishman needed to bury his never-healing grief in duty.

He found that duty in the southern United States where he rejoined Clinton and besieged Charleston—this time, unlike a previous attempt in 1776, successfully. With Charleston secured, Clinton returned to New York, leaving Cornwallis in command, granting him broad powers and instructions to work his way to the Chesapeake after bringing the Carolinas to heel. This Cornwallis swiftly set out to do, reestablishing a loyalist government in South Carolina and then moving to the back country to fight the rebels. He met them at Camden. The rebel commander was General Horatio Gates, a former British army major of common birth and conniving personality. He had served in America in the past, but had only become an American resident in 1772. For all of Gates's experience—and the fact that he had nearly twice Cornwallis's number of guns and men—the nobleman routed the commoner, popping Gates's self-inflated reputation, and capturing all his guns. Gates disgraced himself by abandoning his army and fleeing the field.

An Imperialist in Grief

"This country [England] now has no charms for me, & I am perfectly indifferent as to what part of the world I may go."

Cornwallis, after the death of his wife, in a letter to Sir Henry Clinton, 4 April 1779

Cornwallis believed in seeking out enemy armies and destroying them, but in the South he was confronted by partisan warfare, with loyalists brutalized into submission by patriot guerrillas. The patriots were full of passionate intensity, while the loyalists lacked all conviction—not surprising perhaps because all they wanted was a quiet life and a return to the status quo ante bellum.

The enormous weight the British government put on the presumed loyalist sentiment of Georgia (back in the British fold) and the Carolinas annoyed Cornwallis, usually the most temperate of men. He dismissed the loyalists as "dastardly and pusillanimous"[4] and entirely reliant on his British regulars. The loyalists, however, were neither dastardly nor pusillanimous under the command of Scotch-born Major Patrick Ferguson, a brilliant and courageous British officer, at the Battle of King's Mountain, North Carolina (7 October 1780). They were nevertheless destroyed, their defeat reverberating throughout the South; the allegedly loyalist Carolinas did not seem so very safe for the British.

An Active Senior

"Was there ever an instance of a General running away, as Gates has done, from his whole army? And was there ever so precipitous a flight?... It does admirable credit to the activity of a man at his time of life."

Alexander Hamilton on Horatio Gates's fleeing the field at Camden, quoted in Harrison Clark, *All Cloudless Glory, Volume One: The Life of George Washington from Youth to Yorktown* (Regnery, 1995), p. 467

Cornwallis's chief failing in the Southern campaign was actually to his credit as a human being. He had, as his most prominent biographers have noted, "a soldier's conception of honor and straight dealing. He enjoyed fighting openly against a declared and courageous foe. By the same token he abhorred cruelty, deceit, and dishonesty. Here, however, he found himself in a situation where the last three qualities counted most in winning the war."[5] Luckily, he had the British Legion under the command of Banastre Tarleton, a cavalryman and politically incorrect poster boy who had fewer qualms about cruelty, deceit, and dishonesty. It is hard not to warm to a man like Tarleton—a man who boasted, according to Horace Walpole, "of having butchered more men and lain with more women than anybody else in the army"[6] and who, as a member of Parliament defended the slave trade[7]—but the Americans managed; indeed, his very name was used to frighten children; "Tarleton's quarter" was invoked by the patriots to mean "no quarter"; he was the most feared and hated British cavalryman in the war. While Cornwallis insisted that his officers should behave like gentlemen, Tarleton, a gentleman by birth, was more than willing to mix it up with the partisans on their own terms of terror and slaughter. Cornwallis liked the ambitious young Tarleton, and though he discerned an occasional impetuosity and lack of scruple in his subordinate, he defended him when pressed. He did so even after Tarleton's rashly ordered cavalry charge, while on detached command, led to defeat at Cowpens (17 January 1781)[8]—another serious blow to Cornwallis's campaign, one that he confessed "has almost broke my heart."[9]

But when Cornwallis could bring his army against the colonials in a set-piece battle, even if badly outnumbered, he turned up trumps. He was so eager to catch an American army to fight that he burnt his supply train so that his troops could move faster. It also meant they had to endure more and live off what they could find, whether a turnip patch or a field of corn. As redcoat sergeant Roger Lamb noted, "In all this his lordship participated, nor did he indulge himself even in the distinction of a tent; but in all things

A Not So Gracious South

"The violence and passions of these people are beyond every curb of religion, and Humanity, they are unbounded and every hour exhibits dreadful wanton mischiefs, murders, and violence of every kind. We find the country in great measure abandoned, and the few who venture to remain at home in hourly expectation of being murdered, or stripped of their property."

British general Charles O'Hara on the partisan warfare in the Carolinas, in a letter to the Duke of Grafton 6 January 1781, quoted in Robert B. Asprey, *War in the Shadows: The Guerrilla in History* (iUniverse, 2002), p. 66

An Eighteenth-Century Hannibal

"Be a little careful, and tread softly; for depend upon it, you have a modern Hannibal to deal with in the person of Cornwallis."

Patriot General Nathanael Greene to General "Mad" Anthony Wayne, quoted in Burke Davis, *The Cowpen-Guilford Courthouse Campaign* (University of Pennsylvania Press, 2002), p. 69

partook our sufferings, and seemed much more to feel for us than for himself."[10]

He raced to confront patriot Nathanael Greene at Guildford Courthouse (15 March 1781) in Greensboro, North Carolina, though Greene held an easily defended position on the high ground flanked by covering woods. The patriots outnumbered him more than two to one, but Cornwallis's intelligence reports told him he was outnumbered four to one. He decided to attack regardless, trusting to the steadiness of his British regulars. His confidence and determination were well placed, as his troops charged through rebel militiamen, shot down sharpshooters, and advanced straight through canister fire until their bayonets pricked the Americans into retreat.

The victory, of course, came at a high cost: at least a quarter of his force. Rubbing salt into the wound was that it did nothing to cement North Carolina's allegiance to the Crown or crush the rebels' ambitions. Cornwallis decided his only viable strategy was to plunge into Virginia, despite having only 1,400 men. He hoped to compel Washington and Greene to combine against him; then he could defeat them entire with reinforcements from some of the thousands of troops that sat idle with Clinton in New York. Events, however, betrayed Cornwallis's hopes.

Yorktown

Clinton had sent troops to Virginia, but they were intended to fortify a naval base at Portsmouth. Cornwallis had entirely other ideas. Forts were superfluous to winning the war; what was necessary was destroying the rebel army, and Virginia was the center of gravity of the war in the South;

force its submission and the Carolinas were secured. Clinton, however, remained convinced that New York was the center of the war. Combined French and American forces, he believed, would soon be striking against him; the Southern theatre was essentially a diversionary one. He ordered Cornwallis to locate his troops at either Williamsburg or Yorktown, where British ships could reach him; the plan was not to reinforce Cornwallis but for Cornwallis to reinforce Clinton.

The problem was that it was the French Navy that arrived in Chesapeake Bay—disembarking French troops and rebuffing the Royal Navy. With Cornwallis's men divided between Yorktown and Gloucester (necessary for the defense of Yorktown), he could either try to break out against the French regulars who outnumbered him or he could dig in for a siege. Cornwallis planned for a breakout—until, that is, he received a dispatch from Clinton promising troops. With that promise he decided to stick it out at Yorktown. But now racing down to Yorktown was Washington, who recognized that Cornwallis was trapped and could be destroyed. Cornwallis kept Tarleton sweeping his front and his men furiously building entrenchments; the rival armies traded bombardments; but as the siege tightened and the relief force didn't arrive, the end was inevitable. Cornwallis, pleading ill health, did not meet his conquerors at the surrender ceremony. Instead he sent Brigadier General Charles O'Hara, who tried to present Cornwallis's sword to the French commander the Comte de Rochambeau, who indicated that the honor belonged to General Washington. Washington returned O'Hara's snub by directing him to surrender to his own second-in-command, General Benjamin Lincoln.

A Passage to India

Defeat at Yorktown did not end Cornwallis's career. Not only did he have the frisson of having his voyage home interrupted by a French privateer, but when he did return to Old Blighty he found himself cheered on all sides:

Lord North's government held him blameless, dumping its vitriol on General Clinton; King George found no fault in him; and even the opposition kept its fire on the government for failing to support Cornwallis properly. If his reputation needed a shield it was found in the near universal respect for his probity.

Cornwallis was under parole from the French privateer, but when the war with America ended, he felt free to accept, on 23 February 1786, the positions of governor-general and commander in chief of India. He demanded the positions be unified because he came to India as a broom, sweeping out corruption and choosing as his lieutenants Christian men of brilliance, dedication, and integrity. They were men like John Shore, an old Etonian, cricketer, classicist, and translator of Persian and Sanskrit, who came not to enrich himself in India but to serve the Indian people; William Jones, a lawyer, judge, and linguist who could speak thirteen languages fluently and get by in thirty more, and who appeared to know more about Hindu culture and history than the Hindus themselves; and Charles Grant, a friend of Shore's, sharing many of Shore's virtues and adding to them a masterful knowledge of the commercial workings of the East India Company. Together, they set the Hindu and Muslim legal codes into English, codified a general legal code for British India (the "Cornwallis Code"), and tried to ensure that the justice system lived up to its name (and abolished some of the harsher bits like mutilation as punishment). While they could not abolish slavery, which was still too popular in India, they did threaten to

Arms and the Man

"His appearance gave the impression of nobility of soul, magnanimity, and strength of character; his manner seemed to say, 'I have nothing with which to reproach myself, I have done my duty, and I held out as long as possible.'"

Baron Ludwig von Closen of the Franco-American forces after Cornwallis's surrender at Yorktown, quoted in Burke Davis, *The Campaign that Won America: The Story of Yorktown* (Eastern Acorn Press, 1997), p. 272

prosecute slave traders and prevent the selling of children. They established India's currency, reformed its system of taxation, founded a Sanskrit college for Hindus (still in existence), and, on the whole, followed Cornwallis's admonition that "whilst we call ourselves sovereign of the country we cannot leave the lives, liberty, & property of our subjects unprotected."[11] It is true, as his modern critics will be quick to point out, that Cornwallis established a color bar, requiring that officers and civil servants be not only gentlemen but white gentlemen. His reasons were simple. He thought European men were, in general, more likely to be disinterested and honest and that in the myriad of races, religions, and castes in India only a white man was capable of winning universal authority and respect.

Cornwallis, nevertheless, certainly treated the Indians with respect. A large part of his job was diplomatic (he sent the first Englishman to Tibet). British India at the time was centered on Calcutta, and much of the subcontinent remained in the hands of a variety of rajahs, the residual Mughal empire, the Mahrattas, and others. Cornwallis managed to keep the English peace with one significant exception, when he was called upon to unsheathe his sword against the sultan of Mysore, who was invading neighboring states (and who would eventually be overthrown by Arthur Wellesley, later the Duke of Wellington). In these campaigns, Cornwallis proved a master of tactics and logistics (he was the first English commander to see that elephants were the perfect transport animals for artillery) and brought as allies the Mahrattas and the Nizam of Hyderabad. It is, incidentally, a myth that the eighteenth-century English had a huge technological advantage over their Indian adversaries. In fact, the troops of the sultan of Mysore were at least as well equipped, if not better, than the English. They were, however, neither as disciplined, nor as dogged, nor as well led (some of their officers were French), and the sultan was forced to negotiate a peace.

Cornwallis might not have looked like a soldier to some—he looked more like a portly, grey-haired grandfather—but he certainly conducted himself like one, oblivious to the ping of musket rounds, manifestly competent in his duties, and magnanimous in donating prize money to his troops. He returned to England in 1793, where he was appointed to relatively trifling diplomatic and military duties, including acting as master general of ordnance. In 1798, however, he was sent to do for Ireland what he had done for India. He again combined a political and military role as lord-lieutenant and commander in chief. He put down Irish rebels, staved off a French landing, and in the end, as he noted, found himself the surprised recipient of popular acclaim in Dublin—"Not an unpleasant circumstance to a man who had governed a country above two years by martial law."[12] With Lord Castlereagh he had pushed for and won the Act of Union between Ireland and Great Britain. Union, he thought, was the only hope to bring good government to the Emerald Isle, but union should be concurrent with Catholic emancipation: "Until the Catholics are admitted into a general participation of rights, there will be no peace or safety in Ireland."[13] When the king refused to emancipate the Catholics, Cornwallis resigned.

He returned to diplomatic service, negotiating the peace of Amiens, a brief respite in the Napoleonic wars, and then was reappointed governor-general of India, a post he did not want, and in which he died on 5 October 1805. Like the true servant of empire that he was, he was buried in India (in a grave still maintained by the Indian government) and a monument to his memory was erected in St. Paul's. As one of his biographers has written, "For sound advice and difficult duties, Cornwallis was the man to be approached. He was always ready to do his duty.... If a single man had to be chosen to illustrate the noblest features of the aristocratic ideal in the eighteenth century it might be Cornwallis. He was a true patriot."[14]

Part III

IRELAND AND
JOHN BULL'S OTHER
EUROPEAN ISLANDS

Chapter 7

THE SHAMROCK
AND
THE ROCK

"Ireland, the under-developed country of no importance
except when rebelling or invaded...."

—*Norman Lloyd Williams*, Sir Walter Raleigh[1]

The central fact of Irish history is that Ireland is an appendage of England. Granted, the Irish have not seen it as such—and in their exhaustion with the place, the English have long since surrendered that view. But if England is the cockpit of Great Britain, Ireland is the Lesser Britain (which is how it was known to the ancients) of the British Isles. For most of its history, England regarded Ireland as an uncongenial, barbarous, and mystifying colony—but one necessary for the defense of the realm, because it was an all too convenient jumping-off point for possible invasions. At first the worry was the Spanish or the French or the Jacobites, but the threat continued through both twentieth-century World Wars, in which Ireland played less than stellar roles. In World War I, German U-boats tried to smuggle arms to the Irish rebels; and the farcical, if it hadn't been so tragic, Easter Rebellion of 1916 came while Britain was being bled white in the trenches defending the rule of law in Europe. In World War II, while Great Britain stood at one point alone against the forces of Hitler, Stalin, Mussolini, the Japanese militarists, Vichy France, and their allies, the

Did you know?

♛ The original Norman English invasion of Ireland was approved by the pope—and came at the request of an Irish king

♛ In the nineteenth century, the Irish always formed a disproportionately large percentage of the British army—both officers and enlisted ranks

♛ The idea of an Irish republic came from England

bravely neutral Irish Republic dallied with Adolf Hitler, the Irish Republican Army openly allied itself with the Nazis, and it took all the forbearance British Prime Minister Winston Churchill could muster not to act on rumors that German U-boats were using western Irish ports.

There is much to admire about the Irish, but it is also easy to see why the English, when not regarding them as comical, tended to see them as shiftless, ignorant, stubborn, contumacious, and cruel—though the cruelty cut both ways, for the Protestant Ascendancy in Ireland found it simple to justify extraordinary measures against such a race as the Irish, and the Protestant Orangemen of Ulster, as much as the seething nationalists of the South, gave support to Rudyard Kipling's observation that Ireland's second religion was hate.[2]

The Arrival of the English

It is important to note that the centuries-long conflict between England and Ireland is not primarily a religious one. Religion is merely another shillelagh with which the two sides bash each other. The Catholic faith came to Ireland through an Englishman, St. Patrick, whom Irish raiders kidnapped and enslaved, though Patrick refused to hold that against them. He made the Irish Christians and toppled the old Druidic religion.[3]

When the Englishmen came again, it was in 1169, and many of them spoke French, because they were Normans. The invasion, under the authority of King Henry II of England, was actually made at the request of the ousted Irish king of Leinster, Dermot MacMurrough (Ireland had a plethora of petty kings who were occasionally united under a High King of Ireland). MacMurrough pledged fealty to Henry and so was allowed to recruit an army in Wales. Included in that army was his future son-in-law, the Earl of Pembroke, Richard de Clare, known as Strongbow—one of the first English villains in Irish history, because he had the temerity to marry

MacMurrough's daughter and thus bind Ireland and England together. (The English have always regarded Irish colleens as attractive—a tribute few Irishmen appreciate.) MacMurrough is regarded as a traitor; one moniker for him is "Dermot of the foreigners."

MacMurrough's campaign to recapture his kingdom—and make himself High King of Ireland—began well but was soon stymied by the armies of his rivals. He asked Strongbow to land with reinforcements, which meant not only Welshmen but Normans. The pope had a stake in the campaign as well, because a Norman invasion of Ireland meant a more Catholic Ireland. Irish law—the Brehon laws, adjudicated by a juridical class of *brehons*— remained pagan and countenanced things like divorce and bigamy; more-over, the Church in Ireland was conformed to Rome only insofar as it was conformed to Canterbury (some Irish bishops made a point of being conse-crated there) because the Irish Church was corrupted by secular appoint-ments and clerical indiscipline while the English Church was seen as orthodox.

Though his men were few, Strongbow arrived and conquered Wexford, Waterford, and Dublin. In 1171, Henry II came with an army to check on things for himself. The Irish kings accepted him as their overlord, "the Lord of Ireland," as did the bishops, and the pope confirmed the sanctity of the English invasion. So if the English are interlopers in Ireland, they are inter-lopers whose interloping began in the twelfth century—a fairly long his-torical stake—and with the blessing of the pope.

Despite the arrival of Norman law and order, Ireland remained a strife-torn place—in part because the Normans conformed themselves to many Irish customs and habits. Ireland had never been united, and it remained a land of disparate parts, many of which, in the north and west, remained untouched by the Normans. Subsequent Norman invasions were the doing of enterprising knights who created their own feudal estates that were only later recognized by the Crown.

The Celts Didn't Have a Word for It

In 1921, during negotiations over the creation of an Irish republic, British Prime Minister David Lloyd George (a Welshman who could speak Welsh) reminded the Irish nationalist and Gaelic extremist Eamon de Valera that the Celts had never had a word for "a republic"—it was an idea given to them by the English.

The conversation is quoted in Thomas Jones, *Whitehall Diary: Ireland, 1918–1925*, ed. Keith Middlemas (Oxford University Press, 1971), p. 89

Still, Ireland clearly benefited from Catholic Norman law, where it was imposed, dismantling the vagaries of paganism. The Irish gained other benefits too from their colonization by the English. A year after the Magna Carta was promulgated in England (1215) it became law in Ireland. Before the end of the thirteenth century (1297), Ireland had a parliament of its own.

Going Native

The triumph of English language and law, however, proved deceptive, for not only did the Irish find themselves a part of a greater Gaelic revival, of which the "gallowglasses"—Scotch mercenaries from the Highlands and western isles of Scotland, often the descendants of Vikings—were the sword arm, but the old Norman feudal lords swiftly became culturally Irish themselves. Laws might be passed prohibiting intermarriage, or requiring the supremacy of English language and law, but in truth, the sod of Ireland was fast slipping from a distracted England. Even in "the Pale," the Dublin-centered seat of English authority in Ireland, Irish customs and language were repealing those of England, in practice, if not in juridical rulebooks. The English made feeble attempts to rid the Irish of their recidivist barbarisms, but it was not until the arrival of the Tudor Dynasty (1485–1603) that the Crown began to take things in hand.

Under Henry VII (who reigned from 1485 to 1509), "Poynings' Law" was promulgated, making all acts of the Irish parliament subordinate and subject to the approval of the English parliament; and this time, English supremacy was meant to stick. More serious, though, was King Henry VIII's declaration of himself as head of the Church in England. When this led to an Irish rebellion by the Fitzgeralds, to whom successive English monarchs had delegated authority in Ireland, it was crushed. Henry VIII declared himself not only head of the English Church but King of Ireland and pressed all Irish kings to submit. In exchange, he would give them English titles and full English rights. The Irish assented, but in an Irish way: they took what benefited them from the law and planned to ignore it whenever it collided with convenience.

Religion was now injected into the continual strife of Ireland. In English eyes there were at least three categories of Irishmen: the wild Irish beyond the Pale, the Old English (the Anglo-Norman families who remained loyal to the Catholic Church), and the small section of Protestant English settlers within the Pale. The Irish (including the Anglo-Irish) were proud of their fighting prowess and their ruthlessness against their enemies—and fighting they always were, whether in rebellion against the Crown or in affrays between themselves. There was always some Irishman raising a standard against another, and in their apparent bloodlust the Irish had not advanced in civilization and humanity, in English eyes, since the days of MacMurrough, who had once, in front of his English allies, seized the severed head of one of his hated enemies and gnawed on it, offending the Englishmen's innate sense of moderation—decapitation, okay; gnawing, no way.

Men without Shoes

An example of Gaelic barbarism, of a minor sort, can be seen in a painting (made in 1594) of Sir Thomas Lee, an English officer in Ireland. His upper half is dressed in English finery, but his bottom half is barelegged and barefooted in the appalling Irish style—highlighting the unsettling ways Englishmen could go native, and reminding all men to this day that legs belong in pants and feet belong in shoes.

Ireland: England's Tijuana

Yes, that's more or less how the English saw it. It was cheap to live there, colorful in a way, tantalizingly foreign, but also more than a little sketchy and dangerous—and cheap only if you discounted the risk of crime and mob violence, for the native Irish were not just poor but shockingly lacking in moral scruple. In the words of Sir Henry Sidney, writing at the time of Queen Elizabeth I, "Surely there was never a people that lived in more misery than...[the Irish] do, nor as it should seem of worse minds, for matrimony among them is no more regarded in effect than conjunction between unreasonable beasts. Perjury, robbery and murder counted allowable. Finally, I cannot find that they make any conscience of sin...."[4]

Queen Elizabeth I, wearied by the constant stream of murderous news from Ireland, endorsed this view and discovered in Irish barbarism a scope for English duty: it was necessary "to bring that rude and barbarous nation to civility."[5] Indeed the common view among English observers was that there was no more barbarous land on the planet. If Ireland were ever to be made habitable for civilized people, harsh measures were necessary—and at length, one part of the answer seemed to be the establishment of "plantations," the opening up of Ireland with land grants for English settlers. But the settlements remained precarious. Hugh O'Neill, the Earl of Tyrone, and Rory O'Donnell, the Earl of Tyrconnell, led a fierce rebellion against England, burning out the colonists wherever they could find them. The rebellion lasted nine years (1594–1603)—nine years of fire and bloodshed, disease and famine, killing

The Fighting Irish

"I am with all the wild Irish at the same point as I am with bears and mad dogs when I see them fight: so that they fight earnestly indeed, and tug each other well, I care not who have the worst."

Sir Nicholas Arnold, Lord Chief Justice of Ireland, 1565, quoted in Paul Johnson, *Ireland: A Concise History from the Twelfth Century to the Present Day* (Academy Chicago Publishers, 1996), p. 32

tens of thousands; and it raised for England the haunting specter of Ireland as a seat not only of rebellion but of foreign invasion: an army of four thousand Spaniards had arrived in Ireland to aid the rebels. After enormous hard slogging the English defeated the Irish rebels and granted them lenient terms—they were allowed to keep their lands, if not their private armies and political authority. But after four years of chafing under the restraints of peace and the recusant fines levied on Catholics by the Protestant authorities, "The O'Neill" and O'Donnell fled the country in "the flight of the Earls" (1607), apparently hoping to raise a foreign army to invade Ireland and drive out the English. Instead, their departure allowed King James I of England (who reigned from 1603 to 1625) to declare their lands forfeit. Ulster, which had been one of the most "Irish" parts of Ireland, was now to become an enormous plantation for English and Scotch settlers—complicating the religious differences in Ireland even further.

For the Irish, Catholicism was a matter of principle and identity, even if they might be poorly catechized. For the English, Anglicanism was a matter of state policy; it was the only way to make sure that conflict was avoided and everyone agreed on the same faith (except it wasn't and they didn't) and to guarantee freedom of religion (except for Catholics and some Protestant dissenters). The lowland Scotch Presbyterians were different altogether. They were certain, as Calvinists, that they were saved, just as they were convinced that everyone else was predestined to hell. This could make them uncomfortable neighbors, especially as England fell into a civil war between Anglican Royalists and Puritan Roundheads, with the Catholic Irish becoming allies of the former and targets of the latter.

War, War, and More War

The Irish rose in rebellion—a phrase that could be inserted virtually anywhere in Irish history—under the leadership of Sir Phelim O'Neill and

Rory O'More as putative allies of the king against parliament in 1641, but paradoxically they also pursued the objective of driving the Protestants from Ireland. It is true that the Stuart kings leaned in a Catholic direction (Charles I's wife was Catholic, Charles II was a crypto Catholic, and James II publicly embraced the faith), which made the Stuarts particularly attractive to the "Old English" in Ireland, but it is equally clear that the rebels and the king had separate goals that only sometimes worked in concert. There was no way, for instance, that Charles I could condone or countenance the massacre of the Protestant men, women, and children of Portadown (and elsewhere) by the rebels; and loyalist armies took to the field to fight the Irish, while a Scotch army arrived in Ulster to fight the Presbyterian corner against the royalist Anglicans.

After the execution of Charles I in 1649, Oliver Cromwell, leader of the parliamentary armies, put Ireland in his sites; his enemy was the whole bloody island. Catholics were the enemy, loyalists were the enemy—and indeed they had been one and the same after the Catholic Confederacy (led by Anglo-Irishmen) had made a formal alliance with the Royalists. The whole island needed to be subdued and made Puritan. The result was slaughter on a massive scale: Ireland lost at least a quarter of its population (estimates go as high as half). Some fell by the sword, others fled to find sanctuary. If the rising of 1641 had given Protestants their martyrs, Cromwell's murderous troops gave the Catholics plenty in return—and in Ireland, neither Catholic nor Presbyterian was inclined to forget. Cromwell judged the massacre of Catholic men, women, children, babies, priests, and monks at the town of Drogheda to be God's judgment; other Irish towns rapidly capitulated to avoid the same fate. With Ireland firmly in his hand, Cromwell multiplied the Ulster plantations, exiling Catholic landholders to the west, to the rocky lands of Connacht and County Clare, and waged an unceasing war of persecution against the Catholic Church.

Good Time Charlie and the Siege of Derry

With the restoration of the monarchy under the charming and broadminded Charles II, hope returned to Ireland, but Protestant extremism at home limited Charles's options. While James II, his brother, was much more active in expanding toleration—and even preference—to Catholics, he was a far less savvy politician; James lost his throne in a Protestant coup d'etat mounted by his son-in-law William of Orange. James II then went to Ireland, raised an army, and marched on Londonderry in an event that became an epic in Irish history. The city fathers felt they had no alternative but to let James's army in, until thirteen young apprentices slammed the gates shut ("the Apprentice Boys" are now a Protestant fraternal society famous for its marches in Northern Ireland); the Protestant commander Robert Lundy thought resistance futile and snuck out of the city to escape ("Lundy" is now a term of abuse in Protestant Northern Ireland); and when the besieging Jacobites demanded the city's capitulation, the Protestant answer came back then (and now), "No surrender." Of course another great Protestant rallying cry was "no popery"—though the pope, and the Catholic Habsburgs of Austria, supported Britain's Protestant King William III against the Catholic James II, because the Habsburgs and the Vatican were at odds with James's ally France.

The "Siege of Derry," begun on 18 April 1689, was broken by English ships on 28 July. James's other crippling defeat came at the hands of William himself, who led his army to defeat the Jacobites at the Battle of the Boyne on 12 July 1689. After two more years of hard fighting, the Jacobites were finished,[6] and with defeat came swingeingly punitive anti-Catholic laws—enacted, it is important to note, by the parliament in Dublin, not London. All this was the result of the Irish fighting on behalf of the former king of England. Catholic Irishmen could no longer vote, hold office, bear arms, or even transmit property to their heirs (instead they became tenant farmers for Protestant landlords). From the rebellion of 1641 the proportion of Irish land held by Irish Catholics fell from far more than half (about 59 percent) to an estimated 14 percent in 1695 to only 7 percent in 1714.[7]

Yet eighteenth-century Ireland seemed a country finally beginning to emerge into prosperity. The English landowners built lavish country houses. Dublin was a major and bustling European city. Irish writers (Jonathan Swift, Oliver Goldsmith, Richard Brinley Sheridan) and politicians (Edmund Burke, Lord Castlereagh, the Duke of Wellington) were of the highest caliber. In some ways, the Protestant Ascendancy of Ireland should not have been surprising. As Lord Macaulay noted of Ireland's history,

> The English settlers seem to have been, in knowledge, energy, and perseverance, rather above than below the average level of the population of the mother country. The aboriginal [Irish] peasantry, on the contrary, were in almost a savage state. They never worked till they felt the sting of hunger. They were content with accommodation inferior to that which, in happier countries, was provided for domestic cattle. Already the potato, a root which can be cultivated with scarcely any art, industry, or capital, and which cannot be long stored, had become the food of the common people. From a people so fed diligence and forethought were not to be expected. Even within a few miles of Dublin, the traveller, on a soil the richest and most verdant in the world, saw with disgust the miserable burrows of which squalid and half naked barbarians stared wildly as he passed.[8]

"To this day," Macaulay noted, "a more than Spartan haughtiness alloys the many noble qualities which characterize the children of the victors, while a Helot feeling, compounded of awe and hatred, is but too often discernible in the children of the vanquished."[9] Such was the state of Ireland, though of course on the surface normal life carried on, and relations between the Spartan English and the Helot Irish could be cordial enough, though the imperial English—who would govern races as diverse as the Maoris and the Zulus, the Pathans and the Burmese—would always remain fundamentally baffled by the Irish in a way they were not by more exotic peoples.

Reform and Famine

The Anglo-Irish ruling class was so successful that it soon began bruiting about the idea that it deserved more of a hand in governing, even perhaps an independent Ireland. Indeed, simultaneous with the American War for Independence, the Protestant Irishman Henry Grattan led a movement for free trade and an independent Irish legislature. It is, perhaps, an irony of Irish history that many of the leading calls for Irish independence in the eighteenth and nineteenth century came from Protestants, and that in the twentieth century many of the agitators for Irish independence were half English or at least only half Irish (including Eamon de Valera, the dominant political figure of the Irish republic who was born in New York City to an Irish mother and a Spanish-Cuban father).

Indeed, the hierarchy of the Catholic Church in Ireland (if not all its priests) was almost always on the side of maintaining the Union with England after Parliament began repealing the penal laws against Catholics in the late eighteenth century. As a supranational institution, the Church distrusts nationalism, even Irish nationalism; and the Church condemns secret societies, especially those prone to violence, which meant that, for instance, in the twentieth century, members of the Irish Republican Army were held to be excommunicated. Moreover, since its foundation in 1795, the British government had provided a generous subsidy to the Catholic seminary at Maynooth, and Catholic seminarians took an oath of loyalty to the British Crown. And it did not go unnoticed that so many independence movements were led by Protestants, which made the Catholic hierarchy suspect some devilish heresy was afoot.

The evocatively named Wolfe Tone gave Catholic bishops plenty of reason for pause, despite his pleas for Catholic toleration. He was an Enlightenment radical, which meant, among other things, that he was a Protestant who had imbibed heavy doses of agnosticism; one of his allies, and rivals, was the equally wonderfully named Napper Tandy. Tone led the Presbyterian-dominated United Irishmen, meant to unite Protestant Dissenters and Irish Catholics against England. The French Revolution made Francophiles of Tone and Tandy, and Tone was actually commissioned in Napoleon's army. He returned to Ireland to lead an uprising with the help of the French in 1796 and again in 1798. Both were miserable failures, and after the latter, he was captured. Threatened with hanging, he died of self-inflicted wounds in prison.

These rebellions—however easily stifled—were a reminder that Ireland remained a possible springboard for an invasion of Britain, then embroiled in its long war against Napoleonic France. The logical solution was to hug Ireland closer to the bosom of Britannia, and in 1800, Ireland was integrated fully into the Parliament at Westminster with the Act of Union (effective 1 January 1801). The Union with Scotland (1707) had been a success, and it was hoped union with Ireland would end that unhappy country's endless turmoil. Of course it did not. At first Catholics greeted the Union as they had greeted the restoration of the Stuart monarchy—with hope, for the Irish people, despite their contumacious cussedness, are naturally conservative, and peace and prosperity, such as England might offer, would have been a refreshing change. But they soon found themselves swept up by a charismatic leader who spoke for Catholic emancipation and whose goal was dissolving the Union while keeping Ireland under the Crown in a sort of self-governing commonwealth status. This was the patrician Catholic Daniel O'Connell (1775–1847), a man naturally conservative by his aristocratic birth and political inclination, who became a champion of Irish reform. It was he who created the populist support within Ireland that led the Tory government of the Duke of Wellington (Anglo-Irish himself) to grant toleration to Irish Catholics in the Catholic Relief Act of 1829, allowing them to vote and serve in Parliament.

Though Ireland remained ever turbulent, there were certainly hopeful signs in the prosperity of Ulster and the removal of the penal acts against Catholics. But all this was put at hazard by the Irish potato famine (1845–49), which Irish farmers could not overcome and which British relief efforts could not alleviate to anywhere near a sufficient degree. It is clear, despite pernicious mythmaking to the contrary (mythmaking enshrined in law by the state of New York, which requires that the Irish potato famine be—outrageously—compared to "genocide, slavery, and the Holocaust"[10]) that there was no intentional effort to starve the Irish or inflict genocide on Ireland. There was, however, a misguided sense among some members of the British government that relief efforts that violated laissez-faire would only make matters worse, and it was hard for the British government to comprehend the full extent of the calamity.

The government of Sir Robert Peel responded to the potato blight with the lifting of the Corn Laws—which protected British farmers from free trade and thus kept prices artificially high. Peel's assumption was that free trade would help lift the Irish economy and provide jobs for the poor tenant farmers squeezed unto death between the demands of their landlords and the failed crop. When famine propagandists talk about starving Ireland exporting food to England, this is what they mean—Ireland did indeed export food to Britain, but the money earned from the exports was supposed to create Irish jobs. However misguided the policy, it was meant to help the Irish, and it was so unpopular with the agricultural lobby in England that the Peel government fell.

Along with the Corn Laws (1846), the Navigation Laws were repealed (1847), allowing relief supplies from other nations to go directly to Ireland rather than first being transferred to British ships. In addition, the Peel government imported corn from America specifically to feed the hungry Irish—though the Irish didn't know what to do with the corn, as it required a relatively complicated process to make it edible—and set up a vast, if mismanaged, system of poor relief, which the successor government of Lord John Russell developed into subsidized government works projects that failed to achieve their aims.

The botched response to the famine, when Britain prided itself on bringing good government to Ireland, could only engender bitterness in the Irish who suffered horribly—not only from famine, but from a concurrent outbreak of cholera. There were numerous private charities—endorsed by the Queen—devoted to famine relief, but even these caused resentment; starving Catholic Irishmen did not like having Protestant pamphlets foisted on them with their soup.

There is no telling with certainty how many died, though we know that poorer areas suffered most, and that Ireland's population fell by about two million people between 1845 and 1851. More than half this number was made up of emigrants, many of whom left for America—an exodus that would continue in startling numbers over the next half century. In 1846, Ireland's population was about eight million people. In 1901, it was about four million. There were some, it is true, who took a Malthusian view—that the famine was the inevitable result of Irish overpopulation, or the inevitable result of a hapless, improvident people. But there were many others in England who considered the Irish famine a problem that should have been dealt with by the wealthy Anglo-Irish landowners; to their mind it was the Protestant Ascendancy's failure, not England's. It was nevertheless a catastrophe for the Irish, and a direct repudiation of the advertised benefits of British rule.

Independence: Gladstone and Parnell; Lloyd George and De Valera

The former Tory turned Liberal, William Ewart Gladstone (prime minister 1868–74, 1880–85, 1886, 1892–94) said before his first premiership, "My mission is to pacify Ireland."[11] That, needless to say, appeared a Herculean task, but the great tree feller and prostitute reformer took it upon himself with the vigor of a true Victorian. In 1868 he repealed the article of the Act of Union that made the Anglican Church of Ireland the established church over a largely Catholic people, and he made some attempts at supporting Irish tenant farmers. But the real driver of events in Ireland was the Protestant Irishman Charles Stewart Parnell (1846–91), whose Protestant Ascendancy ancestors had opposed the Union. Parnell led Ireland's Home Rule party and was quite content to make common cause with the murderous Fenians, precursors (along with the Irish Republican Brotherhood) of

Orange and Green Soldiers of the Queen

During the Victorian heyday of the British Empire, the thin red line of the British Army was well colored with Shamrock green and Ulster orange. In 1831, about 42 percent of the British army was Irish (Irish soldiers actually outnumbered English ones), and up until 1910, the Irish were always disproportionately represented in the Army, most of the enlisted men being Catholic and the overwhelming majority of officers being Protestant. Even in 1900, when Ireland had dramatically decreased as a proportion of the United Kingdom's population (to about ten percent), a third of the army's officers were Irish.

See Ruth Dudley Edwards and Bridget Hourican, *An Atlas of Irish History* (Routledge, 1995), pp. 141–42.

the Irish Republican Army. He was, however, disgraced by an adulterous affair. His own party divided over the scandal, just as Gladstone's Liberal Party divided over home rule, and Parnell's efforts for an independent Ireland collapsed. He remains a tragic hero to some Irish nationalists (but not the Catholic Church), and also something of a political enigma (not unusual in Ireland): a radical who considered his natural allies to be the Conservatives.

"Ulster Will Fight; Ulster Will Be Right!"

In Presbyterian Ulster, English talk of Irish home rule was seen as treason, consigning the province to the Catholic South. Lord Randolph Churchill, Winston Churchill's father, taught the Tories "to play the Orange Card" against home rule, to stand fast for the Union, and to rouse the crowds with the threat that, if home rule came to Ireland, "Ulster will fight; Ulster will be right"[12]—and it very nearly happened. Dependent on Irish votes in Parliament, the Liberals passed a Home Rule bill in 1914. But the Ulstermen, led by the distinguished barrister and Member of Parliament Sir Edward Carson, had already raised an Ulster Volunteer Force of more than one hundred thousand men in 1912, and Irish-born or Ulster-sympathizing officers in the British army were preparing to defend Ulster against its absorption into an Irish parliament (where it was doomed to permanent minority status). Gun-running to both the Ulster and the nationalist Irish Volunteers proceeded apace. Ireland came very close not only to civil war between North and South but a war that would have divided the British army between Ulster loyalist officers and those willing to coerce Northern Ireland. (As First Lord of the Admiralty, Winston Churchill was prepared to use the Royal Navy to enforce home rule.)

It is somehow fitting that this pending catastrophe in Ireland was averted by the holocaust of the First World War, which deferred the enactment of home rule and diverted the belligerent energies of the Ulster Volunteer Force and most of the Irish Volunteers (save those in the nationalist Irish Brotherhood) to fighting against the aggressive designs of the Central Powers that put the rights of small countries like Belgium at forfeit. The Irish Volunteers were treated to a speech by the Irish member of Parliament, John Redmond, who was a truly remarkable man. From a distinguished Irish family, of mixed Protestant and Catholic heritage (he was himself a Jesuit-educated Catholic), Redmond was a moderate nationalist and advocate for home rule, but also a liberal imperialist who, in his own words, thought that Ireland's voice should be heard in "the councils of an empire which the genius and valour of her sons have done so much to build up and of which she is to remain."[13] He admonished the Irish Volunteers headed to the front to "account yourselves as men, not only in Ireland itself, but wherever the firing line extends, in defense of right, of freedom, and of religion," which he believed were truly at stake in the Great War in which Ireland was duty-bound to take part.[14] Redmond's goal was to lead the home rule cause to "that brighter day when the grant of full self-government would reveal to Britain the open secret of making Ireland her friend and helpmate, the brightest jewel in her crown of Empire."[15] Such an outcome was devoutly to be wished—and he thought the shared sacrifices of the First World War would help ensure its outcome, as Irishmen, singing "It's a Long Way to Tipperary" boarded the troopships—but the Easter Rising of 1916 put paid to that.

Central as it is to the Irish Republican myth, the rising was a squalid affair led by a small, secretive segment of the nationalist movement. It was despicable in its betrayal of the 1914 Home Rule agreement (which was to go into effect after the war); it was treason (including against the nearly one hundred thousand Irish Catholics fighting the real war in France); and it was an incompetent and miserable failure (its German arms shipments were intercepted by the Royal Navy, the Irish people were resolutely opposed to the gunmen, and the number of active Irish rebels was fewer than a thousand). The Easter Rising set the tone for Irish misery for the next half dozen years as Ireland was held hostage to the politics of the gun, and to reprisals.

The reprisals began with the imposition of courts-martial, which resulted in the execution of sixteen of the traitors, making martyrs of them and undermining the loyalist sympathies of most Irishmen. This political sin was compounded with the threat of imposing conscription on Ireland—not in itself an unjust thing (it was already the law in Britain) but a political line in the sand that it had been presumed the Parliament in Westminster would not cross. In any event, conscription was never enforced on Ireland; the war ended and so, alas, did the dominant position of John Redmond's moderate-nationalist Irish Party. Redmond died in 1918 knowing that the radicals of Sinn Fein were going to seize and ruin his life's work.

The Gunman's Republic[16]

While Sinn Fein candidates won the clear majority of Irish seats in the December 1918 elections, they refused to sit at Westminster and instead, as a show of independence, created their own Dublin-based Parliament, the Dail Eireann, in January 1919. The Dail soon went into hiding, and the Irish Republican Army, led by the boisterous, charming thug Michael Collins, became its militant wing. The IRA fought the British Army, the Royal Irish Constabulary, and the Constabulary's hastily assembled supporting units of discharged British servicemen, the soon to be notorious Black and Tans and Auxiliaries, judged by the IRA to be "super fighters and all but invincible."[17] It is important to remember that throughout the undeclared, small-scale Anglo-Irish War (1919–21) most of Ireland remained at peace, the violence was isolated, and given the hecatombs of the First World War and the cost of other post-war police actions around the globe the death toll was small. It was nevertheless disconcerting, to say the least, to have Dublin patrolled by military units in armored cars, for ordinary citizens to be subjected to searches, for the IRA to punish or kill "collaborators," for a regular pattern to be established of vicious murder and assassination, arson and looting, too often followed by irresponsi-ble reprisals (frequently by the Black and Tans). If the purpose was to drive Britain from Southern Ireland, the IRA succeeded—not by defeating the British militarily but by making them heartily sick of the place, which seemed to make a ghastly mockery of everything Brit-ain thought it stood for: compromise, toler-ance, and fair play. Instead, however small their numbers, the IRA had made Ireland the gunman's republic—and did so to its own cost.

IRA Unity

"Irish republicanism is easily the stupidest political movement in Europe. The claim of Irish republicanism is that it unites Catholic, Protestant and dissenter under the common title Irishman. This is mountebank bluster. In fact, Irish republicanism usually unites peo-ple under the common title, corpse."

Kevin Myers, one of Ireland's best reporters, in "Irishmen of Myth," *The Spectator*, 8 May 2010, p. 38

In 1921, a treaty was reached between the British government and the representatives of Sinn Fein led by Arthur Griffith, an Irish nationalist and monarchist (who, earlier, had rather admired the czar and the kaiser), and Michael Collins. The treaty provided for the partition of Northern Ireland and an Irish Free State within the British Commonwealth owing allegiance to the Crown. The Irish people applauded, but many of their nationalist representatives stubbornly did not—the Dail narrowly approving the treaty in 1922, and the Irish people increasing that treaty-supporting majority in elections that summer. The legacy of the gunman's republic, however, was more violence—an Irish civil war between the treaty's supporters and detractors. Among the dead was Michael Collins, assassinated, as he believed he would be, by nationalists more extreme than himself in 1922. The government of the Irish Free State sent to the firing squad far more Irish nationalist rebels than the British ever did (among those executed was the

English soldier, sailor, airman, novelist, and Irish nationalist Erskine Childers, whose son became the fourth president of the Irish Republic). By 1923, the authorities of the Irish Free State had imprisoned more than eleven thousand IRA supporters. Proscribed and hunted by the Irish Free State, the IRA lost the war in the South, leaving it with no better cause than terrorism in Northern Ireland and against the British government that honored Ulster's desire to remain within the United Kingdom.

Irish Peace at Last

Britain calmly accepted the new constitution Eamon de Valera wrote in the 1930s. The British did not much care how the Irish governed themselves as long as they remained in the Empire (Ireland did not become a full republic and leave the commonwealth until 1949); and in fact the Irish governed themselves much along British parliamentary lines, though Ireland's professed neutrality in the Second World War was an obvious source of bitterness made to look all the worse by the tremendous loyalty of the farmers, industrial workers, and soldiers of Ulster. Belfast shipbuilders launched more than 170 ships during World War II, and 120,000 American troops trained in Northern Ireland.

After the war, Northern Ireland was relatively prosperous—so much so that when the IRA tried to ignite a sectarian border war (1956–62) they found themselves utterly unsupported by Catholics in the province. Though discriminated against to an appalling degree by the Protestant majority, Catholics remained loyal to the Crown and were content

How the Ulstermen Won D-Day

"Without Northern Ireland, I do not see how the American forces could have been concentrated to begin the invasion of Europe."

General Dwight David Eisenhower, quoted in John Ranelagh, *Ireland: An Illustrated History* (Oxford University Press, 1981), p. 257

with a standard of living better than they could expect in the Irish Republic. But even Northern Ireland was not immune from the turbulent mood of the late 1960s that drove Republicans, wrapping themselves in the civil rights movement, and Unionists, reacting virulently against even modest reforms, to political extremes. British troops were dispatched to Northern Ireland to protect the Catholic minority in 1969—only to see their peacekeeping seized upon as an excuse for violence by the militant Provisional IRA, which worked diligently at a campaign of terrorism, including bloody attacks on the British mainland (one such attack being an attempt to assassinate Prime Minister Margaret Thatcher). The IRA hoped to deepen the sectarian divide and drive the English out of Northern Ireland. But given that the Parliament at Westminster was actually a moderating influence on the Ulster Unionists this would have been a Pyrrhic victory. In any event, by the 1970s the Provisional IRA was simply another branch of international terrorism, with arms coming from Libya and support coming from other leftist terrorist groups. The regular IRA, itself now thoroughly Marxist, gave birth to splinter movements, none of which represented traditional Irish Catholics. Indeed, it could be argued that the British government did a better job of that with its Anglo-Irish agreement of 1985 that gave the Irish Republic a consultative role in Northern Irish affairs.

But what really advanced the cause of peace in Northern Ireland were the dramatic 11 September 2001 terrorist attacks on the United States. These convinced the Provisional IRA to more fully cooperate with Anglo-Irish agreements on decommissioning arms, because it seemed unlikely that even the most sentimentally misguided Irish-Americans could any longer in good conscience support the terrorist IRA. In Ireland, it often takes a war to prevent a war—a bellicose attitude that seven centuries of English involvement in the Emerald Isle never managed to erase. The English left Ireland language, laws, and parliamentary government, but did nothing to tame the stubborn pugnacity of Ireland's Celts.

Gibraltar, Malta, Cyprus, and the Ionian Islands

If Southern Ireland is lost, and Northern Ireland is as attractive to most Englishmen as a mother-in-law, there is still Gibraltar, the Rock, seized by the British from Spain in 1704 and officially surrendered to Great Britain by the Treaty of Utrecht in 1713. Gibraltar remains, despite Spanish protests, a British possession—and a durable one that has weathered Spanish attempts at reconquest, the Napoleonic wars, and two World Wars, giving the Royal Navy a base at "the Pillars of Hercules" guarding the Mediterranean. As with the Falklands and Northern Ireland, the people of Gibraltar want no other sovereign than the British Crown; so the British are obliged to hold on—and, the story has it, they will stay for as long as Gibraltar's famous monkeys, the Barbary Macaques, do.

The British took Malta from the French in 1800, during France's Revolutionary wars, and became the defender of the Catholic Church and Catholic Maltese (who asked to be annexed by the British Crown) against French anti-clericals. The British introduced a free press, secret ballots, and a modest dose of democracy. In World War II, Malta heroically endured massive bombing by Nazi Germany; and in 1942, the island was awarded the George Cross (it is now part of the Maltese flag), Britain's highest award for civilian courage—the only time it has been given to an entire country. Malta gained its independence in 1964, the last British forces withdrew in 1979, and though it annoyingly declared itself a "non-aligned nation" the following year, preferring not to choose sides in the Cold War, it remains in the Commonwealth.

Cyprus offers the least happy story, because, as sometimes happened in the Empire, the British were left in the middle between competing forces they could not control. The British inherited Cyprus as a protectorate from the Ottoman Empire in 1878, and then annexed it in 1914 after the Ottomans joined the Axis Powers in World War I. More than three-quarters of Cyprus's people were and are Greek (the minority being Turks), and during the First

World War Britain offered Cyprus to Greece if the Greeks would take a more active role on the side of the Allies, but the Greeks refused. After that Britain's interest in Cyprus was to defend the minority Turks, block political movements of union with Greece, and preserve its military bases on the island (which were particularly important after the British left Egypt in 1956). But it is never a good idea to place oneself between a Greek and a Turk, and after the usual nationalist-terrorist campaign (the nationalist party was fronted by a Greek Orthodox archbishop, Makarios III, bearing a striking, bearded resemblance to Peter Sellers), the British finally came up with a compromise solution that guaranteed the island would neither be partitioned between Greek and Turk nor absorbed by Greece; and both peoples were guaranteed power in the government. The British granted Cyprus independence in 1960, all the wonderful guarantees the British had written into the Cypriot constitution were repealed by the Greek majority, and the country eventually ended up partitioned—with Turkey invading north Cyprus in 1974 and annexing that part of the island. Still, Britain retains its bases in Cyprus, which is the important thing, so that at least a small reservoir of good sense is always available on the island.

As for the Ionian islands, we will save them for later, when we meet an eccentric British general who once held them as his own little dominion.

Chapter 8

SIR WALTER RALEIGH
(1554–1618)

"It is my last mirth in this world. Do not grudge it to me.
When I come to the sad parting you shall see me grave enough."

—Sir Walter Raleigh[1]

Dost Americans think of Sir Walter Raleigh as the founder of the doomed colony of Roanoke, or perhaps as the courtier who lay down his cape for Queen Elizabeth to tread upon, or possibly as the founder of a chain of seafood restaurants, and so might be surprised to find him here, in the section on Ireland—but Raleigh was an Irish land-owner and, the story has it, the man who brought the fabled spud to the Irish masses. He was also by any measure a remarkable man in a time of remark-able men. He was born into a prominent Protestant family of modest means but with numerous connections at court and with relatives involved in soldiering and merchant adventuring. Like a true Elizabethan, Raleigh was both gentleman and brawler, poet and sailor, soldier and queen's favorite.

He grew up in Devon amongst fishermen and farmers, where tales of the sea lit his imagination. In his early teens he could have joined his half-brother Humphrey Gilbert who was fighting for civilization and profit in Ireland, but he chose instead, at the age of fourteen, to join the wars in France, fighting with a detachment of English on the side of the Huguenots.

Did you know?

♛ Raleigh popularized smoking (for which he is much beloved by North Carolina tobacco growers)

♛ He set out twice to find El Dorado

♛ He was executed to appease Spain

France was a sophisticated place and if he was to learn the art of war, better to learn it there than among the kerns of Ireland. What exactly Raleigh did in France, or even how long he was there, is uncertain, though he did return to England a veteran—and by eighteen was off to Oxford and after a few years there moved to London, where he successfully avoided studying law, though registered at the Middle Temple, an Inn of Court that he treated (as many young gentlemen did) as a club.

In his middle twenties, after an aborted voyage to the New World, Raleigh went a-soldiering to Ireland. Humphrey Gilbert had set the tone for fighting in Ireland by lining the pathway to his tent with the severed heads of his enemies. Ireland was that sort of place. Raleigh recognized the especial cruelties of war in Ireland (his cousin was ambushed and murdered in August 1580, shortly after Raleigh landed in Cork), but he also believed that an industrious Englishman could make something out of the Irish bog if he had strength and stamina enough to reduce the bogtrotters.

It was a matter of national security, as well as personal advancement. Ireland was in rebellion (or parts of it were), and aiding the rebels was a small contingent of Spanish and Italian soldiers sent with a papal blessing. Not knowing how to fight in Ireland—the Irish were guerrillas—and not knowing the language, the Italians and the Spanish proved a hapless enemy, built themselves a fort, awaited an English siege, surrendered without much ado, and then were cut down to a man (a few women were hanged, as were some Catholic priests, though they were tortured first). Captain Raleigh was among the officers charged with executing this duty—which was by our lights inexcusable, but customary at the time, though it did spark outrage in Catholic Europe.[2]

Raleigh the swashbuckler was better displayed in another incident of the Irish war. He was crossing a river, pursued by Irish bushwhackers who outnumbered him at least ten or perhaps twenty to one. Raleigh calmly sat his horse in the river, aiding a fallen comrade. Armed only with a pistol and staff, he stared down his Irish pursuers who rode away shouting insults and abuse. Raleigh wrote: "The manner of my own behaviour I leave to the report of others, but the escape was strange to all men."[3]

Raleigh was a clever officer, and not shy about offering advice to his commander or to the queen (through her secretary of state, and spymaster, Sir Francis Walsingham) on how the situation in Ireland could be improved. He left Ireland in December 1851, having gained, with the grudging permission of the Lord Deputy of Ireland (the Puritan Lord Grey), a burnt-down castle (Barry Court). He went to London, to the queen's court, and with the panache for which he was famous—and which made him many enemies— he "had gotten the Queen's ear in a trice, and she began to be taken with his elocution, and loved to hear his reasons to her demands. And the truth is, she took him for a kind of oracle, which nettled them all."[4]

Being a queen's favorite brought with it money (through monopoly licenses), prestige (including an appointment as a member of Parliament from Devon), and special privileges (such as leasing digs at Durham House, a palace confiscated by the Crown from the bishop of Durham). It also gave Raleigh what he really wanted, a royal patent to go discovering in the New World. In 1584, he set out on a scouting expedition that landed in what is now North Carolina and returned to England with two natives to show off, along with glowing reports about the prospects for planting a colony there. In January 1585, Raleigh was knighted, and a coat of arms was awarded to "Walter Raleigh, Knight, Lord and Governor of Virginia."

Virginia's Founder

The establishment of the Virginia colony (most likely named by Raleigh after his patroness, the Virgin Queen) was Raleigh's grand passion. But to his enormous disappointment, the queen would not let him join his next outfitted expedition. So it left without him in 1585, and instead of exploring the New World he was employed as the Lord-Lieutenant of Cornwall and Admiral of the West. He was also, in the English fashion of the time, an investor in piracy, which, as one of his biographers notes, would have made him a wealthy man independent of royal favor;[5] if he had not been a court favorite, Raleigh would almost certainly have been a pirate himself. He was, after all, a handsomer, smoother, lither, more intellectual version of Sir Francis Drake; the sort who would equip his expedition to Virginia with a scientist to make the establishment of his colony a true act of discovery.

The colony began well, with the local Indians gracious because they assumed the Englishmen were gods, or at least higher beings of some sort.[6] The Englishmen, however, were fatally dependent on the generosity of the Indians, whose economy was based on sufficiency rather than surplus and trade. The English had come expecting to find treasure. They were ill-prepared to become farmers in a land that required hard work. The friendly Indians became less so; other, hostile tribes begrudged the arrival of the English interlopers; and inevitably there was fighting, which was bad for the Indians because if the English were poor farmers, they were far better soldiers. The disappointed colonists returned home to England.

Raleigh, however, was determined to make a go of it and recruit a sturdier group of settlers. He wanted to attract families, people who would stick it out and not give up in the absence of easy riches. He also took to smoking tobacco from an Indian pipe, demonstrating one of the comforts, and products, of a Virginia colonial life. The new settlement would be at Roanoke, the settlers of good birth, and two of the settlers were pregnant, one with a child who would be named Virginia Dare, the

The Sixteenth-Century Anti-Smoking Movement

It is said that when one of Raleigh's manservants first saw him smoking, he doused him with water thinking his master had caught fire.

first child of English blood to be born in the Americas. But Roanoke proved no permanent settlement, except in legend.

In the meantime, Raleigh continued to advance at court, becoming Captain of the Guard. He was one of the queen's most intimate friends— which of course made him many enemies. But to the queen he was an exciting conversationalist, a flattering and clever poet (his poems for the most part hold up rather well), and a dynamic man of action (which now included dabbling in espionage against Spain). She was pleased to make use of these capacities. She was also pleased to give him forty-two thousand acres in Munster, Ireland, to found an English colony there. The lands had been confiscated from the Earl of Desmond after his failed rebellion, and the goal was to establish a colony that would bring with it all the benefits of English civilization and guard the island from foreign invasion. As for the native Irish, they were regarded as the American settlers later regarded Indians—the farther away one was from them, the more sympathetic one might be to their plight; the closer one was, the more one took the view that pushing these poor, unproductive, and occasionally savage people out of the way was a simple act of advancing civilization. Though much of the time he managed his Irish estates from afar, Raleigh proved singularly adept at populating his colony with the families, farmers, skilled workers, and tradesmen, not to mention potatoes, the land needed to be profitable and self-sustaining. In Ireland, he struck up a friendship with Edmund Spenser, another expatriate and a fellow poet.

Raleigh's main home remained Durham House, and there he gathered men with active, educated, restless minds, pushing the boundaries of current knowledge, and worrying some with their philosophical speculations—because, having jettisoned Christian orthodoxy of more than a millennium, it was not so large a step to dispense with the new Protestant orthodoxy for free-thinking speculation. Liberals call this process "the

Enlightenment"; enemies of Raleigh called it atheism; and while it is clear that Raleigh travelled some distance in the direction of free-thinking, it is equally clear that he retained his Anglicanism. Anglicanism was a religion of patriotism, and patriot he surely was. Especially as his sovereign robbed one of her bishops (in the Tudor style) to give him a country estate at Sherborne.

And Raleigh did his duty. He supervised the execution of Jesuits (though he was no Jesuit-hunter), and his great privateer warship, the *Ark Raleigh* (given to the queen and rechristened the *Ark Royal* in 1587) led the English fleet against Spain's armada in 1588. Raleigh himself was obliged to organize the defenses of the West Country for an invasion that never took place.

What did take place was a marriage, in secret (most likely in 1592), between Raleigh and Bess Throckmorton, a maid of honor to the queen—a sacrament that, when discovered, had them struck off the roles of palace favorites and even landed Raleigh confinement in the Tower of London and Bess into a sort of house arrest. It was only after Elizabeth gouged the spoils from one of Raleigh's privateering ventures (and left him to take a loss on his investment), that she freed him (and later Bess). Though he had profited from royal favor, he chafed at its constraints. Marriage gave him some independence; so, ironically, did his fall into the queen's displeasure. Raleigh had often proposed overseas adventures that Elizabeth allowed—while keeping him in England. Now, with his mind fastened on the prospect of finding El Dorado, she was disposed to let him go.

In Search of El Dorado

The rumored city of gold was said to be in the jungles of Guiana, and Raleigh was committed to finding it, and carving an English colony off the Spanish Main. Raleigh set sail in 1595. On his way to El Dorado, he liberated

Trinidad's Indians from the hated Spanish (English imperialists have always had a taste for putting themselves at the heads of native armies to overthrow presumed oppressors; in this case, the capture of St. Joseph, Trinidad, also helped secure Raleigh's rear flank before he embarked for Guiana). The Indians celebrated their annexation to the great white queen and remembered Raleigh as a hero for generations after. They also confirmed for Raleigh the existence of El Dorado, and agreed to help him find it. Raleigh and a hundred Englishmen then rowed into the mysterious, humid, mosquito-heavy jungle, the swamp of the Orinoco delta. If one wants to understand the making of the British Empire one can see it here: why should a financially well-established forty-year-old man plunge into trackless jungle in search of gold and patriotic glory? The answer: that is what Englishmen did.

They could also be taken in by the locals. As they plowed the creeper-laden swamps to the mountain country where they presumed El Dorado to be, they were told stories of Amazons and a tribe of people who had their eyes in their shoulders and their mouths in their chests—stories that were met with merry, debunking guffaws when Raleigh dutifully reported them on his return to England. But the Indians apparently believed these stories themselves, for some volunteered to go with Raleigh to fight and take El Dorado. That fight did not happen, of course, but Raleigh did not leave Guiana without making preparations for another expedition. He even left behind a teenage member of his crew, whose task was to learn the Indian language. That, Raleigh thought, would be a great help when next he returned to Guiana—which, in the event, would be twenty years later.

In the meantime, he tried his own hand at singeing the beard of the king of Spain. The Spaniards appeared to be preparing another armada; Raleigh wanted to cut them off with a mighty preemptive strike of cutlass-wielding Englishmen, and his advice was taken. A great fleet was prepared to attack the Spanish port of Cadiz. The Englishmen and their Dutch allies struck in June 1596, with Raleigh one of the fleet commanders. He was brave and intrepid and one of the most inspiring commanders in battle (his first sea action), but he was also badly wounded in the thigh (which gave him a permanent limp). He largely missed out on the month's worth of sacking that followed Cadiz's capture. Where others made a profit, Raleigh, in his own words, gained "naught but poverty and pain."[7]

After a botched attack on the Azores (botched by the Earl of Essex—a longtime rival, later executed for treason; Raleigh was once again gallant in action) he increasingly busied himself, of necessity, with business and parliamentary affairs. Business in Ireland was bad. The ever rebellious natives had despoiled his estates, and he eventually conceded there was little profit to be made in that soggy, contumacious island. In Parliament he proved himself a commonsensical and generous representative of the people's interests. But when his great patroness Elizabeth died Raleigh found himself in disfavor with the new king, James VI of Scotland, now James I of England. Raleigh was accused of involvement in a Catholic plot

Raleigh the Scholar's Martial Judgment

"If therefore it be demanded whether the Macedonian or the Roman were the best warrior, I will answer, the English.... If any man ask, how then it came to pass that the English won so many battles.... I may, with best commendation of modesty, refer him to the French historian; who ... useth these words: 'The English[man] comes with a conquering bravery, as he that was accustomed to gain everywhere, without any stay.'"

Quoted in Norman Lloyd Williams, *Sir Walter Raleigh* (Cassell Biographies, 1988), p. 227

to overthrow the new monarch—a charge ludicrous on its face but potentially deadly in its consequences. Though he defended himself with wonderful rhetorical art, he was found guilty. His death sentence was suspended by the king who kept him imprisoned in the Tower of London for thirteen years.

These were not wasted years. Though life expectancies were shorter, men dreamed big in those days, and Raleigh still dreamt of gold mines in Guiana. His thoughts turned to religion too, and he became something of a moral philosopher, his philosophy deeply grounded in the Bible and a waxing Christian faith. He devoted himself to calculations mathematical and to conducting scientific experiments—chemical and medical mostly—and to writing a massive (and unfinished) history of the world, focused on the history recounted in the Bible, as well as the history of ancient Greece and Rome, and the history of England. The king's wife liked him and was wont to intercede for him, as did the king's son, to whom he became a sort of informal tutor and adviser.

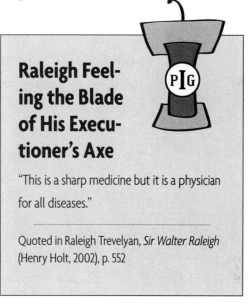

Raleigh Feeling the Blade of His Executioner's Axe

"This is a sharp medicine but it is a physician for all diseases."

Quoted in Raleigh Trevelyan, *Sir Walter Raleigh* (Henry Holt, 2002), p. 552

For thirteen years, Raleigh was considered legally dead (though he was animated enough to father another son with his wife Bess). When he was finally resurrected, in 1616, it was to sail again for Guiana. But El Dorado would be his undoing. The sixty-two-year-old adventurer came down desperately sick, and his scapegrace but brave son Wat died leading his men into battle—a battle against Spaniards that it would have been politic to avoid, for the king of Spain demanded Raleigh's head for the outrage. As Raleigh was an already condemned man, it was an easy diplomatic solution for King James to put Raleigh on trial again, have him condemned, and this time send him to the chopping block. Raleigh showed an impressive, Christian calm before the executioner—so much so that the axeman seemed paralyzed and unable to do his duty. Raleigh called out to him: "Strike, man, strike!" and the blade crashed down once, and then again to finish the job.

It was poor payment for a patriot, and a man of talent. But England has always been careless of these; sending out privately educated gentlemen to tame savage tribes, in which duty, Kipling noted in his poem *The Arithmetic of the Frontier*, "Two thousand pounds of education" could drop "to a ten-rupee jezail" bullet. The British Empire always trusted that more gallant, ingenious men would come springing up—and they did, and they were put to good use.

Chapter Nine

ARTHUR WELLESLEY, THE 1ST DUKE OF WELLINGTON (1769–1852)

"My ugly boy Arthur is food for powder and nothing more."

—the assessment of Arthur Wellesley's loving mother[1]

Arthur Wellesley, the man who would become the "Iron Duke," the 1st Duke of Wellington, was born in Dublin to a family that had come to England with William the Conqueror, and to Ireland with its subsequent Norman conquest. It was a noble family. His father was an earl and a member of the Irish House of Lords, his mother the daughter of a viscount. The Anglo-Irish aristocracy of which he was a part was bred to lead—especially to lead men into battle.

Arthur was sent to Eton, where he remained a rather lonely figure, an outsider in all except bloodlines. His mother then took him to Brussels to learn French. The one, and possibly only, talent he showed at this time was a facility with the violin, something he had inherited from his (now late) father. His eldest brother was in the Irish House of Lords and had a seat in Parliament at Westminster. His second brother was a former naval man elected to the Irish parliament. His younger brother appeared to have brains and piety sufficient for the church, and his youngest brother was aiming for an army career. Only Arthur seemed to be without prospects or ambition. This would change.

Did you know?

- ♛ Wellington, an accomplished musician, burnt his violin to concentrate on being a soldier

- ♛ The "Iron Duke," renowned for his self-control, wept over battlefield losses

- ♛ It was Wellington, the arch-Conservative, who carried Catholic Emancipation

He spent a year at the French Royal Academy of Equitation at Angers, a finishing school for gentlemen and potential officers. When he returned home at the end of 1786, even his mother was impressed at his transformation—the awkward boy was now handsome, sometimes mischievous, sometimes reserved, and still to grow into his full dignity, but to his admirers at least he was a charming young man. The following year, before he turned eighteen, he was commissioned an infantry ensign. Soon promoted to lieutenant and stationed in Ireland, he became a member of the Irish House of Commons at the age of only nineteen.

In 1794, the future Iron Duke finally got what he wanted—overseas service and action. In preparation he had resigned his seat in the House of Commons and given up two of his vices: gambling and the violin (the latter, he said, took up too much of his time and was not a soldierly occupation[2]). He was utterly committed to excelling as an officer of infantry. He came to the Netherlands a twenty-five-year-old lieutenant colonel—his promotions accelerated by purchasing ranks, as was common in the case of young noblemen—eager to fight against the French revolutionaries who had overthrown the *ancien regime* (which he had come to respect from his schooling in France) and who had declared war on England. But the action he saw was cold and wet and taught him little more than that generals seemed to approach battlefields as absentee landlords—no one ever accused Wellesley of that.

He was destined for India—and for a lad who had not been studious, he packed an impressive library of books to take with him, everything from Plutarch to Hume's *History of England* and Adam Smith's *Wealth of Nations*; from books on India and its wars, the East India Company and Egypt (along with grammars to teach himself German, Persian, and Arabic) to a plethora of books on the military arts; from divertimentos like the works of Jonathan Swift, Dr. Johnson's *Dictionary*, and Voltaire to Blackstone's *Commentaries on the Laws of England* and a selection of works from John Locke and

Viscount Bolingbroke. (He packed a voluminous library on his return trip, too, though it leant more heavily on romantic novels.) In a hard-drinking age, British officers in India were known to drink even harder; but Wellesley, while far from abstemious in drink (though he was always a light eater with an intentionally dull palate), did not want to fritter away his time with a bottle; he wanted action, and if he couldn't get it, he studied to make himself a master of Indian affairs: civil, economic, geographical, agricultural, and military. He soon had an ally in his yearning for active service; his brother Richard, the future Marquess Wellesley, was named India's governor-general, and Arthur became, de facto, his chief military adviser. Britain's portion of the Indian subcontinent—which was not yet unified under the British Raj—was now in the hands of the Wellesleys.

In 1798, Arthur helped lead the conquest of Mysore—whose Muslim sultan had been conspiring with the French—and was rewarded by being named governor of the state ("I must say that I was the *fit* person to be selected"[3]). He had no affection for the Indians—he thought them absent of redeeming qualities—but he respected their customs and ruled with a temperate, conciliatory, and responsible hand, smiting warlords and brigands and punishing his own troops when they misbehaved. As he put it, the British army was "placed in this country to protect the inhabitants, not to oppress them."[4] He also put his study of Indian languages to good use. Once in conversation with a rajah, he caught out an Indian interpreter mistranslating what he said.

In 1802, promoted to major-general, he led the campaign to restore the pro-British ruler of the Mahratta confederacy and depose his usurper. With that achieved, in early 1803, it became apparent that two Mahratta chieftains, with French-trained armies, were committed to causing trouble. At the village of Assaye, on 23 September 1803, he met the enemy. Wellesley's force was a mere 7,000; he was outnumbered in infantry by six to one, in artillery by at least five to one, in cavalry twenty to one, his men had marched more than twenty miles, and his guides informed him there were no fords across the river that blocked his way. But Wellesley did his own scouting and found the ford. He brought his men across it and in the subsequent battle was everywhere in the fighting, directing troops into line, ordering a flanking maneuver, having two horses shot beneath him, ever maintaining a cool disposition and a steady nerve. The result was a smashing victory, if at a heavy cost. Wellesley considered it his finest performance in the field; and a bloodier battle for the numbers, he said, he had never seen. There was plenty of courage to admire that day, including that of one British cavalry officer who charged into combat with his horse's reins between his teeth (he had lost an arm in previous combat; his other arm was broken but grimly trying to raise a sabre). Wellesley suffered in excess of 1,500 casualties, more than a third of them Britons, and inflicted nearly four times as many. He pursued the enemy and, with the capture of the Mahratta fortress of Gawilghur, brought the British victory in the Second Mahratta War (1803–05).

Wellington in Love

He had pledged his troth to Kitty Pakenham, thirteen years before, but had been thwarted by her family. Now that he had returned from India a man of some wealth, they were to be married. But when he clapped eyes on Kitty for the first time in more than a decade—at their wedding ceremony in 1806—he turned to his brother Gerald, the priest presiding, and muttered, "She has grown ugly, by Jove!"

This famous quote can be found in any Wellington biography, but Elizabeth Longford's authoritative *Wellington: The Years of the Sword* (Harper and Row, 1969, see p. 122) is best; the second volume is *Wellington: Pillar of State*. Longford married into the Pakenham family; one of her daughters is the historian Lady Antonia Fraser

Napoleon's Nemesis

Wellesley spent eight years in India, and though he returned home with his brother in 1805 a hero and was made a Knight Companion of the Order of the Bath, he was happy to be done with the subcontinent. India could be profitable, but Indian service was not highly regarded at Horse Guards or in Whitehall. The real enemy was Napoleon; the main battle front was Europe, and Wellesley wanted to be a part of it.

There were also political battles to fight. Wellesley, as a member of Parliament, spoke most often on matters where he had some expertise—India, military affairs, the defense of his brother's administration. But his primary goal was to return to command. The British government was looking to attack Napoleon and his allies at any vulnerable point. There was even talk in the cabinet of seizing Mexico from Spain, then France's ally, though Wellesley had to advise against it, as he also advised against supporting revolutions in Latin America, thinking it a terrible responsibility to stir up civil strife: as an arch-Tory nothing was more hateful to him.

Instead of fighting in the land of sombreros, he became chief secretary for Ireland. Though an Anglo-Irishman himself, Wellesley recognized that the mood in Dublin had changed—or at least was far different from how he remembered it. The Irish were almost uniformly oblivious to the benefits of union with Britain and were all for independence, which convinced him of the need for firm government. Independence was impossible; Ireland was already a target for landings by the French; and without a British government in Ireland, the back door to the invasion of England was left wide open. He was equally firm in his belief that sectarian discord had to be undone, that Protestants and Catholics had to be treated as indistinguishable subjects of the Crown.

His political service in Ireland did not keep him from military service abroad. He took part in the hugely successful invasion of Denmark and capture of Copenhagen, which was done to seize the Danish fleet and keep it from Napoleon's hands. More important for the Wellington legend was the popular revolt (1808) against the Napoleonic occupation of Spain, followed by a revolt in Portugal. If India had been Wellesley's training ground, the Peninsular War is where he honed his talents into a form of genius, proving that he understood the political considerations of strategy, the need to make do with the resources available, how to handle allies, the crucial importance of supply, and how to maneuver and arrange his troops (well-positioned, dogged infantry was his specialty, artillery was used to support them, and he was almost contemptuous of cavalry[5]). He told his friend John Wilson Croker that he had seen French troops in action before and they were "capital soldiers." Moreover, "a dozen years of victory under Buonaparte must have made them better still. They have besides, it seems, a new system of strategy which out-manoeuvred and overwhelmed all the armies of Europe." But, he added, "if what I hear of their system of manoeuvre is true, I think it is a false one as against steady troops. I suspect all the continental armies were more than half beaten before the battle was begun—I, at least, will not be frightened beforehand."[6]

Landing in Portugal in 1809, Wellesley delivered a smashing victory at Vimeiro and was halted from charging on to Lisbon by one of his superiors, though Wellesley thought the capital could be had in three days. Another such superior, Hew Dalrymple, then negotiated a French evacuation of such sweeping generosity that it became a matter of parliamentary investigation (which rightfully cleared Wellesley of any blame—he had not been involved in the negotiations and had been taken aback when he read the terms).

The Bare Necessities

"If I had rice and bullocks I had men, and if I had men I knew I could defeat the enemy."

Wellington's recipe for success in the Peninsular War, quoted in Christopher Hibbert, *Wellington: A Personal History* (Addison Wesley, 1997), p. 69

The Fighting Irish, Not the Worshipful Irish

In Portugal, Wellington was insistent that his troops give due respect to the Catholic Church. Officers were to remove their hats in Catholic churches and were to treat the Host as Catholics treat it, as the Body and Blood of Christ, sentries presenting arms when the Host passed by during religious processions. He noted, however, that although "we have whole regiments of Irishmen, and of course Roman Catholics, nobody goes to Mass.... I have not seen one soldier perform any act of religious worship, excepting making the sign of the cross to induce the people of the country to give them wine."

On a different, earlier occasion, he dismissed the idea that Napoleon's mistreatment of the pope would dampen Irish ardor for the French, because, he said, Irish Catholics were entirely "indifferent upon the fate of their religion" and would even admire Napoleon all the more for his cocking a snook at the papacy.

Quoted in Christopher Hibbert, *Wellington: A Personal History* (Addison Wesley, 1997), p. 70, and in Andrew Roberts, *Napoleon and Wellington: The Battle of Waterloo and the Great Commanders Who Fought It* (Simon & Schuster, 2001), p. 31

The political investigation compelled his attendance in London. When he returned to Portugal in 1809, his chief supporter in the cabinet—a fellow Anglo-Irish Tory, Lord Castlereagh—had won him supreme command. Wellesley, always outnumbered, shoved the French out of Portugal and Spain. His string of victories, "Vimeiro, Busaco, Torres Vedras, Talavera, Badjoz, Fuentes de Onoro, the Arapiles, Vittoria and the battles of the Pyrenees—these names," writes the historian Geoffrey Treasure, "so glorious in British military history, were but the great landmarks in six years of campaigns; there were to be arduous trials and sharp setbacks, but no defeats."[7] The victories were capped by his being made a duke in May 1814, the year Napoleon abdicated.

His military work apparently done, Wellington, as he now was, became Britain's ambassador to France,[8] and then a representative at the Congress of Vienna (filling in for his ally Lord Castlereagh). He advocated magnanimity towards the French, who had their own important role to play in the Concert of Europe. The performance of that concert, however, was temporarily delayed by the return from exile of Napoleon—until Wellington thrashed him definitively in the Battle of Waterloo (1815). He then set himself to the erection and maintenance of a conservative monarchical Europe that would squash revolutionary sentiment. The Concert of Europe, which he helped conduct, preserved Europe from any continental conflagration for a hundred years—until the First World War.

Pillar of State

At home, he was equally conservative. In 1828 he became prime minister and carried through the 1829 Catholic Relief Act, which allowed Catholics elected to Westminster to take their parliamentary seats. This, he trusted, would help reconcile Ireland to its union with Britain. As a rule, though, he was opposed to the idea of "reform," saying, "Beginning reform is beginning revolution."[9] Wellington was adamant against extending the franchise or weakening the veto power of the House of Lords; just as he was opposed to abolishing flogging or the purchase of commissions in the Army. As an Anglo-Irish aristocrat, he had a firm belief in the aristocratic principle and also in the dreadfulness of the lower orders of humanity (whose depravity he had seen all too vividly displayed when his officers lost control of their men, and let the "scum of the earth" get drunk and pillage). Yet he was, unlike some of his colleagues, a realist and a pragmatist, a hard-line conservative of moderate sentiments who knew when to bend rather than break.

He was, all in all, a perfect imperial Englishman: unflappable amidst shells and musket fire; imperturbable (but showing emotion, though with shame, when he surveyed the carnage of a battlefield and wept over the dead, as he did at Badjoz); immovable against threats ("publish and be damned," as he famously told a courtesan trying to blackmail him[10]); certain of the inferiority of foreigners, yet solicitous of the welfare and respectful of the customs of those under his protection; clipped, brief, and direct in speech; a man of firm prejudices based on experience and disdainful of ideology; an authoritarian in politics but with the goal of preserving Britain's liberal constitution. As he himself put it, he believed in maintaining "the prerogatives of the Crown, the rights and privileges of the Church and its union with the State; and these principles are not inconsistent with a determination to do everything in my power to secure the liberty and promote the prosperity and happiness of the people."[11] That, to the best of his ability, is precisely what he did wherever he served the British Empire.

Chapter 10

SIR CHARLES NAPIER
(1782–1855)

"What a life he has led, what climates he has braved, how riddled and chopped to pieces with balls and bayonet and sabre wounds he is!"

—Lord Dalhousie on Sir Charles Napier[1]

C harles Napier once described himself as "so thin, so sharp, so black, so Jewish, so rascally, such a knavish looking son of a gun,"[2] though he was neither black nor Jewish, and was the son of a duke's daughter and a grandson of the Sixth Lord Napier. His father, Colonel George Napier, was of "the finest specimen of military manhood,"[3] and his mother was a beauty so renowned that the king himself had proposed to her. Blue blood flowed on both sides of his family—and so did eccentricity; in an army rich with characters, Napier ranks as one of the most interesting, with his wire-rimmed glasses (he was seriously short-sighted, so much so that he once marched his troops directly into the French lines); leonine long hair (worn in honor of his Cavalier ancestors, it was said); flowing whiskers; a slight facial twitch (the result of a musket ball that blasted through his nasal passages and had to be yanked from his jaw bone—leaving him with periods when he felt he was suffocating); scars from other musket balls, bayonet thrusts, a crashing sabre to the head, and slamming gun butts; a limp stemming from another wound; a hooked nose; a passion for women

Did you know?

- ♛ Napier was a political liberal who loathed Whigs, admired Wellington, reveled in military glory, and was an ardent imperialist

- ♛ Lord Byron almost convinced him to take command of the Greek rebellion against the Ottoman Turks

- ♛ He abolished the Hindu custom of widow-burning

(and marriage to dowagers); and a firm Christian faith (notwithstanding his two daughters being born out of wedlock to a Greek mistress).[4] His liberal opinions were violently expressed, yet tempered by experience: he opposed flogging, for instance, but thought it satisfactory punishment for blackguards. Napier was a radical, but his patron and military idol was the arch-Tory Duke of Wellington. Multiple times wounded fighting the French in the Peninsular War, he nevertheless regarded Napoleon as a hero, both as a soldier and a politician. A gadfly critic of Britain's imperial methods, he was the Empire's willing executioner, defended British rule as better than the alternative, and was absolutely convinced that he could dramatically improve any land of which he was made a benevolent despot.

The family was prolific—he was one of eight children—and it thrived on military glory. Napiers studded the army. His brothers George and William made lieutenant-general and were knighted for their services. William became a prominent military historian and Charles's biographer. George lost an arm in action at Ciudad Rodrigo and later become governor-general and commander in chief of the Cape Colony, South Africa. Brother Henry became a naval captain and a historian of Florence (in six volumes), and the brothers' first cousin Charles was an admiral.

Napier grew up in Ireland, in a small town outside Dublin, in a warm-hearted (if cash-poor) Protestant family. His father had fought in the American war (as well as against the French and Irish rebels). With a giant, strapping, handsome English father and his remarkably beautiful English mother, it was odd that Charles turned out rather short, slight, and, in his own words, Jewish and rascally-looking. He *was* a bit of a rascal, with a violent temper and a large vocabulary for cursing, but he neither drank nor smoked nor gambled, and by his own lights (if not others', for he was a hugely contentious fellow), he treated no one badly. Thomas Carlyle, who professed to know something about heroes, pegged Napier as "a lynx-eyed, fiery man, with the spirit of the old knight in him. More of a hero than any modern I have seen for a long time; a singular veracity one finds in him, not in his words alone, but in his actions, judgments, aims, in all that he thinks, and does, and says...."[5]

He was sent to a school full of Catholics and embraced Catholic emancipation, which later stood him in good stead with his troops, who were overwhelmingly Irish. Commissioned at the age of twelve in the regiment of Arthur Wellesley, the future Duke of Wellington, his actual service began at age seventeen and saw him putting down Irish rebels, occasionally serving as an aide-de-camp, and clashing with the French in Portugal and Spain (from 1808 to 1812) in the Peninsular War where his brothers saw service and were wounded with him. Of one battle, Napier remarked, "George was hit in the stern and I in the stem. That was burning the family candle at both ends."[6] When he was shot in the face, he had the presence of mind, while carried away on a stretcher, to wave his hat in salute to Wellington.

The Paths of Glory Lead but to the Grave— Hurrah!

"Who would be buried by a sexton in a churchyard rather than by an army in the hour of victory?"

General Sir Charles Napier, quoted in Colonel Sir William F. Butler, *Sir Charles Napier* (Cornell University Library Digital Collections, no date, reprint of Macmillan's 1894 edition), p. 101

He had brief stops in Bermuda, in the War of 1812, at a military college in England, and on the Continent after Napoleon escaped Elba. In 1818, he was made inspecting field officer of the Ionian Islands, then under British possession, and toured Greece where he, unofficially, advised Greek rebels in their fight against the Ottoman Turks (he liked the Greeks because they reminded him of the Irish). In 1822, he was made Military President of Cephalonia, the largest of the Ionian Islands. It was one of those peculiar imperial postings that suit peculiar geniuses. In Cephalonia, he acted as a sort of king and put into action a program of civil engineering works that had him draining marshes, building roads, constructing bridges, and generally tidying up the place with manic Victorian energy. He fathered two daughters with a wild young Greek woman named Anastasia. When he left Cephalonia, he left her too, though he provided money to her, her parents, and his daughters, and took custody of the latter when Anastasia abandoned them and married a Greek. It was also while he was reigning over Cephalonia that he met Byron, who nearly convinced him to take command of the Greek rebel forces against the Turks. His happy days in Cephalonia ended when Major-General Sir Frederick Adam became high commissioner for the islands. Napier, who found few superiors to his liking, immediately fell into a blistering dispute with Adam and lost his post in 1830. He was offered another Ionian island, Zante, but turned it down. His Greek idyll was over.

Napier, the Soldier as Diplomat

"As to the people of every part of Germany, honour to Caesar for killing so many of them; stupid, slow, hard animals, they have not even so much tact as to cheat well."

Quoted in Lieutenant-General Sir William Napier, *The Life and Opinions of General Sir Charles James Napier, G.C.B.* (John Murray, 1857), vol. I, p. 346

So apparently was his career. He rejected a posting to Canada (too cold for his wife, a semi-invalid widow more than a decade his senior) and a governorship in Australia (by which time he was widowed himself). Had he gone to Australia—and he came to regret that he had not—Napier would have assured "that the usual Anglo-Saxon method of planting civilisation by robbery, oppression, murder, and extermination of natives should not take place under his government." Instead, on half pay, he lived in exile in France writing books. Still, he was promoted and knighted (and remarried) and in 1838 was returned to active duty in the North of England. His duty was unsympathetic. Amongst the urban, industrial poor, he had to guard against riots by the Chartists—a radical movement of political reform, whose goals (including universal manhood suffrage) he supported, even if he could not support the Chartist leaders (whom he called "demagogues of evil") or their violent methods. He was contemptuous of the Whigs (the liberals), for their truckling to the mob, and fearful of a possible Tory crackdown. Though he did his duty well, the work was, he felt, morally debilitating: "A man is easily reconciled to act against a misled people if he has an honest plan of his own; but if he is only a servant of greater knaves than those he opposes, and feels he is giving strength to injustice, he loses the right stimulus to action."[7]

Peccavi

In 1841 he was rescued by an invitation to command in India. He did not immediately accept—India, he thought, was no place for his wife or his daughters—but the chance for military glory was always a great goad to him, and there were mercenary reasons as well: "All I want is to catch all the rupees for my girls; and then die like a gentleman."[8] But once in harness he was less concerned about dying like a gentleman than in the marvelous prospect of leading troops to victory. He had his opportunity in Sind, a southern gateway from India to Afghanistan. Britain had a treaty with the emirs (the Baluchi rulers of Sind), but the emirs had not abided by it, and

Better Us than Them

"They are tyrants, and so are we, but the poor will have a fairer play under our sceptre than under theirs.... We have no right to seize Scinde, yet we shall do so, and a very advantageous, useful, humane piece of rascality it shall be."

General Sir Charles Napier on the prospect of toppling the emirs of Sind, quoted in Byron Farwell, *Eminent Victorian Soldiers: Seekers of Glory* (W. W. Norton & Company, 1988), p. 85

they were certainly opposed to the more stringent treaty that Napier was empowered to present them. Napier despised the emirs and looked forward to annexing Sind, because "Peace and civilization will then replace war and barbarism. My conscience shall be light for I see no wrong in so regulating a set of tyrants who…have in sixty years nearly destroyed the country."[9]

His blood up—and expecting the emirs to strike—he struck first at the Battle of Meanee; or, actually, the first thing he struck was the head of a native beating a camel (cruelty to animals, of course, being something that no Englishman can tolerate). With that hand throbbing with pain (and holding his horse's reins), his other gripping his father's sword, the sixty-year-old general led his men into battle outnumbered ten to one, and brought them charging to victory in fierce hand-to-hand combat; a battalion (almost entirely Irish) of the 22nd Regiment cheered him during the action and after, which became one of his proudest memories. Having defeated more than 22,000 Baluchis at Meanee (17 February 1843), a month later he smashed another 26,000 at the Battle of Hyderabad (24 March 1843) and sealed his conquest, immortalized by *Punch* with the caption *"Peccavi"* (Latin for "I have sinned"), which is what much liberal opinion in England believed Napier had done. Everything Napier did was steeped in political controversy, but his conquest of Sind, which was duly annexed, was undeniably a first-class bit of soldiering.

Even better, having shattered the power of the emirs (who had dreamt of parading Napier in chains), he was given Sind to govern: "Now I shall work at Sind as in Cephalonia, to do good, to create, to improve, to end destruction and raise up order."[10] Napier's justice was not impartial; he made it a rule always to favor the poor. His sharp sense of irony and mordant

The Napier Way

"The great receipt for quieting a country is a good thrashing first and great kindness afterwards: the wildest chaps are thus tamed."

General Sir Charles Napier, quoted in Lieutenant-General Sir William Napier, *The Life and Opinions of General Sir Charles James Napier, G.C.B.* (John Murray, 1857), vol. III, p. 34

humor usually saved him from platitudes, but not always. Sometimes his liberalism got the better of him, as in this peroration:

> People think, and justly sometimes, that to execute the law is the great thing; they fancy this to be *justice*. Cast away details, good man, and take what the people call justice, not what the laws call justice, and execute that. Both legal and popular justice have their evils, but assuredly the people's justice is a thousand times nearer to God's justice. Justice must go with the people, not against the people; that is the way to govern nations, and not by square and compass.[11]

Which is all very well and good, but Napier, the champion of the people's justice, later exclaimed—after a countryman killed Napier's dog and a jury of the countryman's peers refused to convict him—"Trial by jury is a farce!"[12] So much for the people's justice.

What really suited Napier was not the people's justice, but Napier's justice executed on the people's behalf. Indeed, he often dreamt of unlimited power and what he would do with it, as a potentate of the East or dictator of Ireland, in which he would both champion freedom of the press—and hang editors who opposed him! But Napier's justice could also be glorious, as when he abolished suttee, the Hindu tradition of burning widows on the funeral pyres of their husbands. Imposing the British Christian value on women— rather higher than the 200-rupee price he believed was the going rate for a woman in Sind—wasn't easy: "There is only one crime I cannot put down— wife killing! They think to kill a cat or a dog is wrong, but I have hanged at least six for killing women: on the slightest quarrel she is chopped to pieces.... I will hang 200 unless they stop."[13] In part to make sure they did stop, his government was in essence a military government, staffed with fellow officers, because Napier distrusted old India hands among the civil servants—he thought them sleek careerists gone native. But he couldn't buck them entirely because he was himself employed by the British East India Company, the de facto ruler of much of India. It was a relationship doomed to fail, not only given Napier's inevitable impatience with restraint and superiors, but because of his utter contempt for men driven by profit rather than the martial virtues and the Napier vision of justice.

Napier credited his success in pacifying Sind to six factors: he put down crime; he showed the people who had fought against him that he respected their military prowess (a very British imperial notion this, that the best fighters against you are the ones you respect and want at your side); those who surrendered had their property restored to them (sometimes with interest); the poor were given justice; the emirs' flunkeys were retained, though strictly supervised; and British power was made manifest so that it was clear that any rebellion would be instantly quashed.

The recipe was good, but his years governing Sind were not nearly so satisfying as those spent in Cephalonia (Napier once said that he "would rather have finished the roads in Cephalonia than have fought Austerlitz

Multiculturalism, Napier-Style

Napier to Brahmin priests protesting his ban on widow-burning: "This burning of widows is your custom; prepare the funeral pile. But my nation also has a custom. When men burn women alive we hang them, and confiscate all their property. My carpenters shall therefore erect gibbets on which to hang all concerned when the widow is consumed. Let us all act according to our national customs."

Quoted in Byron Farwell, *Eminent Victorian Soldiers: Seekers of Glory* (W. W. Norton & Company, 1988), pp. 93–94

or Waterloo"[14]) and were tinged with disappointment (missing the First Sikh War), frustration with the East India Company bureaucracy, and tragedy (a cholera epidemic among whose victims was his nephew). In 1847, dogged by his old wounds and new disabilities and his wife's ill health, he resigned and returned to England (after a recuperative period in the South of France).

He wasn't home long. When news of the Battle of Chillianwala (13 January 1849 in the Second Sikh War) reached England as either a narrow, costly victory or an embarrassing setback, there was a clamor for a new commander to succeed General Sir Hugh Gough. The Duke of Wellington, against the fervent opposition of the East India Company, recommended Napier, telling him finally, "If you don't go, I must."[15] Napier went. But by the time he arrived, gallant old Sir Hugh (himself sixty-nine years old) had recovered matters and pounded the Sikhs into submission and the Punjab was annexed to Britain (as Napier thought should have been done at the end of the First Sikh War). The Sikhs then became among the best and most loyal troops the British had.

Napier, having missed the action, nevertheless arrived as commander in chief for India. Inevitably, having first struck up a liking for the governor-general Lord Dalhousie, he chafed under his supervision, and resigned his command in 1850. Napier died in England in 1853. He provided his own best epitaph towards the end of his service in India, when he dreamt of returning home, writing that he would look at his "father's sword, and think of the day he gave it into my young hands, and of the motto on a Spanish blade he had, 'Draw me not without cause; put me not up without honour.' I have not drawn his sword without cause, nor put it up without honour."[16] Indeed not—and while Napier's justice might have been idiosyncratic and rough and ready, to his mind it was the administration of such justice that vindicated the British Empire and that made him, in good conscience, its military servant.

Part IV

INDIA

Chapter 11

THE JEWEL IN THE CROWN

The British East India Company (or John Company, in its popular moniker), was the sort of company you'd like to work for—it had its own army, its own navy, its own Anglican church, its own courts, its own ambassadors and civil service, and it governed a fifth of the world's population. It was a curiosity and a wonder, as was recognized even at the time by such observers as Thomas Babington Macaulay, member of Parliament, man of letters, and one of the most important figures in the shaping of British India. He had it precisely right when he addressed the House of Commons in 1833:

> It is strange, very strange, that a joint-stock society of traders...should be intrusted with the sovereignty of a larger population, the disposal of a larger clear revenue, the command of a larger army, than are under the direct management of the Executive Government of the United Kingdom. But what constitution can we give to our Indian Empire which shall not be strange.... That Empire is itself the strangest of all political anomalies. That a handful of adventurers from an island in the Atlantic should have subjugated a vast country divided from the place of their birth by half the globe; a country which at no very distant period

was merely the subject of fable to the nations of Europe; a country never before violated by the most renowned of Western conquerors; a country which Trajan never entered; a country lying beyond the point where the phalanx of Alexander refused to proceed; that we should govern a territory ten thousand miles from us, a territory larger and more populous than France, Spain, Italy, and Germany put together, a territory, the present clear revenue of which exceeds the present clear revenue of any state in the world, France excepted; a territory inhabited by men differing from us in race, colour, language, manners, morals, religion; these are prodigies to which the world has seen nothing similar. Reason is confounded. We interrogate the past in vain. General rules are useless where the whole is one vast exception. The Company is an anomaly; but it is part of a system where every thing is anomaly. It is the strangest of all governments; but it is designed for the strangest of all empires.[1]

This strangest of all empires is what most people now think of when they think of the British Empire—they think of the British Raj, the jewel in the crown, pig-sticking and curry, Kipling and the Great Game, railroads and vast white palaces, tea and polo, sunburnt majors and sundowners on the verandah. It was all that and more. Bliss was it in that dawn to be

The British East India Company Defined

"How was the East India Company controlled? By the government. What was its object? To collect taxes. How was this object attained? By means of a large standing army. What were its employees? Soldiers, mostly, the rest, civil servants. Where did it trade to? China. What did it export from England? Courage. What did it import? Tea!"

Dr. (and eventually Major) C. Northcote Parkinson (of Parkinson's Law fame), quoted in Brian Gardner, *The East India Company* (Dorset Press, 1971), p. 11

alive, but to be a Briton in India—if you survived the tropical diseases, the mutiny, the Thugs, and the rebellious tribesmen—was very heaven. And it all started with a merchant company granted a royal charter in 1600 by Queen Elizabeth. The East India Company sought trade throughout East Asia, particularly the Spice Islands, and competed (and fought) against rival merchant powers, including the Portuguese and the Dutch; later, the French and even the Danes and the Swedes (in the eighteenth century) were involved.

India was ruled (for the most part) by the Islamic Mughal Empire whose emperors—Turko-Mongol by blood, Persian by culture, governing a largely Hindu people—granted British merchants trading rights and the right to establish outposts on the Indian subcontinent. The British were not the first to have such footholds: Portugal had been on the subcontinent for a century and the Dutch for a few years before the British. Over the course of the seventeenth century British outposts came to include Surat, Madras, Bombay, and Calcutta. It was England's jolly King Charles II who gave the East India Company a new charter that set it on its unique course, granting it virtually unlimited powers to trade, govern, and expand its Indian holdings. Seventy years later, long after the crown had shifted from the Stuarts to the House of Hanover, an unlikely hero took full advantage of what King Charles had ordained.

An American in India

The American-born Elihu Yale (1649–1721)—the financial benefactor who left his name to Yale College (now Yale University)—spent twenty years in the British East India Company and was governor of Madras.

Avenging the Black Hole of Calcutta

By the beginning of the eighteenth century the Mughal Empire was in manifest rapid decay. Filling the breach, when it was not filled by anarchy and warlords, were the good offices of the British East India Company, the French at Pondicherry, as well as a variety of Hindu princes and confederacies of Mahrattas in central India, Jats in Rajasthan, and Sikhs in the Punjab. In 1739, Persians invaded India and occupied (and massacred the inhabitants of) Delhi, even stealing the famed peacock throne of the Mughal emperors; and Afghans repeatedly rampaged through northern India.

With dominance in the subcontinent up for grabs, princely states allied with each other or with the British East India Company or the French East India Company (which gained concessions of land for lending troops and officers) in wars of conquest. Sometimes the French and the British fought each other directly with Indian allies. Mahrattas, Afghans, and others hired themselves out as mercenaries; and European officers found themselves in demand as mercenaries for the princely states, which might have artillery and muskets like the Europeans, but could not match their military discipline or leadership (though some of them did try to copy their uniforms). One dramatic instance of European officer prowess came from Captain Eustachius De Lannoy of the Dutch East India Company, who was captured by the maharajah of Travancore after the Battle of Colachel in 1741. The maharajah spared the Dutchman's life in exchange for the captain's commitment to train and lead the maharajah's men in the Dutch way of war, which "the great captain," as he came to be known, did with notable success, helping the maharajah to expand his holdings in southwest India.

But the most important adventurer in India at this time was a lowly clerk named Robert Clive of the East India Company, soon to spring to renown as "Clive of India" for his military genius and accession to wealth as an Indian nabob. Without formal military training, he took part in the company's military actions against the French, and proved himself a courageous soldier and capable leader of Indian troops. In 1751, he captured the city of Arcot and then held it, vastly outnumbered, against a fifty-day siege by French-allied Indians. Clive had entered the action as a clerk who doubled as a soldier. He left it as a hero.

He was a hero soon called upon by the Company. In 1756, the young Muslim, anti-British (and not much liked by his Hindu subjects) Nawab of Bengal, Siraj-ad-daula, sacked Calcutta; his officers stuffed 146 prisoners—Englishmen, Anglo-Indians, and one woman—into a dark cell fourteen feet wide and eighteen feet long. There was no space to move, for much of the time no water to drink, temperatures soared to over a hundred degrees, air seemed scarce and eventually so too did any chance of surviving. The prisoners were kept in the suffocating heat for ten hours before the nawab could be roused to order their release. By that time, there were only twenty-three survivors, three of whom were held to extract ransom from the East India Company.[2]

Vengeance was called for, and Clive was asked to deliver it. Calcutta was regained New Year's Day 1757; next for Clive was toppling

A Good Man in India

"Good God! How much depends on the life of one man!"

Major John Carnac on the battlefield heroism of Major Thomas Adams during the conquest of Bengal. Quoted in Lawrence James, *Raj: The Making and Unmaking of British India* (St. Martin's Press, 1997), p. 41

the nawab. On 23 June 1757, at the Battle of Plassey, Clive brought 3,000 men, two-thirds of them sepoys, against more than 50,000 troops of the nawab and utterly routed them. Siraj-ad-daula was killed by the new British-approved nawab, and the East India Company had become the kingmakers of Bengal.

When a successor nawab prepared to attack the British, the Company struck first, and at the Battle of Buxar (22 October 1764) won another smashing victory. The British were outnumbered more than two to one and facing modern artillery manned by European mercenaries. But British audacity, bravery, and intrepidity—and dogged, disciplined infantry—won the day. If Plassey made the East India Company kingmakers, Buxar made Bengal a company province.

An Evolving Empire

By the end of the Seven Years' War (1754–63), France's position in India was reduced to a few trading enclaves that existed under British toleration. The real question was whether the East India Company or Parliament should rule India. For what had begun as another free market imperial adventure had become admixed with a sense of British responsibility. The East India Company paid a subvention to support the Royal Navy, but more important was extracting a commitment from the Company to govern according to British principles. Parliament wanted to ensure the Company did not topple native despotisms only to put its own rapacity in their place (the nouveaux riches nabobs were a bad advertisement for the Company); and Parliament did not want the native corruptions of the East to become the acceptable corruptions of Englishmen who served there.

To this end, the India Act of 1784 merged the authority of the East India Company with that of Parliament through a Board of Control. It brought some government regulation and supervision, but the burden on the Company was light. It was, in fact, largely moral. The goal was to ensure that British rule in India was conducted with probity and honor, and with a respect for Indian traditions and civilization, the study of which became an avocation of the more scholarly of the Company's men.

The Company believed its power rested on its prestige—especially as there were so few Englishmen and so many Indians—and that prestige was secured by military victories that swayed rajahs; the policy was "no retreat," which in fact became a forward policy of annexation when native rulers misbehaved, and there were plenty of French mercenary officers about to encourage them to misbehave. Tipu Sultan, the Tiger of Mysore, was fiercely anti-British and did not need much encouragement; he styled himself a Muslim warrior and an ally of Revolutionary France.[3] Fittingly, Tipu was given his just deserts by, among other serving officers, Arthur Wellesley—a dab hand at subduing both rebellious Indians and revolutionary and imperial French.

British India grew with the conquest of Nepal (1816), the defeat of the Mahrattas in central India (1818), and peace-keeping operations from Burma to Afghanistan. Aside from keeping native rulers in check, there developed "the Great Game"—the rivalry between Britain and Russia in Central Asia. The British, ever wary of Russian inroads into India, especially through the Khyber Pass, kept up an extraordinary network of spies and soldier sahibs who could pass for natives—and pass sometimes alarming news to the British governor-general.

One consequence of the Company's "forward" policy—encapsulated by Clive's admonition that "to stop is dangerous, to recede is ruin"—was that India's borders kept advancing—north all the way to Kashmir, bordering China; west all the way to Aden where the Arabian Sea meets the Red Sea; south to Ceylon; and east to Burma. One particular sore point was Afghanistan—a potential Russian invasion route. The Afghan emir Dost Muhammad worried the British by dallying with the Russians, and a Russian-Persian attack on western Afghanistan seemed proof of Russia's aggressive intent. In 1839, British troops invaded the raucous tribal state to punish Dost Muhammad and warn off the armies of the czar.

Conquering Afghanistan and installing a new puppet emir proved easy—another remarkable feat of British arms, and one which did indeed seem to cause the Russian bear to retire. But holding Afghanistan proved a good deal harder. The sullen Afghans refused to support Dost Muhammad's usurper. Being Afghans, they expressed their displeasure with jezails and knives, ambushes, assassination, and guerrilla war to the point that evacuation became a necessity. Among the assassinated was Sir William Hay Macnaghten, a political agent and de facto governor-general of Kabul—killed while negotiating with Dost Muhammad's son, Akbar Khan, who in typical Afghan fashion believed that an annoying interlocutor is often best stabbed to death.

Akbar Khan did, however, consent to the peaceful withdrawal of the British army and its camp followers (about 4,500 soldiers and 12,000 civilians) through the Khyber Pass back to India. They were commanded by the fifty-nine-year-old General Sir William Elphinstone, a veteran of Waterloo, whose enduring fame rests not on his role in Bonaparte's defeat but in leading one of the great epic disasters of the British Empire. Of the 16,000-plus Britons and Indians who entered the Khyber Pass in January 1842 only one, Dr. William Brydon, emerged alive. After promising them safe passage, the Afghans had treated the retiring Britons and Indians as a subject of violent sport, picking them off as they struggled through the frozen pass. The Britons' last stand was at the Battle of Gandamak (13 January 1842) when about 65 officers and men formed a square in the snow and battled the Afghans to the end, Captain Thomas Souter wrapping himself in the colors.

This, of course, could not be the end. The British stormed into Afghanistan, occupied Kabul, destroyed the villages of those responsible for the massacre, liberated hostages, and then called it a day. Vengeance achieved, the troops marched back to India, and Dost Muhammad returned to his throne. The British had made their point and the Afghans had made theirs. The Duke of Wellington, unperturbed by the Russian threat (Russian numbers, he thought, were no match for British officers), was worried, indeed, by the disaster in the Khyber Pass. "There is not a Moslem heart from Peking to Constantinople which will not vibrate when reflecting on the fact that the European ladies and other females attached to the troops at Kabul were made over to the tender mercies of the Moslem Chief who had with his own hand murdered Sir William Macnaghten."[4]

But only a year later another million Muslims were brought under British rule with the conquest of Sind in 1843. In 1849, the Punjab was annexed, and the martial Sikhs filled the ranks of the British Indian army. The conquest of the Punjab was particularly impressive because the Sikhs met the Company's army not only with a larger force (that was usual; the odds this time were four to one) and with more artillery, but with an army just as well-trained (by Europeans) and well-equipped (by Europeans) as the British, who were led by the redoubtable Sir Hugh Gough, an angular, grey-haired, fearless, blustering, red-cheeked, sixty-six-year-old Anglo-Irishman who led from the front wearing his white "fighting jacket" and believing the only thing necessary to victory was to charge the enemy with the bayonet. This simple tactic did not recommend itself to finer tactical minds, which distrusted the chances of "cold steel" against artillery and musket fire; the British press chalked it up to Gough's being Irish—but it worked. As Gough himself pointed out, the British army had achieved what Alexander the Great could not: the conquest of India.

In the latter half of the nineteenth century, the British population in India hovered at about 100,000, compared to more than 250 million Indians. The British believed they ruled in India not only by power—whether military (Britons and Indians were agreed that white officers were the key) or possibly divine providence (God being an Englishman)—but by force of personality. Nothing else could explain how so few could govern so many over so great an expanse. The essentials were British pluck, fortitude, and courage, without which nothing could be done, and British justice, decency, and fair play, which justified the entire endeavor.

The moral side of the British Empire in India developed gradually. The Company was obviously out for profits. Many of its employees were not only free market buccaneers but quite willing to entertain Indian mistresses (or wives), though never to the extent that the French or Portuguese did (the general term for Eurasians was, in fact, "Portuguese"). The first pressures to reform were imposed by governor-generals like Lord Cornwallis and Lord

Wellesley who brought the aristocratic cult of the gentleman and made it part and parcel of company practice; then came evangelicalism and, just as important, the arrival of English wives.

Always kept in balance were the conservative's respect for native traditions and the liberal's reforming zeal. Conservative and liberal might unite in demanding the abolition of the Hindu practices of widow-burning and killing first-born girls, or the Thugs' murder cult of Kali, the goddess of death (even when such efforts failed, as they did in trying to overcome Muslim and Hindu traditions allowing the marriage of prepubescent girls to older men). Both could unite, for the most part, even on the idea that India might eventually be largely self-governing after sufficient British tutelage. But there were differences too. The conservatives generally preferred governing through the existing Indian ruling classes—speaking as British lord to Indian noble—with little interference in native affairs; liberals preferred a more aggressive, progressive, rationalist approach. Conservatives upheld Christianity as an integral part of British civilization and superiority, but generally thought it best to let Hindus and Muslims be rather than risk religious war. Evangelicals, needless to say, took a different tack entirely; and evangelicalism was the engine of reforming (and soon secularized) liberalism.

Not on the liberal side of the ledger, but an instrument of reform nevertheless, was the Army; and for all the licentious customs that Evangelicals associated with Indian culture, religion, and art (and that British civil servants associated with the decadent Indian princes they had to keep in line), to be a British officer in India in the latter half of the nineteenth century was essentially to take a religious vow—to one's regiment rather than the Church, though the regiment offered just as varied a supply of rituals and orders. When it came to marriage, the catechism for officers had long been, in the famous formulation, that subalterns *must not* marry, captains *may* marry, majors *should* marry, and colonels *must* marry. Certainly after the triumph of Victorian morality at home, a young officer's life was often, as Francis Yeats-Brown (*The Lives of a Bengal Lancer*) noted, writing of his experience in early twentieth century India, "as sexless as any monk's.... What is good for the Roman priest is (I suppose) good for the Indian cavalry subaltern, who has work to do (like the priest) which he could scarcely perform if hampered by family ties."[5] There was a bit of philandering in the hill stations, but less than is sometimes supposed.[6] The real diversion, or indeed obsession, for officers was sport. It doubled as training for war.

The Great Indian Mutiny

The importance of being British—of being cool in a crisis, courageous, a natural leader of men—became even more pronounced after the Sepoy Rebellion of 1857, the seismic event in the history of the British Empire in India. It began with a growing suspicion in some Indian regiments that the British were going to attempt the obliteration of caste and a mass conversion to Christianity; for evidence of Britain's disregard for the beliefs of Hindu and Muslim soldiers one had to look no further than the cartridges for the new Enfield rifle, which were rumored to be greased with cow and pig fat. The Company was quick to ensure that only ungreased cartridges were issued and that they could be greased according to the religious predilections of the greaser, but this did not assuage the sepoys, who distrusted the cartridges, nurtured gripes about pay and pensions, and feared the Army was intent on enrolling lower castes and forcing Hindus to serve overseas where they might lose caste.

The mutiny was not exclusively a military affair. It was joined by disaffected Indian nobles, Indians who distrusted British schools, Indians who resented British interference with their traditions, and the mob that welcomed any excuse to riot and pillage. The revolt was largely confined to north-central India, but it was fearsome nonetheless.

It began with a rumble: a mutinous individual sepoy here, a contumacious regiment there, a series of fires set by arsonists; the British officers responding with quick and effective courts-martial, threats of force, and disbandment of untrustworthy units. But the fuse was really lit in May 1857 when members of the 3rd Bengal Light Cavalry based in Meerut sprang from prison sepoys who had refused (some tearfully, claiming they were loyal but could not violate their religion) to fire the new cartridges. The cavalrymen rode through the city rousing the people to join the revolt. It was Sunday, and though some British officers had been warned of the impending trouble by loyal sepoys, they had not taken the warnings seriously. British soldiers and civilians, including wives and children, were set upon and murdered. The mutinous cavalry rode to the eighty-two-year-old Bahadur Shah, the Mughal king of Delhi, whom they proclaimed the rightful ruler of India. He, rather befuddled by opium, accepted. The rapine that had been inflicted on Meerut was now repeated at Delhi, and the mutiny was in full charge: jihad for some, pillage for others. Most communities were divided; it was not a nationalist revolution or a sectarian revolution (except in the sense that it was anti-Christian and anti-British). The rebellion divided both between and within classes, races, and sects. Some of the mutineers wavered before they made their choice and even escorted their British officers and families to safety before throwing their lot in with the rebels.

Standing by the British were the martial Sikhs and Gurkhas (among many others); Indians who benefited from British law and commerce; loyal rajahs (most Indian princes stayed loyal); and Indians who were intimidated both by the Company's fearsome reputation for battlefield success and by the reinforcements that arrived with bagpipes skirling. The British, however, were still stretched perilously thin. They were besieged at Lucknow and at Cawnpore (where they were lured out by an offer of safe passage and then massacred). The British in turn besieged the mutineers' capital at Delhi. When British retribution came, it was indeed swift and fierce, fired by the rebels' treachery and their murders of women and children. British generals Sir James Outram, Sir Henry Havelock, and Sir Colin Campbell (commander in chief of India), among other commanders, cut through the enemy with avenging swords and Enfield rifles, erecting gibbets to hang surviving traitors; they were slowed only by a shortage of troops.

The rebellion was not fully quashed until early 1859, though the outcome was never in doubt from the summer of 1857. Delhi was regained in September, and the purported rightful ruler of India, Bahadur Shah, sent into exile. Lucknow was fully regained in March 1858. The rest was hunting down miscreants who were shot out of hand. The British had, as usual, been outnumbered in every major battle; they had fought disciplined troops they themselves had trained—troops that could match them, or nearly (the Enfield rifle had its advantages), in weaponry. But they had again emerged triumphant—a fact that impressed itself forcibly on the Indians. The soldier sahibs were to be obeyed.

The Mutiny led to the East India Company's dissolution and the formal annexation of India to the Crown in 1858. Evangelicalism was muzzled—it was a great source for shaping honest, hard-working builders of empire, but it was a dangerous irritation to the Indians. Conservatism was ascendant. The government looked to rule through local, traditional Indian leaders, respecting Indian customs. The hand of government was kept light even as in pomp and ceremonial it was meant to impress (on terms the maharajahs well understood). Universities and elite public schools were created for Indian students to build up a class of Indian gentlemen on the British model.

The British were also devoted to public works improvements—systems of irrigation, canals, the linking of railroads that were meant not only to improve Indian life and agricultural production (and tax revenues) but also to help stymie the periodic famines that could scythe through India like a juggernaut—and which, ironically, anti-colonialists blame on the British, who tried to make all these improvements while never numbering more than 0.05 percent of the Indian population. That was not all the British did either: they strung telegraph poles, began a massive inoculation program against smallpox, and pursued other public health projects. India was the

Making Indians Englishmen

"It is impossible for us, with our limited means, to attempt to educate the body of the people. We must at present do our best to form a class who may be interpreters between us and the millions whom we govern; a class of person, Indian in blood and colour, but English in taste, opinions, morals, and in intellect."

Thomas Babington Macaulay, "Minute on Education," 1835

jewel of Britain's imperial crown not only because it was vast—incorporating the subcontinent from the eastern border of Afghanistan to the western border of Siam—and profitable, but because, in the eye of the imperialist public, it was a gleaming example of how manly Britons with rolled up sleeves were working to advance civilization, peace, and progress. Progress of course was not necessarily popular—native uprisings inevitably targeted Western institutions and technology—but if English schools, programs of medical hygiene, and public works weren't always welcomed, there was always cricket to teach Indians how to play up, play up, and play the game.

Kim's Commission

"The Great Game" itself was still being played in the ever restive Northwest Frontier, where the British continued to fear an invasion combining Cossack ferocity with Islamic fanaticism. The Great Game was a matter of spies (and of course the great spy novel of British India is Rudyard Kipling's *Kim*), but it was also a matter of war, as in the Second Afghan War (1878–80) in which General Frederick "Bobs" Roberts invaded Afghanistan after the emir had entertained an (uninvited) Russian delegation but refused to accept a British one. Such bad manners had to be punished. When British officers blooded themselves on punitive expeditions against turbulent tribes on the frontier, they were usually small-scale affairs, enjoyed by both sides as a bit of martial sport (killing people was what Pathans did—and why the British liked them and enlisted them when they could: "We must gradually convert to our way of thinking in matters of civilization these splendid tribes," in the words of Lord Salisbury[7]). The Second Afghan War, on the other hand, was mounted as a large-scale military operation, with an army of 40,000 men invading the country, occupying the seat of government, and squelching the emir's attempt to enlist Russian help. In 1879, the emir's son and successor signed the Treaty of Gandamak, allowing the British to annex small portions of Afghanistan (along its eastern borderlands) and run the country's foreign policy. This amicable arrangement folded when only a few months later Britain's man in Kabul was assassinated, and Afghans flew into rebellion. Roberts then marched into Afghanistan, crushed the various rebellions, installed a biddable emir, and reaffirmed the Treaty of Gandamak, though this time no British officials were left behind as targets for assassination. The British returned to India, and everyone was more or less happy…at least until the next Afghan War (1919), when the Afghans invaded India and were repulsed. In exchange for their promise of good behavior, the British allowed them to conduct their own foreign policy (which they were doing anyway).

In 1903–04, Russophobia led to the British invasion of Tibet, where, it turned out, there were no Russians. The campaign was over in six months, and the British were eventually apologetic about the misunderstanding (the Tibetans compared the British favorably to the Chinese in this regard). The military commander of the expedition, Francis Younghusband, a doughty great-gamer, was apparently touched by the high altitude, as sometimes happened to spiritually inclined officers, becoming a mystic of amalgamated New Age and Victorian beliefs (while at least maintaining the appearance of a grey-moustached, tweed-waist-coated English gentleman).

To the east, in Burma, which had been progressively absorbed from the 1820s to the fall of Mandalay in 1885, there was no great game against a rival imperial power—at least until World War II and the invasion by the Japanese—but there were extraordinary adventures in the jungles with

British officers leading small detachments of troops (often Gurkhas) to hunt down dacoits, dodge poisoned arrows (not to mention slithering leeches and malarial mosquitoes), and stamp out nasty old Burmese habits like child sacrifice and slavery, customs the British were still fighting between the World Wars.

But the Northwest Frontier and Burma were the wild peripheries of the empire. In what we might think of as India proper, the word for the dawning twentieth century was nationalism. India, a land of two thousand languages and two hundred castes, had never been a unified nation, but Britain had given its educated classes a common language, it had provided them with freedom of the press (and Indian newspapers could publish the most inflammatory rubbish), it had offered them places as lawyers and junior civil servants, and it had given them English ideals, including the ideal of representative democracy. The question was not whether the Indians would be given a greater say in their government but when and how.

All that was put on hold, however, when the guns of August 1914 erupted and Britain went to war against the Central Powers. Indian princes pledged their loyalty. The Empire was united, and the Indian army, all volunteers, contributed more than a million men—virtually none of them, it should be noted, from the educated elite—who served from Mesopotamia to the shell-rocked trenches of France. Despite the efforts of a variety of nationalist agitators and a Turkish-German campaign to inspire a jihad against the British, the Indians, with few exceptions, stayed loyal.

Gandhi versus Churchill

It was generally agreed that India's loyalty merited some reward. For a conservative like the former viceroy Lord Curzon that meant gradually increasing the Indians' role in what he liked to call "responsible government." Liberals and socialists (in the Labour Party), however, wanted to

Mahatma Gandhi: Recruiting Sergeant for the Empire

"An Empire that has been defending India and of which India aspires to be the equal partner is in great peril [in World War I], and it ill befits India to stand aloof.... India would be nowhere without Englishmen. If the British do not win, [to] whom shall we go for claiming equal partnership.... [W]hereas the liberty-loving English will surely yield, when they have seen that we have laid down our lives for them."

Quoted in Lawrence James, *Raj: The Making and Unmaking of British India* (St. Martin's Press, 1997), p. 456

push for full Indian self-government. Conservatives were cautious not only out of imperial principle but because of the new danger of Bolshevism. The Bolsheviks had as their top foreign policy goal the destruction of the British Empire. To that end, though atheists, they called Muslims to jihad, and their seditious hand was seen behind nationalist Indian riots and protests.

Another agitator for Indian nationalism was a wizened, eccentric lawyer and holy man, Mohandas Gandhi, who had inexplicably—to both educated Indians and the British—become a prominent political figure. He and other Indian leaders called for protests against new anti-terrorist laws that stripped normal judicial protections from criminals accused of sedition. The protests, despite Gandhi's entreaties, inevitably turned violent. The agitation spread across India, absorbing other grievances and giving mobs an excuse for a rioter's holiday in what was supposed to be a program of passive disobedience. Many in the British Raj felt that now was not the time to show conciliation. The pressures on the Raj blew up at Amritsar.

In April 1919, Brigadier General Reginald Dyer arrived in Amritsar to find a city in the grips of an Indian mob. Europeans had been killed, a white female missionary had been knocked off her bike and assaulted, and European women and children had been forced to seek shelter at a fort, while gangs of Indians burned and pillaged. Everything he saw outraged him, and rightly so. Dyer was a hero of the old school. He had been born in India and spent his childhood there before being educated in Ireland and at Sandhurst. He had a gallant record that extended from service in the Northwest Frontier to Burma. He knew India well and spoke several of its languages in addition to Persian. Most of all, he was a man who stood by the British imperial principles of justice, fair play, and decency—delivered by force if necessary—and who believed that a mob that attacked women and threatened children deserved condign punishment. Amritsar was put under martial law, and Dyer ordered that, for a five-day period, any Indians wishing to go

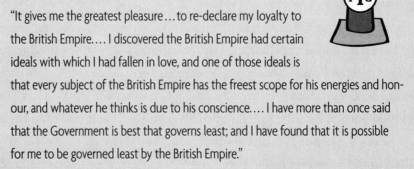

Gandhi: British Imperialist

"It gives me the greatest pleasure...to re-declare my loyalty to the British Empire.... I discovered the British Empire had certain ideals with which I had fallen in love, and one of those ideals is that every subject of the British Empire has the freest scope for his energies and honour, and whatever he thinks is due to his conscience.... I have more than once said that the Government is best that governs least; and I have found that it is possible for me to be governed least by the British Empire."

Mahatma Gandhi in 1915, quoted in C. F. Andrews, *Mahatma Gandhi's Ideas, Including Selections from His Writings* (Pierides Press, 2008), p. 219

down the street where the missionary had been attacked had to crawl on their bellies, because in Dyer's Christian, British, chivalric view "We look upon women as sacred, or ought to."[8]

Dyer was charged with keeping order over more than three thousand square miles of the Punjab, not to mention Amritsar (the population of which was 150,000 in 1919). He had fewer than 1,200 troops. He ordered a complete ban on public protests and gatherings of any kind in Amritsar, stating explicitly that any public demonstrations would be fired upon. The message was broadcast throughout the city. But on 13 April 1919, 15,000 to 20,000 Indians gathered in a bordered area called the Jillianwala Bagh, near the Sikh's Golden Temple of Amritsar. Dyer brought fewer than a hundred troops (mostly Gurkhas), not all of them armed with rifles, to confront the mob, many of whose members were armed with metal-tipped sticks. Dyer ordered his men into line and without delay gave the order to fire: 379 Indians were killed and more than 1,000 were wounded. The mob was dispersed—and so was the feared rebellion in the Punjab.

Dyer became a hate figure to anti-colonialists, and was repudiated by liberal opinion and the British government at home. But he was praised by old India hands, the conservative press (which linked the Indian rebellion to international Bolshevism), and the lieutenant governor of the Punjab, Michael O'Dwyer (who was assassinated by an Indian terrorist in 1940). Perhaps more telling, Dyer's actions were supported by many Indians, especially businessmen, who feared the mob; Dyer was even made an honorary Sikh.

Called by some "the savior of India," he was nevertheless an embarrassment to the British government. He was stripped of his command and shoved into forced retirement. His enemies (who included Winston Churchill, though privately he held some sympathy for Dyer) believed that he had betrayed every element of justice for which Britain stood. Dyer believed he had only done what was necessary to restore peace to Amritsar and the Punjab. He did not deny the horror of the massacre, but he took a frontier soldier's view that doing harsh and terrible things was sometimes necessary to preserve the peace. In retirement, he was battered by a succession of strokes, and the day before he died (in 1927) he said that he had no desire to recover, "I only want to die and know from my Maker whether I did right or wrong."[9]

Gandhi meanwhile continued to preach non-cooperation with the British government. The political vehicle he had made his own, the Indian National Congress, began expanding its reach from the Indian lawyer class to the peasants, who garlanded Gandhi as a sort of mystical savior who would overturn their eternal lot—though Gandhi's goal was somewhat different: a nation of self-sufficient spinners untainted by industrialism and Western influence (he opposed Western medicine and vaccinations as well). Indians tended to read into Gandhi what they wanted to find, which was why, again, his campaign of peaceful non-cooperation degenerated into violence in practice: the mob wasn't interested in the finer points of Gandhi's philosophy of *satyagraha*, and it—sometimes joined to a combination of Islamism and Bolshevism with which it had very little in common—became an excuse for riot and insurgency. As the death toll stacked up, Gandhi was imprisoned for sedition in 1922 (he served two years of a six-year sentence). The British Raj, relying on loyal Indian princes, brave British officers, and reliable Indian soldiers, police, and civil servants, endured.

Gandhi continued to preach his gospel of primitive self-sufficiency, homeopathic cures, and alleged religious enlightenment that would cure all political evils. In 1930, his program of professedly peaceful protests again roiled India with violence. The British viceroy negotiated with Gandhi; concessions, it appeared, had to be made to Indian nationalism. Opposing this tide was Winston Churchill, who was convinced that Britain alone spared India communal bloodshed and granted it the benefits of humane, liberal government. It was during this period of British appeasement of

Gandhi and the Indian National Congress that Churchill made his famous comment: "It is alarming and nauseating to see Mr. Gandhi, a seditious Middle Temple lawyer, now posing as a fakir of a type well known in the East, striding half-naked up the steps of the viceregal palace, while he is still organizing and conducting a defiant campaign of civil disobedience...."[10]

British policy was to lead India to becoming a self-governing dominion, an exotic version of Canada. There were elections giving Indians a greater voice in the government, but that voice was hardly united. A Muslim League, calling for an independent Muslim state, rose as a rival to the largely Hindu Indian National Congress. The princely states tried to isolate themselves from a nationalism of which they wanted no part.

By 1939, of course, the British were somewhat distracted by a World War against Nazi Germany, Mussolini's Italy, and imperial Japan. Gandhi advised that the British should foil the Nazis by surrendering unconditionally to them and thus defeat them through moral example. Gandhi's nemesis Winston Churchill (who became prime minister in May 1940) had other, more robust ideas. As in the First World War, Indians flocked to the colors: the Indian army, all volunteers, grew to number more than 2,644,000 men—and this despite the opposition of the Indian National Congress (the Muslim League supported the war, as did the Indian princes).

The Indian National Congress, inspired by Gandhi (who would soon be imprisoned again) sponsored an anti-British "Quit India" campaign that called on Indians to act as saboteurs, blowing up trains, cutting telegraph wires, and rioting in the streets (in one such riot, two Canadian pilots were murdered). There was also Subhas Chandra Bose, an Indian nationalist of a more militant stripe, who tried to raise a pro-Nazi Indian Legion from Indian soldiers captured by the Germans and Italians. This proved a bust, but when he took his appeal to the Japanese he found a cleverer audience. The Japanese immediately segregated Indian prisoners and pumped them full of propaganda about how Asians should unite to crush the British. They had some takers, enough for Bose to form an "Indian National Army." Bose, however, found that the Japanese held a lower opinion of Indian soldiers than did the British—in fact, they were far more racist, delegating the Indians to the most menial of roles, including labor details. They even put Bose under arrest. But he labored on, dubbing himself the *führer* of the "Provisional Government of Free India" and as such declared war on Britain and the United States. (His government was recognized by President Eamon de Valera of the Irish Republic.) The low Japanese opinion of the Indian National Army proved well-founded; numbering about 40,000 troops at its height, it was plagued by desertion and its men proved no match for the loyal British Indian Army, whose troops took a special pleasure in gunning them down. With the Japanese empire collapsing and Burma regained by Britain, Bose attempted to flee to Soviet Russia and lead a Soviet invasion of India. Instead, he died from petrol burns suffered after his plane crashed.

Of the Indian National Army prisoners of war, the British deemed that most were merely dupes. Some were reinstated into the army, many were simply discharged; fewer than 6,200 were deemed true traitors; fewer than twenty faced courts-martial; and none was given a death sentence. The British authorities feared making martyrs of traitors whom Gandhi was praising, and for whom parts of India were rioting. Indian nationalists took this as a sign of weakness, and it appeared they were right, for the British had had enough of India. Conscript Britons wanted to go home, and Indian agitators wanted the British out of India—apparently so they could get on with the business of killing each other. The Muslim League of Mohammed Ali Jinnah, demanding an independent Pakistan, launched a "Direct Action Day," which became the excuse for sectarian violence. Gandhi and the Indian National Congress continued to fan the flames of mutiny and rebellion, and India's fissiparous tendencies found expression in the Sikhs' claiming a right to an independent Khalistan. The old idea of an India of diverse peoples and 565 princely states united in one federated dominion with a limited central government run by peacekeeping Britons was rapidly giving way to the noxious modern politics of violent, segregated nationalisms. A new viceroy was appointed in February 1947, Lord Louis Mountbatten, who declared that India would be granted its independence on 15 August 1947. The Raj was packing up, giving in to Indian lawyers like Gandhi (University College London, Inner Temple), Jawaharlal Nehru (Harrow, Cambridge, Inner Temple), and Ali Jinnah (Lincoln's Inn), that it had educated and trained.

The princes did not want to be absorbed into a nationalistic India or Pakistan, but their pleas were ignored, the British voided their treaty obligations to the states and left them to the sufferance of India and Pakistan, which had far less toleration for princely sovereignty than the British had. As the princely states were partitioned so was the Indian Army, to which so many British officers had devoted their lives and careers. One such, Field Marshal Sir Claude Auchinleck, commander in chief of the Indian army, was given the melancholy task of severing the institution he loved along the ethnic and religious lines that would soon demark India and Pakistan.

Winston Churchill had warned that an independent India would degenerate into communal carnage; he was right. Hardened British officers, used to the slaughter of war, found themselves unable to stomach the sadistic mutilations and mass murders that followed independence and partition—with Sikh, Muslim, and Hindu each trying to outdo the other in preying upon refugees, desecrating women, slitting babies from their mothers' wombs, and killing or mutilating upwards of a million people. The Pax Britannica was no more, and not even Gandhi survived the chaos he helped unleash; he was assassinated by a Hindu nationalist.

The India of the British Raj was a glorious thing, uniting a subcontinent under a benign, tolerant, and liberal administration that strove to improve the lot of the people it served, providing justice, and ruling with a light hand

Films about British India That Anti-Colonialists Don't Want You to See

The Lives of a Bengal Lancer, 1935, with Gary Cooper and Franchot Tone. Good evocation of what life could be like for a young British officer in India.

The Charge of the Light Brigade, 1936, with Errol Flynn and Olivia de Havilland. The history's a little off—the Cawnpore massacre, accurately enough depicted, is misappropriated as a precursor to the Crimean War—but enjoyable nonetheless.

The Drum (also known as *Drums*), 1938, with Sabu and Roger Livesey. Filmed in India, an adventure spectacular set in the early twentieth century.

Gunga Din, 1939, with Cary Grant, Douglas Fairbanks Jr., and Victor McLaglen. *The* great Indian adventure film; Rudyard Kipling (an actor portraying him, that is) makes a guest appearance.

Northwest Frontier (also known as *Flame over India*), 1959, with Kenneth Moore and Lauren Bacall. A nifty little thriller that nicely captures how a well-meaning British officer might do his duty in terrific style, and yet earn "the blame of those ye better / The hate of those ye guard."

The Man Who Would Be King, 1975, with Sean Connery and Michael Caine. Based on the Rudyard Kipling short story. Two British soldiers decide to set up a kingdom of their own.

and through local rulers wherever possible, showing the mailed fist only to keep the peace, and with an army drawn from the subcontinent's own "martial races." From its ashes at least something has been saved—Britain's democratic principles; English language and literature, and the idea of a free and popular press; the shared games and food; and a nostalgic affection in many circles, including Indian ones, for what once was.

Chapter 12

ROBERT CLIVE,
1ST BARON CLIVE
(1725–1774)

"Our island, so fertile in heroes and statesmen, has scarcely ever produced a man more truly great...."

—*Lord Macaulay on Robert Clive*[1]

Robert Clive—Clive of India, a man who would conquer a subcontinent for the British Empire (and also predict the Americans would create an empire of their own rather than stay loyal to Britain)—was a boy who loved fighting. His uncle tried to cure him of it, saying that "I do what I can to suppress the hero,"[2] but as time would prove, the hero would win out. Clive led a gang of young hooligans who threatened shopkeepers in a year-round version of trick or treat; in this case: pay up or we smash your windows.

He was not lowly born, but rather came from the respectable middle class (his father was a middling country squire turned London lawyer and a member of Parliament). Clive wasn't much of a student, however, and his youthful high spirits eventually congealed into a dour visage. He seemed a young man without bright prospects until his father introduced him to a director of the East India Company, with whom he signed on as a clerk. The job was in Madras, India.

Did you know?

- Clive learned Portuguese while stranded in Brazil on his first trip to India, but never learned an Indian language, despite leading Indian armies into battle, creating the British Empire in India, and serving as India's governor-general

- At the Battle of Plassey, Clive with 3,000 men defeated an army of more than 50,000

- His death remains a mystery

The passage took him through storms and bad seamanship, the loss of many of his belongings, and an unexpected nine-month idyll in Brazil where he taught himself a smattering of Portuguese. Though he would later lead sepoys into battle, Clive never bothered to learn any of the native languages of the subcontinent. But Portuguese was useful with the traders in India, and perhaps it was useful with the young ladies of Brazil. From there he sailed to South Africa and then to Madras where, in June 1744, he was confronted by the heat, smells, and jostling humanity of India. He was not happy. He was lonely, and that little corner of England which was the East India Company's Fort St. George left him feeling stifled. He whiled away his spare hours drinking, and, more important, reading. The unstudious ruffian became an autodidact. His repressed energies yearned for an outlet greater than acting as a clerk for the company. He soon found one—and if he had not he might very well have killed himself. He confided to a friend that he had put a pistol to his head and twice pulled the trigger with no result, convincing him that destiny had something in store for him. That thing was war.

From Clerk to Hero

In 1746, in a spillover from the Austrian War of Succession, the French seized Madras. Clive was imprisoned—but not well guarded. Disguised as Indians, he and three of his colleagues escaped to the nearest English settlement (though it was fifty miles away), Fort St. David. Burning with a young man's desire for revenge, he enlisted in the Company's army. In terms of prestige, this was a catastrophic plunge from being a clerk, but it suited both the circumstances and his temperament. Clive was meant to be a soldier—indeed he so distinguished himself in the defense of Fort St. David that he was commissioned an ensign.

His courage extended beyond the battlefield. At a game of cards he accused an officer of cheating. This led to a duel. Clive, with the first shot, missed. The officer told Clive that if he retracted his accusation, he would not fire. Clive responded, "Fire and be damned. I said you cheated, I say so still and I will never repay you."[3] The flabbergasted officer lowered his pistol and that was the end of it—proving if nothing else that Clive had a remarkable facility for avoiding bullets; a talent that is essential for any hero. He dodged them in action after the siege of St. David and showed an equal facility for ducking and weaving his way through slashing sabres while campaigning on behalf of the rajah of Tanjore. He was hot-headed and used his cane to strike men who questioned his courage or the courage of the Company's troops.

Clive, now a lieutenant, would gladly have continued his military career, but the Company was more interested in profits than military glory and conquest (though these kept coming) and took a heavy scalpel to the defense budget. Clive returned to civilian employment but at a much higher level and with the goal of making his fortune. He was a rising young man.

He had a French counterpart, twenty-eight years his senior, haughty, clever, quite brilliant, scheming, and ambitious—Joseph Francois Dupleix, the governor-general of French India who aimed to have India entire by alliances with Indian princes. The British, watching French influence sweep southern India, drew a line in the sands of the Carnatic (southeastern India), backing a rival nawab. The result was a jolly, reputation-making war for Clive.

But it didn't start in a very jolly way. Clive was relegated to supplying the army rather than leading a portion of it. That wouldn't stand—especially as the Company's initial efforts to support its rival nawab, Muhammad Ali, were feeble and embarrassing in the extreme. Clive demanded the rank of captain and said he would serve without pay. It was an offer that no businessman—and the East India Company was a business after all—could refuse. Duly commissioned, he took the field and soon slipped through enemy lines to the besieged city of Trichinopoly where Ali's forces were outnumbered ten to one (20,000 against 2,000), and 60 Britons stood against 800 French.

Ali and Clive contrived a scheme to break the siege by hitting the nawab Chanda Sahib at Arcot, the capital of the Carnatic. The twenty-six-year-old Clive, raising troops at Fort St. David and Fort St. George, marched from Madras with an army of 200 Europeans and perhaps 300 to 500 sepoys. They were a ragamuffin bunch; their eight officers were men like Clive—civilians turned soldiers; only two or three had seen action. Clive set his men a terrific pace, for he hoped to surprise the Arcot garrison. He didn't do that, but his forced march through drenching thunderstorms convinced the nawab's army to flee. Clive's troops, they thought, must be supermen; Clive entered Arcot as a liberator.

Clive worked to stay on the good side of the city's inhabitants, but he and his men knew better than to trust to the goodwill of Arcot's people; they would surely turn from friend to foe if interest so dictated. The city appeared indefensible given the number of men he had, and it surely housed thousands of Chanda Sahib loyalists who might turn their hands to murder or insurrection. Still, Clive was resolved to hold it. He harried Chanda Sahib's men camped outside Arcot and did what he could to better supply and defend the city's fort. His manpower resources were dwindling, as he had to send troops back for the possible defense of Madras. He had no more than 320 effectives to hold the city.

On 23 September, an army of at least 10,000 men attacked Arcot, quickly breaching the crumbling city walls. Clive and his men held the fort in the city center; and while the enemy expected him to be cowed, Clive led his troopers charging to seize the enemy's big French guns. They failed but again stunned Chanda Sahib's men with their audacity. A lieutenant stopped a sniper's bullet meant for Clive, and as the siege progressed, snipers riddled the parapets, slotting Clive's men but never striking home on Clive himself.

Heavy French artillery repeatedly reduced the walls to rubble; and just as repeatedly Clive's men shored them up. The besiegers had swelled to 15,000 men and planned to make their final attack on a Shia Muslim holy day. The vast, frenzied army came charging before dawn on 14 November, with giant iron-helmeted elephants ready to batter the walls. Clive directed musket fire that acted as mice among the pachyderms, scattering the elephants, and kept up waves of volleys that broke up Chanda Sahib's attacks. Frustrated, the enemy tried to reduce Arcot by bombarding it. The crash and rattle of artillery continued until two in the morning. When dawn arose, Clive's men stiffened for the next attack, but saw the field was deserted. Chanda Sahib's officers knew a British relief force and hostile Mahratta mercenaries were on their way.[4] Clive had held the city for two and a half months, and withstood the full power of the besieging enemy for more than seven weeks. It was like the Battle of the Alamo (which of course had not yet happened)—except the defenders won.

The indefatigable Clive now took an army, including the Mahrattas, and harassed the retreating enemy. Always outnumbered, he nevertheless defeated Chanda Sahib's forces repeatedly, building a reputation as an invincible commander, and convincing Indian princes that it was better to be for Clive than against him. Muhammad Ali, still besieged at Trichinopoly, had seen his forces grow to 40,000 men in the wake of Clive's victories—they now outnumbered their besiegers. But no commander had stepped forward to attack the enemy. Clive arrived and changed all that, breaking the siege in April 1752, then penning Chanda Sahib's remaining troops on the island of Srirangam and compelling them to surrender in early June. Chanda Sahib was beheaded by his Indian enemies, and Britain's ally Muhammad Ali became nawab of the Carnatic.

The Prize of Plassey

Clive returned to civilian life and found himself a wealthy man; his earnings as a company steward and commissary officer had stacked up while he was in the field. Celebrated for courage and martial genius, and now with a fortune as well, he nevertheless did not settle down immediately. Indeed, he took a commission to fight the French again, which he did with his usual cool head and reckless courage, spurring on his green troops by constantly exposing himself to the enemy's fire—which continued to miss him.[5] He returned victorious once more, married in February 1753, and embarked for England where he won election to Parliament at the age of twenty-eight.

The victory, however, was short-lived. Clive's election was affirmed by a Parliamentary committee as free from irregularities, but the prime minister, the Duke of Newcastle, and the opposition Tories voted against the committee and denied Clive his seat. Their common interest was keeping Clive's patron, James Fox, from becoming first minister of the Crown. Clive's political ambitions thwarted, his fortune dwindling faster than he expected, he accepted the Company's offer to return to India.

Nominally, Clive was deputy governor of Madras; more important, he was a lieutenant-colonel of the Company's armed forces. His goal was to absorb all of French India. His first adventure was reducing a pirate stronghold at Gheria.

In 1756, Clive was appointed commander of Fort St. David—it was here that he learned that Calcutta had been attacked by the despicable nawab of Bengal, whose lethal imprisonment of nearly a hundred and fifty Britons in the "Black Hole of Calcutta" was an outrage that had to be avenged—and Clive, naturally, was the man selected to do the avenging. He did so with his usual efficiency. In the words of Macaulay, "Nine hundred English infantry, fine troops and full of spirit, and fifteen hundred sepoys, composed the army which sailed to punish a Prince who had more subjects than Louis the Fifteenth."[6] Macaulay gave a generous estimate of British strength; the troops available to Clive were cut by more than a third when some of the ships carrying them had to turn back in stormy seas. Nevertheless, Calcutta was abandoned at his approach—as was discovered when a drunken British sailor wandered out of camp and decided to breach the city walls. He chased off a handful of Muslim soldiers and declared, "The place is mine!"

But delivering Calcutta from the notorious Nawab Siraj-ad-daula was not enough to restore British prestige and preserve the company's position. Clive saw that what was required—and what was possible—was the annexation

Nearly 1,000 Englishmen against more than 55,000 soldiers of the nawab of Bengal = advantage England

"Forty thousand infantry, armed with firelocks, pikes, swords, bows and arrows, covered the plain. They were accompanied by fifty pieces of ordnance of the largest size, each tugged by a long team of white oxen, and each pushed on from behind by an elephant. Some smaller guns, under the direction of a few French auxiliaries, were perhaps more formidable. The cavalry were fifteen thousand, drawn not from the effeminate population of Bengal, but from the bolder race which inhabits the northern provinces; and the practiced eye of Clive could perceive that both the men and the horses were more powerful than those of the Carnatic. The force which he had to oppose to this great multitude consisted of only three thousand men. But of these nearly a thousand were English; and all were led by English officers, and trained in the English discipline."

Lord Macaulay on the Battle of Plassey, *Essay on Clive* (Longmans' English Classics, Longmans, Green and Co., 1928), p. 52

of Bengal; and it was to that task that he set himself. The first step was the destruction of the nawab's army, which was achieved at the Battle of Plassey (23 June 1757) where Clive and 3,000 men routed the more than 50,000 troops of the nawab.

The campaign continued as France, providentially, was at war with England and had allied itself with the nawab, which gave Clive every pretext he needed to fight both. The Company's navy took the lead against the French Bengalese city of Chandernagore, which Clive besieged from the landward side. It fell to the British on 23 March 1757.

But it was not purely force of arms that defeated the nawab; Clive also engaged in a diplomatic conspiracy, supporting a coup against the nawab and deceiving a greedy, two-faced wealthy Bengali merchant who had tried to play both sides and threatened to reveal the plot unless he was given five percent of the nawab's treasury. With an entirely clear conscience, Clive went to the extent of drawing up a fake treaty and forging a signature on it to fool the merchant. The coup was successful, and the merchant, when he discovered that his dreams of avarice had been foiled, lost his mind and become a pathetic simpleton (at least according to Lord Macaulay). Some of Clive's biographers (like Macaulay) condemn Clive for his diplomatic duplicity, accusing him, in essence, of going native rather than upholding British standards—and indeed, years later Clive would face parliamentary questions over his conduct; there was always strong suspicion in Parliament against nabobs, whom it was assumed had cut corners to achieve their riches. Of course, Clive has had his defenders, both at the time and later among some of his biographers (like Robert Harvey). Clive did not interfere when the former nawab was put to death, and he accepted a fortune as a gift from the new nawab—and while this too has come under scrutiny, Clive could have demanded much more; as an employee of the British East India Company there were no bars to his seeking profit from princes. The company, meanwhile, made him governor of Bengal, a country of 40 million people.

For three years he drove himself hard, reinforcing his conquests, dispatching subordinates to smash French or Dutch upstarts, militarily defending the cowardly, corrupt, and conniving new nawab of Bengal against all rivals (while not backing him too much, knowing how conniving he was), and solidifying Britain's hold on most of India. It was demanding work, but financially rewarding. When he returned to England in 1760, Clive was an extraordinarily wealthy man.

Ennobled but Not Respected

In India, he was regarded as an invincible soldier and an authoritative lawgiver. In England, while he entered Parliament (and eventually became Baron Clive of Plassey), he proved inept as a politician (the cynicism he learned in Indian politics being readily ridiculed as lack of principle) and was quickly dismissed as a typical nabob—all new wealth and no finer qualities. It seems poor recompense for a man who had been inarguably heroic in his battles in India; but he also feuded with the directors of the East India Company, which made him appear a man primarily motivated by pecuniary self-interest, though this was not true. Clive was generous with his family, he purchased estates, but for all the wealth he obtained, it seems clear that wealth itself was never his object. Clive was driven much more by a yearning after greatness, for himself and for his country.

How valuable he was in India became manifest after his departure. Muslims and Hindus who had accepted Clive as a disinterested lawgiver were

An Empire Built by Veracity More Than Valor

"English valour and English intelligence have done less to extend and preserve our Oriental empire than English veracity. All that we could have gained by imitating the doublings, the evasions, the fictions, the perjuries which have been employed against us, is as nothing, when compared with what we have gained by being the one power in India on whose word reliance can be placed."

Lord Macaulay, *Essay on Clive* (Longmans' English Classics, Longmans, Green and Co., 1928), pp. 56–57

appalled by the new administration of Henry Vansittart, which seemed driven by greed and was utterly incompetent at keeping the balances of power Clive had maintained between rival Indian rulers. The result was insurrection, mutiny, and war; and while British arms won the day as usual, there was only one man who could restore the political order of Bengal: Clive.

Winning his power struggle against the chairman of the company, Clive returned to India in 1765 as governor with full power to restore the Pax Britannica, root out corruption, and revive the Company's fortunes. All this he did with an ardor as if to prove that he was an idealist after all and devoted to the honor of England. He received from the Mughal of India official title for Britain's holdings on the subcontinent, he reformed the civil service, and he restructured the army. In 1757, with British India furbished and solidified, he returned to England.

But after every such whirlwind of activity Clive paid a price. For all his cool-headedness in battle, his clear-sighted ability to navigate Indian politics, the forcible energies of his personality—once he was expended, he collapsed into depression of a deep and shocking sort, worsened by occasional recurrences of malaria. Though reunited with his wife, and blessed with a happy marriage, Clive found England a gloomy place. In India, he was the man who would be king; in England he was a second-rater: useful abroad, but otherwise a trumped-up parvenu. Indeed, his enemies in the Company and in parliament conspired to portray Clive as avaricious, plundering, and worthy of censure, and used an outbreak of famine in Bengal (caused by drought) as an excuse to excoriate him. In 1772, he took to the floor of the House of Commons to defend himself and did so with an outburst of oratory that astonished his listeners (for he was not known as a speaker). A parliamentary committee investigated him, and during the investigation he made his most famous statement about the riches that had been held out before him after the Battle of Plassey: "An opulent city lay at my mercy. Its richest bankers bid against each other for my smiles. I walked through vaults which were thrown open to me alone, piled on either hand with gold and jewels. By God, Mr. Chairman, at this moment I stand astonished at my own moderation."[7] His final appeal to the House was "leave me my honour, take away my fortune!"[8] Clive was vindicated by parliamentary vote in 1773, but only after the most dreadful attacks had been made upon him.

Advice to a Young Noble-man from King George II

"If he wants to learn the art of war, let him go to Clive!"

Quoted in Mark Bence-Jones, *Clive of India* (Book Club Associates, London, 1974), p. 169

In 1774, in the midst of depression, a severe cold, and recurrent, debilitating stomach pain, he died—though whether of apoplexy, or from an accidental overdose of laudanum, or of a pen knife stabbed into his throat (either by himself or by someone else) is unclear. He was forty-nine and was buried in an unmarked grave in an English church in the small village of Moreton Saye, near where he was born and near to Market Drayton, to whose shopkeepers he and his small gang of child ruffians had threatened broken windows. If the Battle of Waterloo was won on the playing fields of Eton, the Battle of Plassey was won on the streets of Market Drayton. Clive had, at last, truly returned home.

Chapter 13

GEORGE CURZON, 1ST MARQUESS CURZON OF KEDLESTON (1859–1925)

"My name is George Nathaniel Curzon,

I am a most superior person,

My cheek is pink, my hair is sleek,

I dine at Blenheim once a week."

—a bit of doggerel presumed to have been written by two of
Curzon's contemporaries at Balliol College, Oxford[1]

The four lines above are the most quoted lines about Lord Curzon. He was indeed a most superior person, addressing his fellow members of Parliament as "a divinity addressing black beetles."[2] He was perhaps the most widely traveled man of his day: through Europe, the Levant, Central Asia, and the Far and Near East most especially (writing massive volumes on Russia and Central Asia, the Near East, and the Far East). His father, in fact, once asked him, "Why don't you stay at home and be quiet?"[3] That had been the Curzon way for centuries, a noble family without ambition. But George Curzon, while a conservative in politics (and in many of his tastes; he was a great conservator, for instance, in matters architectural), could restrain neither his ambition, nor his self-improving travels, nor his eager and witty tongue. Arrogant, he was nevertheless charming. He cut a swath through women, though never violating his gentleman's code of not

Did you know?

- ♛ Curzon worked to conserve and restore Indian architecture (including the Taj Mahal)

- ♛ He was an early environmentalist in India

- ♛ Curzon believed that Britain stripped of its empire would be "a sort of glorified Belgium"

behaving like a bounder, never despoiling a maiden, and restricting himself, more or less, to the aristocratic wives of complaisant husbands (as was the case with one of the great loves of Curzon's life, Sibell, Lady Grosvenor, whose husband Lord Grosvenor was "a fragile epileptic whose chief passion was steam engines"[4] rather than his wife).

His arrogance had been with him since his schooldays (at Eton and before), in which he was often contemptuous of his instructors, preferring to teach himself—and then humiliating his ignored tutors by scooping up all the academic prizes. He could, from this description, easily be seen as a snooty, sophisticated, rank (albeit high-rank) bastard that women might love (because they do rather like that kind) but that men despise. Yet that would be to take away the wrong impression. No one ever doubted Curzon's self-regard—but they also didn't doubt his talent, or his industry, or, for that matter, his creativity, his wit, and his loyalty in friendship. He was never short of sincere and devoted friends.

Though born to wealth and position at Kedleston Hall, he was raised by sadistic governesses and a father more famous for removing unnecessary coal from fires than for any warm paternal affection. Though energetic, Curzon lived in pain all his adult life because of a riding injury that forced him to wear a metal back brace. The greatest shock of his young life was not that injury, but instead taking a second-class rather than a first-class degree in the second half of his classics course at Oxford (divided into "Mods" and "Greats"; he had taken a first in "Mods")—a shortfall he redressed by setting himself to win two prestigious academic prizes, which he did, and a fellowship to All Souls.

His ultimate goal was not academic, but political. In 1885 he became private secretary to the prime minister, Lord Salisbury, leader of the Conservative Party. In 1886, he entered Parliament himself, though he seemed far less interested in constituency matters than in his global travels. In 1895, he married an American, Mary Leiter, heiress to a department store fortune;

their engagement was kept secret for two years, during which time she rarely saw him or heard from him, so that he could undertake dangerous travels in the East. He then settled into work in the new Conservative government as the parliamentary under-secretary for foreign affairs. In 1898, the thirty-nine-year-old Curzon became viceroy of India.

The Great Viceroy

Curzon, whose global travels put him in a position to make apt comparisons, judged the British Empire "under Providence, the greatest instrument for good that the world has seen."[5] In India, he set about immediately to make sure that such a judgment could be main-

> ## Great Moments in British Imperial History
>
> In 1894, during a singular visit to the Northwest Frontier, in the region of the Pamir Mountains, along the Oxus River, Curzon came riding along the grassy plains of Mastuj and was overcome with an overwhelming desire for a beer. As the desire waxed he saw in the distance a horseman bearing towards him. The man pulled rein just before Curzon, identified himself as the servant of Captain Francis Younghusband, and held out a bottle of Bass Ale.

tained. He reformed and improved the already high standards of the Indian Civil Service; created an imperial cadet corps to provide military training and special commissions for Indian princes; and worked assiduously to reconcile the tribes of the northwest frontier and block Russian penetration into British areas of influence. An ardent imperialist in foreign policy, he was a paternalist in domestic policy and saw his role as helping to improve the lot of the Indians. He also devoted himself to his architectural passion, most especially the restoration of the Taj Mahal, which he adored.

Aristocrat that he was, he felt a kinship with the poor (*noblesse oblige*) and with the native aristocracy, but disdain for the Indian commercial classes and most especially the Babus, the educated Indians of Bengal, who were full of fruity, overblown rhetoric and personal and nationalistic aspirations that he opposed. Still, he was India's defender, both in his relations with the British government and in his belief in the value of its ancient civilization. If the British position was to be justified, Britons in India had to behave with honesty and justice; if they didn't they would be punished; and Curzon made no exceptions for British merchants, planters, or soldiers. Like many Englishmen, he respected Islam, though he was less certain of Hinduism. He was an opponent of Christian missionaries, thinking them meddlesome and unhelpful to the Empire. Macaulay had wanted to create a class of Indian Englishmen. Curzon wanted to leave Indian civilization alone and govern through the British Raj and the native aristocracy. In this, he felt, there was stability, order, and a hope for continuity and permanence in maintaining British India.

He built more railroads than any other governor-general (or viceroy) in India. He advanced agrarian reforms to help Indian peasants maintain their

The Viceroy on His Charge

"I do not see how any Englishman contrasting India as it is now with what it was, and would certainly have been under any other conditions than British rule, can fail to see that we came and have stayed here under no blind or capricious impulse, but in obedience to what some (of whom I am one) would call the decree of Providence, others the law of destiny—in any case for the lasting benefit of millions of the human race. We often make great mistakes here: we are sometimes hard, and insolent, and overbearing: we are a good deal strangled with red tape. But none the less, I do firmly believe that there is no Government in the world (and I have seen most) that rests on so secure a moral basis, or that is more freely animated by duty."

Curzon, viceroy of India, in a letter to John Morley, Liberal member of Parliament (and a future secretary of state for India), in the summer of 1900, quoted in David Gilmour, *Curzon: Imperial Statesman* (Farrar, Straus and Giroux, 2003), p. 166

land. He promoted massive new irrigation projects, hoping to prevent a replay of the horrific famine that followed the drought of 1899. He toured every hospital he could find, generally pleased at the efforts of British doctors and civil servants and unimpressed by the fatalistic attitude of the native Indian officials.

It became his habit to work himself into a state of physical collapse—in part because he thought he could do everyone's job better himself, and proceeded to do so; in part because of his physical disabilities, most particularly his bad back, which suffered from the overwork and lack of exercise; and in part because when he was bedridden he could accomplish even more, writing letters, dispatches, and reports, so collapse could be considered a positive good to a man who wanted to be judged by what he had achieved for the Indians. He meant to achieve a lot—so much, in fact, that when his name was bruited about as a potential foreign secretary or even prime minister, he poohed-poohed the suggestion. His path to achievement was as viceroy of India.

Curzon was an Orientalist—he loved Asia, and wanted it preserved in all its rough, exotic glory, and he spent enormous amounts of time, money, and effort restoring historic Indian buildings—even booting Britons out in the process. India's historical architecture had no better friend than Curzon. He was also something of a conservationist, showing a rare concern for the preservation of Indian wildlife.

Running through all this was Curzon's belief in British aristocrats running India with the assistance of Indian aristocrats who, if they went to Oxford or Cambridge, would only return to India despising their own people and picking up the worst habits a wealthy young man could pick up in such surroundings—an excessive taste for drink and a proclivity for dissipation. Curzon preferred princes on elephants to princes gambling in Monte Carlo and maintaining European mistresses. He considered it part of his duty to lecture the princes on their family affairs—and, as might be surmised, he was very fond of lecturing other people. While Curzon believed in the cult of the English gentleman and saw Christianity as an important source of Western superiority, he did not believe that Christianity was an exportable commodity or that Indian princes should be English gentlemen rather than Indian ones. It was to this end that Curzon reformed the Indian colleges and set up an Indian officer-training program. The princes were still taught English ways and tastes, but at least they learned them in India, and military training and discipline was the one way to shore up the moral fibre of princes who might otherwise unravel with wine, women, and song.

While Curzon remained a mighty force in India—when his wife fell sick in England he received messages of sympathy from all the Indian princes—his abortive second term as viceroy (1904–05) helped to ruin his reputation. Curzon authorized the administrative partition of Bengal—a province designed by British line-drawers and now amended by them, but to the dismay of the Bengalis, who had taken fiercely to the "nationality" given them by the British; they would not have it redrawn away, and the new lines were eventually scrapped (in 1911). More immediately important to Curzon was his conflict with the new commander in chief of the Indian Army, Lord Kitchener. Kitchener successfully conspired against Curzon to concentrate all military authority in his own hands (stripping it from the Military Member of the Viceroy's Council, who represented the Military Department and acted as both an adviser to the Viceroy and the commander in chief). In consequence, Curzon resigned.

An Empire of Good Taste

"After every other viceroy has been forgotten, Curzon will be remembered because he restored all that was beautiful in India."

Jawaharlal Nehru, first prime minister of independent India, quoted in Kenneth Rose, *Curzon: A Most Superior Person* (Weidenfeld and Nicolson, 1969), p. 239

Righteous Viceroy

"A hundred times in India have I said to myself, Oh that to every Englishman in this country, as he ends his work, might be truthfully applied the phrase, 'Thou hast loved righteousness and hated iniquity.' No man has, I believe, ever served India faithfully of whom that could not be said. All other triumphs are tinsel and sham.... I have worked for no other aim. Let India be my judge."

From Lord Curzon's farewell speech at the Byculla Club in Bombay, 16 November 1905, quoted in Sir Thomas Raleigh's collection of Curzon's viceregal speeches, *Lord Curzon in India* (Adamant Media Corporation, 2005), pp. 589–90

At home, and despite enjoying the king's favor, Curzon's political career went on the skids, without a parliamentary seat and denied a peerage. In 1906 his wife Mary, who had given him three daughters, died. She was only thirty-six, but the last two years of her life had been blighted by sickness. Despairing after his wife's death, Curzon wrote, "Every man's hand has long been against me, and now God's hand has turned against me too."[6]

Curzon's Age of Lead

Curzon had lost an empire and had yet to find a role. He busied himself in the meantime with a myriad of architectural projects and with micro-managing every responsibility to which he could turn his hand, believing that he (assisted by his daughters) was better at weeding than any gardener, better at dusting books than any housekeeper, and better at devising the curriculum for his girls' schooling than any governess. He became a chancellor at Oxford and was elevated to the House of Lords, where he became a defender of its prerogatives, while also being a champion of reform. He showed himself ahead of his time in his opposition to female suffrage.

But really, until the First World War, it seemed that Curzon's star had fallen. He certainly felt so; at the outset of the war he felt sadly unemployed, lamenting that "a man who at 39 was thought good enough to rule 300 millions of people—and did rule them—is apparently useless at 55 when the existence of his country is at stake."[7] He took a special interest in supporting India's military units (ensuring, for instance, that they were all supplied with massive water boilers—paid for out of his own pocket—for tea), harbored the Belgian royal family on his estates, and was an active opponent, again, of Lord Kitchener, who argued for an all-volunteer force while Curzon believed in the necessity of conscription.

In December 1916, the new prime minister, David Lloyd George, leading a Liberal-Tory Coalition government, brought Curzon into the War Cabinet. Curzon was easily the best-informed cabinet member on questions involving India and the Middle East, but his advice was routinely ignored. He opposed occupying any more of Mesopotamia beyond the port of Basra; he opposed promising the Arabs their own state or carving states out of the defeated Ottoman Empire, and he was opposed to the Balfour Declaration of 1917, which put the British government on record supporting a Jewish state in Palestine. His arguments were, in each of these cases, dismissed, which resulted in an enormously costly campaign in Mesopotamia, competing promises to the Arabs and the French, and the sowing of greater enmity between Arabs and Jews in the Middle East. His great fear was that the Allies would negotiate a peace in the West in exchange for giving Germany a free hand in Eastern Europe—though this hardly seems the nightmare Curzon imagined it to be.

Curzon accepted that Allied war rhetoric inevitably meant concessions on self-government for India, but he was quick to insist that self-government could only be successfully achieved under British tutelage and supervision, which could last for centuries. Many of his parliamentary colleagues, however, were impatient to speed things along. Curzon accepted that nationalism seemed an unstoppable consequence of the war, and that some people preferred to be badly governed by their own rather than well governed by another. But independence, to which he thought hasty reforms inevitably led, would in his view be a tragedy for the Indians *and* the British—putting the interests of politicized Bengali lawyers over the interests of the Indian people as a whole and relegating Britain to a second-rank power.

In 1919, he became foreign secretary, a position that had once seemed inevitable but that he finally achieved only by lobbying Lloyd George. Curzon drew the border between Poland and the Soviet Union (the Curzon Line) and rebuffed the secretary of state for war, Winston Churchill, who wanted to crush the Russian Bolsheviks, because Curzon feared the White Russians would more seriously threaten British interests in central Asia. He also defeated Churchill on the matter of Egypt, over which Lloyd George and Churchill wanted to maintain the British protectorate that had existed under the Ottoman Empire, while Curzon insisted on recognizing Egyptian independence (albeit under British supervision and military defense).

That victory, if such it was, had to compensate for the unraveling agreement he thought he had reached with Persia. Curzon had agreed to guarantee Persia's independence, while flooding it with British assistance— political, military, technical, and commercial—in exchange for securing British rights to Persia's oil fields. As Curzon conceived the agreement, it neatly welded Persian self-interest to the interests of the British Empire. To his dismay the agreement was never formally ratified in Tehran and was then repudiated by the new Persian government (taking power in a military coup) in 1921, though the Persians still wanted British aid and assistance. His amour-propre badly wounded by Persian ingratitude—and the indifference of his Cabinet colleagues who were far more interested in retrenching British commitments than extending them—he vowed never to negotiate with the Persians again.

He was also determined, despite his Persian setback, not to resign again. His resignation as viceroy had cast him into the political wilderness, and though he felt forever at odds with Churchill and Lloyd George (who opposed him on Greek and Turkish policy; they being philhellenes, he being pragmatically pro-Turk), he was determined to stick it out. Indeed he stuck it out even after the Conservatives came to power and he was passed over, to his immense disappointment and even shame, as prime minister—that prize going to Stanley Baldwin. But in January 1924, Labour took power and Curzon was out at the Foreign Office. When the Conservatives were returned to power later in the year, Baldwin kept him as leader of the House of Lords but denied him the Foreign Office, offering him in recompense the chairmanship of the Committee of Imperial Defence.[8] He died a few months later, prematurely aged from overwork.

> ## Curzon's Definition of British Imperialism
>
> "A discipline, an inspiration, and a faith." Without the empire, Britain would no longer be a world power, but would become "a sort of glorified Belgium" with "no aspiration but a narrow and selfish materialism."
>
> Quoted in David Gilmour, *Curzon: Imperial Statesman* (Farrar, Straus and Giroux, 2003), p. 363

Curzon had spilled out his life for the cause of the Empire—and most particularly for India. But by the time he died, his ideals had faded from a Britain that was more democratic, less imperialistic, and even capable of electing a socialist government. He was not a man easy to like, but he was a dedicated patriot all the same. Churchill's epitaph for him has never been bettered: "The morning had been golden; the noontide was bronze; and the evening lead. But all were solid and each was polished till it shone after its fashion."[9]

Chapter 14

LOUIS MOUNTBATTEN, 1ST EARL MOUNTBATTEN OF BURMA (1900-1979)

"The only man I have ever been impressed with all my life is Lord Mountbatten."

—*Muhammad Ali Jinnah, first governor-general of Pakistan, 1948*[1]

I f nothing else, Mountbatten looked the part—handsome, patrician, tall and striking in uniform, perfect casting for a modern viceroy of India, even if his inevitable role was to preside over an epic tragedy. He was born a German prince—Prince Louis of Battenberg—though his place of birth was Windsor Castle and his eventual moniker of choice was Dickie. His father, also styled Prince Louis of Battenberg, had become a British subject when he joined the Royal Navy at the age of fourteen—an idea recommended to him by two of his English cousins, who happened to be the son and daughter of Queen Victoria.

Dickie's father had grown up speaking German, French, and English; and Dickie—the youngest, by eight years, of four children—was expected to do the same, which was easy enough because as a young boy he holidayed in Germany and spent time with his cosmopolitan Russian cousins, the Romanovs. His father rose to become an admiral and eventually (1912) First Sea Lord, a position he resigned in October 1914 as his health declined under the stress of the First World War and the mob's demand for the scalp of the "German" Battenberg. In July 1917 he renounced his

Did you know?

♛ Mountbatten's cousins were the Romanovs, executed by the Bolsheviks

♛ Noël Coward's famous film *In Which We Serve* is based on the wartime service of Lord Mountbatten

♛ Mountbatten advocated the creation of iceberg-based aircraft carriers

German titles and changed the family name to the more English-sounding Mountbatten.

Young Mountbatten

Dickie, unlike his father, had no foreign accent, and thus was freer to live the serene life of an English aristocrat (he was in fact, properly, "His Serene Highness Prince Louis"); he was cheerful in demeanor, diligent in his studies (he had to be, as he was not naturally clever), and eager, even if not gifted, on the playing field. There was no question as to his career—he was bound for the Navy, supposing he could scrape by on his mathematics. He was twelve, nearly thirteen, when he entered the Royal Naval College at Osborne; the First World War began while he was a cadet, and he was there when his father was forced to resign as First Sea Lord. His ambition crystallized: he would take his father's place. The next step was to the Royal Naval College at Dartmouth in January 1915, and then on to the Naval College at Keyham where he surprised by graduating top of his class. By July 1916 he was a midshipman aboard the battle cruiser HMS *Lion*, the flagship of the Admiral of the Fleet, Sir David Beatty, the hero of Jutland. Beatty became commander in chief of the Grand Fleet and Dickie transferred to the flagship of the fleet, HMS *Queen Elizabeth*. It was aboard the *Queen Elizabeth* that he learned that his surname had been changed and he was now Lord Louis Mountbatten. He ended the war a sub-lieutenant and executive officer of a patrol boat. In 1919, the Navy sent him to attend Cambridge.

This proved to be a bad idea. Mountbatten had been raised with a simple creed: do the right thing. It had been reinforced by the Navy. It provided what moral ballast there was to his agnostic Anglicanism. As he had no greater philosophical resources—and also had a tremendous fondness for gadgets, inventions,[2] and new technology; in short, for "progress"; he was vulnerable to the conceit—fed to him by a cultured, leftist subversive named Peter Murphy—that the Left was on the side of justice and progress. The Bolsheviks who murdered the Russian royal family, his cousins the Romanovs, might have gotten carried away, but on the whole, the Left's goals were enlightened. Mountbatten might glory in his bloodlines (his best friends at Cambridge were the Prince of Wales and the future King George VI), his cultural tastes might be conservative and traditional, he might be a career Navy man pledged to the defense of the realm, but in his politics he always assumed that the Left spoke for the future and for what was morally right. Nevertheless, when he accompanied the Prince of Wales on his trip to India in 1921, Mountbatten had no sympathy for Indian nationalists—his mind was focused more on mastering the great game of polo (to which he became devoted) than on the rumbling independence movement.

If Mountbatten made a mistake in befriending Peter Murphy at Cambridge, he perhaps compounded it by marrying Edwina Ashley (the Prince of Wales approved of her, but then again, he was a famously disastrous judge of women). Edwina had loads of cash from her maternal grandfather, Sir Ernest Cassel, a German Jew who had come to England as a young man and become an extraordinarily successful financier, friend of King Edward VII, and Catholic convert. Her father was Lieutenant-Colonel Wilfrid Ashley, a Conservative M.P. Edwina, however, was no conservative. An opinionated flapper, she shared Mountbatten's left-wing politics but was impatient with Mountbatten's desire for a traditional marriage, had a taste for extramarital affairs, and left an ever-understanding Mountbatten to do most of the raising of their children— while resenting and trying to prevent his closeness to them. Like many a high-living socialite she proved her merit when danger threatened, working with the St. John's Ambulance Brigade during the war, and easing the suffering of Indians amidst the carnage and misery of India's partition. She died in 1960 while inspecting hospital facilities in Borneo; Mountbatten never remarried.

Mountbatten survived the swingeing cuts to the armed services after World War I—and while some attributed this to royal intervention on his behalf, there was no doubt that he was a dedicated, energetic, industrious officer who knew how to handle men (he made a point of memorizing a biographical profile of every man under his command). As at school, he possessed no extraordinary talent, but he did have the gift of charm, a determination to succeed, a natural capacity for detail and hard work, and an ability to teach and inspire young officers.

He excelled as a signals officer, qualified as a French translator, and commanded a destroyer before being appointed to the Fleet Air Arm at the Admiralty. He was no mere pencil pusher but an active proponent of myriad improvements from acquiring better guns to adopting the Typex enciphering machine. In London, and with his social connections, he became the close friend of two Tory politicians, Anthony Eden and Duff Cooper—all three of them sharing strong anti-fascist sentiments and opposition to a policy of appeasing Hitler and Mussolini. Captain Cosmo Graham wrote this assessment of Mountbatten on his departure from the Admiralty in 1938: "He possesses a naïve simplicity combined with a compelling manner and dynamic energy. His interests incline mainly towards the material world and he is, therefore, inclined to be surprised by the unexpected; he has been so successful in that sphere that he does not contemplate failure. His social assets are invaluable in any rank to any Service. His natural thoroughness is extended to sport. Desirable as it is to avoid superlatives, he has nearly all the qualities and qualifications for the highest commands."[3]

Mountbatten as Commander of HMS *Kelly*

"I want to make it clear to all of you that I shall never give the order to 'abandon ship,' the only way you can leave the ship is if she sinks beneath your feet."

Quoted in Philip Ziegler, *Mountbatten: The Official Biography* (Collins, 1985), p. 128

With a second World War imminent, he was about to test his mettle.

In 1939, he became commander of the destroyer HMS *Kelly*, and quickly earned a reputation for dash, daring, and fearless and inspiring leadership. The *Kelly* evacuated troops from Norway, fought German U-boats and bombers, battled in the Mediterranean, and survived (at least for a while, thanks to gallant seamanship) wounds that should have sunk her. Churchill, ever appreciative of a well-born swashbuckler, became one of Mountbatten's wartime champions. When Ger-

A Broadminded Fellow

"Isn't it grand news that the Russians are fighting on our side? The original Bolsheviks murdered most of our relations and I never thought the day would come when I would welcome them as allies, but we must on no account let the Nazis win, must we?"

Letter from Lord Louis Mountbatten to his daughter Pamela, 14 July 1941

man bombers finally sank the *Kelly* during the battle for Crete in 1941, Mountbatten was last to leave the ship—indeed almost went down with her—and then swam to help others as German machine guns strafed the water. They were rescued by HMS *Kipling*. The *Kelly*'s story became the (officially unacknowledged) basis of Noël Coward's film *In Which We Serve*, with Coward playing the captain based on Mountbatten (they were friends).

With the *Kelly* at the bottom of the ocean, in August 1941 Mountbatten was assigned to command HMS *Illustrious*, then being repaired in Norfolk, Virginia, giving him an excuse to make a triumphal tour of the United States (where his two daughters had been evacuated). He not only met with the president but toured Pearl Harbor—and was appalled at how vulnerable it was to a possible Japanese attack. While in America he received an urgent message that his appointment to HMS *Illustrious* had been canceled. Churchill wanted him to organize combined operations. Promoted to commodore, Mountbatten was ordered to prepare everything necessary—from landing craft to men—for raiding the coast of France, though in fact Mountbatten's first raid was in Norway. (Mountbatten also backed an extraordinary

No False Humility

"My task is probably the biggest and most difficult which any Englishman has been given in the war. To reconquer Burma, Malaya, the Dutch East Indies and all the places in which the British Empire's present forces received an unparalleled series of defeats on land, at sea, and in the air. Particularly as no one seems to have done anything about it until now!"

Mountbatten writing to his daughter Patricia about his appointment as Supreme Allied Commander of the Southeast Asian Theatre, 26 August 1943

project to make unsinkable iceberg aircraft carriers—an idea, developed by some of his boffins, which collapsed because of the enormous expense involved.)

Just as Drake had singed the beard of the king of Spain, Mountbatten's task was to singe the toothbrush moustache of the führer of the Reich. In March 1942, his men destroyed the dry dock at St. Nazaire. Though these and other raids pleased Churchill and raised Allied morale, they often came at a high cost in casualties for the gains made. Churchill made Mountbatten an acting vice admiral and chief of combined operations.

As combined operations chief, Mountbatten organized the ill-fated raid on Dieppe where Canadian commandos took nearly seventy percent casualties—though Eisenhower said the hard lessons learned at Dieppe made success at Normandy possible, and Churchill's confidence in Mountbatten was unabated. In October 1943, Churchill appointed Mountbatten Supreme Allied Commander in Southeast Asia, leading the campaign to reclaim Burma. In that role Mountbatten had to manage such difficult customers as the Anglophobic, misanthropic American General "Vinegar Joe" Stilwell—one of whose nicest names for Mountbatten was "glamour boy" and who was officially his deputy—and Generalissimo Chiang Kai-shek, the leader of the Chinese nationalist government. The end result was victory over formidable obstacles of geography and disease and a fanatical enemy.

Mountbatten saw British victories in Southeast Asia as a triumph of civilization over the depraved barbarism of imperial Japan. He believed that

Britain's colonies welcomed the return of the Union Jack (which for the most part they did),[4] while also believing it necessary to accommodate nationalist, and usually leftist, native forces. For Britain's Labour government (elected in July 1945), Mountbatten's position and progressive sympathies made him the natural choice to replace Lord Wavell as viceroy of India in 1947.

Wavell had given up trying to reconcile India's Hindus and Muslims. After the Hindu-dominated Congress Party refused to accept a federated India—and Muslims responded with sectarian massacre—Wavell thought Britain was left with two unpalatable choices: scuttle and run, or massively reinforce the Indian army and put off independence for another decade and a half. Mountbatten's assignment was to guide the subcontinent into independence, and to do so swiftly.

Labour's Viceroy

Mountbatten was already well-regarded by Indian nationalists. Jawaharlal Nehru, who had met him in Singapore, had remarked to Aung San, the Communist-nationalist leader of Burma, that Mountbatten was "a very noble speciman of British imperialism."[5] He was sworn in as viceroy in March 1947 with a deadline of 1 June 1948 to bring India to independence. There were two main parties to the negotiations: Nehru, leader of the Congress Party, whom Mountbatten found congenial and willing to negotiate, and Muhammad Ali Jinnah of the Muslim League, whom he found cold and intransigent—Jinnah had plumped for partition, for an independent Muslim Pakistan. As Jinnah would not budge, and as the deadline was inexorable, it was a fait accompli, in Mountbatten's opinion, that British India would not become independent whole and entire. The major loser in this was the Indian people themselves, as millions were forced to flee their homes and hundreds of thousands were killed as Muslim and Hindu butchered each other freed from the constraints of effective British peace-keeping.[6] Another casualty was the Indian princes whose rights, privileges, and semi-autonomous status were crushed by the governments of India and Pakistan. The Hindu maharajah of Muslim-majority Kashmir delayed declaring his loyalty to either side for as long as possible. He hoped against all evidence that Britain would stay. When he finally declared he would join India, it sparked the first Indian-Pakistani War in 1947–48, leading to Kashmir's own partition between the two states.

Churchill held Mountbatten partially culpable for the disaster of independence—and for the death knell it sounded for the British Empire. The result might have been inevitable, given the policy of the Labour government, but Churchill was appalled that Mountbatten would lend his hand to it, and only with the passage of time could he reconcile with his former favorite. Churchill well knew the difficulties Mountbatten faced, yet could but mourn in 1947 that "We are of course only at the beginning of these horrors and butcheries, perpetrated upon one another, men, women, and children, with the ferocity of cannibals, by races gifted with capacities of the highest culture and who had for generations dwelt side by side in general peace under the broad, tolerant and impartial rule of the British Crown and Parliament."[7] Churchill did not see how the removal of that broad, tolerant, and impartial rule—to be replaced by fanatic sectarianism—could possibly be a good thing.

Mountbatten believed that history—no less than the praise he received from Nehru, Jinnah, the Labour government, and much of the liberal press—would vindicate his viceroyship, if for no other reason than that he had contrived to bring both India and Pakistan into the British Commonwealth. If that seems a trifling bauble today, it was thought to be worth much more in 1947 (so much so that Indian nationalists suspected it and British politicians and civil servants fretted about it overstretching British resources and commitments). In Mountbatten's vision, India and Pakistan would join

Australia and Canada as real and lasting allies of Britain, tied to the Mother Country by mystic chords of memory. Mountbatten was as sentimental in his progressive liberalism as Churchill was in his nostalgic conservatism; both thought Britain and India (and Pakistan) belonged together.[8] As a reward for his service, Lord Louis became Earl Mountbatten of Burma.

There were other consolations. His nephew, and fellow naval officer, Prince Philip took on his maternal grandparents' surname of Mountbatten and married Princess Elizabeth, future queen of the United Kingdom of Great Britain and Northern Ireland; Mountbatten became a mentor to the couple's first-born son, Prince Charles. And there was the sea and his career as a naval officer, which reached its apotheosis in his elevation to First Sea Lord (1955–59), after a stint as commander in chief of the Mediterranean Fleet, and promotion to the highest naval rank, Admiral of the Fleet. It was followed by his appointment as Chief of the Defence Staff (1959–65), his last military posting. He was instrumental in Britain's adoption of nuclear-powered submarines, advocated nuclear arms reductions (but not unilateral nuclear disarmament), pushed for interservice cooperation, and argued for a mobile British strike force based on aircraft carriers.

In his retirement, Mountbatten acted as an unofficial ambassador for Britain, devoted himself to a vast number of worthy organizations and charities, and became president of United World Colleges, which were meant to spread the progressive spirit of internationalism. The denouement of Mountbatten's life was appropriately, if unfortunately and gruesomely, imperial. He kept a summer home in Ireland, from which he enjoyed boating. On 27 August 1979, the IRA blew up his boat, killing Mountbatten, his grandson, another young boy, and an eighty-three-year-old woman, as well as seriously injuring three others. It was a typical pointless and bloodthirsty act of murder by the IRA, timed to coincide with an ambush on a British patrol in Northern Ireland that left eighteen paratroopers dead. Mountbatten might have appreciated the irony that, in assassinating him, the IRA had killed an impeccable liberal who actually, if privately, supported the idea of a united Ireland.

Part V

AFRICA

Chapter 15

THE DARK CONTINENT

The irony of the British Empire in Africa is that while it started with slave ships tapping into the millennium-old slave trade of the Dark Continent, Britain became the most powerful force in the world for ending slavery and the slave trade, and the anti-slaving campaign drove the expansion of the British Empire.

British slave ships plied the Atlantic in the sixteenth, seventeenth, and eighteenth centuries, bringing their human cargo to work the plantations of the West Indies and continental North America. But by 1807, Britain's parliament had banned the slave trade, and in true imperial nanny fashion prohibited it for everyone else too, declaring slavery a crime—like piracy, at which the British had also formerly excelled. The Royal Navy now had as one of its chief and most dangerous duties the patrolling of West Africa against the slavers. As the British flag traveled across the continent, so too did its mission to squelch the slave trade, convert the heathen, and deliver law, ports, and roads. In addition, in southern Africa the British unearthed diamonds and gold; in eastern Africa they established farms and ranches; in northern Africa they took command of the Suez Canal; and everywhere in Africa they were motivated by something else: a desire for discovery— most famously, to find the source of the Nile.

Did you know?

- ♛ Britain's primary interest in Africa in the mid-nineteenth century was abolishing the slave trade

- ♛ Sub-Saharan Africans never invented the wheel or a written language (the British gave them both)

- ♛ Jan Smuts, a South African who fought against the British in the Boer War, became a British field marshal and a leader in the creation of both the League of Nations and the United Nations

Ashanti

Britain's West African colonies—the Gambia, the Gold Coast (modern Ghana), Nigeria (which didn't become an official British protectorate until 1901), and Sierra Leone—were established as outposts for the Royal Navy's anti-slavery missions, with Sierra Leone set aside as a colony for freed slaves. West Africa was dangerous largely because of disease, but there was also the danger of hostile tribes—the conflict with one such tribe created the epic conflict of British West Africa, the Ashanti Wars.

The Ashanti, the great inland kingdom of the Gold Coast, had fought the British repeatedly (with long intervals of peace), largely over strips of shoreline where the British protected coastal tribes. Sir Charles MacCarthy (1764–1824), an Irish soldier-of-fortune whom the British made governor of Sierra Leone, was one of the Ashanti's most celebrated early victims.

In 1821, the British Crown absorbed the Gold Coast from the British African Company of Merchants, which was judged too feeble in suppressing the slave trade. It was put under the jurisdiction of MacCarthy, who fought slavers and established schools for children orphaned by the slave trade. But for all his good works he came into conflict with the Ashanti, and in a punitive expedition against them he was killed; his corpse was decapitated, and his skull, gold plated, became a goblet for the Ashanti king.

But the great Anglo-Ashanti War is reckoned to be the one of 1873–74, which pitted the Ashanti Empire and its 100,000-strong army (though only 40,000 took the field) against a British force led by Garnet Wolseley. The immediate cause of the war was the British Empire's acquisition of another strip of the Gold Coast, this one formerly held by the Dutch. The Ashanti refused to recognize Britain's claims. The British—eager to avenge the decapitation of MacCarthy and, among other frustrations, punish the Ashanti kingdom's refusal to countenance free trade—braced themselves for the Ashanti assault.

The Ashanti army was well-organized and led, and equipped with ill-aimed (actually not aimed at all) muskets that the warriors seemed to value as much for their gunpowdery bang as for anything else. For the British troops, the Gold Coast was known as the "white man's grave," made such by tropical disease. But Wolseley, a forty-year-old major-general—the modern major-general of future Gilbert and Sullivan fame—was, as ever, prepared: his troops were issued quinine and a pamphlet on tropical warfare, written by Wolseley himself, which was chock full of tips for keeping bugs and disease at bay.

When Wolseley's force of 1,500 British and 700 black troops arrived ashore in January 1874, the Ashanti were already withdrawing, racked by sickness. So the chase was on—the Ashanti hoping to lure Wolseley into the interior and sure defeat; Wolseley looking to strike hard and fast so that he could crush the Ashanti quickly before disease caught up with his men. The first engagement, the Battle of Amoaful, was fought in dense jungle. Wolseley had made allowances for the terrain, dividing his army into small units, each led by an officer. The British came "creeping through the bush...gaining ground foot by foot...pouring a ceaseless fire into every bush which might conceal an invisible foe." As war correspondent G. A. Henty (later a famous author of adventure stories for boys) observed, "Nothing could have been better than Sir Garnet Wolseley's plan of battle.... Where [the enemy] attacked us he found himself opposed by a continuous front of men...."[1] The British juggernaut cut through to the Ashanti capital of Kumasi, torched it (in lieu of finding anyone with whom to negotiate), and then quick-marched to the coast in hopes of keeping the sick list from exploding. The Ashanti had troubles of their own—not only had British martial vigor surprised them, but subject tribes had risen in rebellion against the Ashanti king. Ashanti ambassadors caught up with Wolseley, agreed to the principle of free trade, and signed a peace treaty.

Wolseley called the Ashanti war "the most horrible war I ever took part in"[2] (and he took part in quite a few, stretching from Burma to Canada, India to South Africa, China to Egypt, and the Sudan). British casualties—dead, wounded, or invalided home—amounted to more than 40 percent of his force, and more than 70 percent were sick over the course of the two-month campaign. In January 1896, the British formally (and forcibly) annexed the Ashanti kingdom into the British Empire (among those leading troops on that campaign was Robert Baden-Powell, founder of the Boy Scouts). The final act of the Ashanti wars was an Ashanti rebellion, the so-called "War of the Golden Stool," the stool being the sacred throne of the Ashanti monarchy. The Ashanti royal family was exiled to the Seychelles, but the golden stool was hidden and not rediscovered until 1920. In the interest of peace, the British let the Ashanti keep it.

Lord Lugard and "Indirect Rule"

The crucial figure in the development of British West Africa was Frederick Lugard (who was made a baron for his service, though like all too many empire-builders he left no heir to his title). The son of a clergyman (an army chaplain), Lugard started life as a soldier. He was educated at Sandhurst and saw duty in Afghanistan, the Sudan, and Burma, though soldiering did not—or so he believed—suit him; he thought of himself as having a "*woman's* character,"[3] too emotionally soft to be a soldier. Nevertheless, he hired himself out to fight against slavers in Nyasaland—hoping to get himself killed as a cure for a broken heart, but instead only managed to get badly wounded.

He found his niche as an imperial troubleshooter, conqueror, and administrator. It was a role Lugard first took up with the Imperial British East Africa Company, which hired him to open Uganda to British trade and influence. He did this with aplomb and a single Maxim gun.

Lugard was a model Victorian—serious, active, with a deep moralistic strain. His methods were sometimes harsh, he was an imperialist of the most ardent stripe, but he also recognized the Empire's hold on Africa would be temporary: "For two or three generations we can show the Negro what we are; then we shall be asked to go away. Then we shall leave the land to those it belongs to, with the feeling that they have better business friends in us than in other white men."[4]

The key phrase was "we can show the Negro what we are." Lugard was the man who shaped the British civil service in West Africa, and he shaped it in his own upright, paternalistic image. A District Commissioner had to be courageous and strong, a man with moral force and a Maxim gun to back it up: "we do not intend to be fooled...we come like men that are not afraid,"[5] as he said when he marched into Uganda. The District Commissioner had to be a fair and disinterested dispenser of justice, and he had to advance the cause of civilized standards and economic development and enterprise.

Lugard's method was indirect rule—ruling through local elites who had been won over to the imperial cause—which was a common enough British imperial strategy but one that he developed, expounded, and made his own as a practical political philosophy. It meant that the hundred disparate tribes of Nigeria could be governed in ways that preserved their traditions and cultures, while a British representative was kept on hand to make sure that all due obeisance was given to fair play, free trade, and the requisite moral decencies (though these sometimes required a sliding scale, as even

Sorry, Anti-Colonialists, You're Wrong

"The merchant, the miner, and the manufacturer do not enter the tropics on sufferance or employ their technical skill and energy and their capital as 'interlopers' or as 'greedy capitalists,' but in the fulfillment of the mandate of civilization."

Sir Frederick (later Lord) Lugard, governor of Nigeria (and earlier of Hong Kong), quoted in James Morris, *Farewell the Trumpets: An Imperial Retreat* (The Folio Society, 1992), p. 323

the anti-slavery-minded Lugard tolerated, up to a point, the limited practice of slavery in Islamic northern Nigeria).

Lugard envisioned African self-government at a local level, leading eventually to self-government at a regional level, and after some considerable time at the highest level in independent states. Africa was his passion, but unlike later liberals he did not clothe the Africans with any sort of inherent moral superiority; on the contrary, his view, based on his long, adventurous experience on the continent, was a justification for imperial paternalism. The average African, he said, tended to be a "happy, thriftless, excitable person, naturally courteous and polite, full of personal vanity, with little sense of veracity...his thoughts are concentrated on the events and feelings of the moment, and he suffers little from apprehension of the future or grief

The Missionary with Only One Convert

Among the soldiers and explorers and Randlords of Britain's African empire, perhaps the most famous imperialist of all was a Protestant medical missionary, Dr. David Livingstone (1813–73). As a missionary in Central Africa, Livingstone cured the sick; tried (and failed) to interest the natives in a non-polygamous religion (he made only one partial convert); and became an ardent African explorer—believing this was his true calling, and one not unrelated to preaching the gospel. As a Scotsman, he had also absorbed the teachings of Adam Smith and believed in the holy trinity of Christianity, commerce, and civilization: commerce required navigable rivers, increased trade with Britain might displace the slave trade, and as more of Africa became explored more missionary stations could be established. His life was certainly adventurous—he was once mauled by a lion, frequently tread where no white man had been before, and was famously lost and presumed dead in darkest Africa, until found by Henry Morton Stanley: "Doctor Livingstone, I presume." He died, his body ravaged by African diseases, while searching for the source of the Nile. His African attendants cut out his heart, so that it could be buried in African soil, before transporting the body back to Britain.

for the past."[6] It was the Empire's role to guide such men in the ways of honesty, industry, and sobriety.

Alas, the sun set on British West Africa sooner than it should have—at least if the goal was to create parliamentary institutions. These were the inheritance of Ghana (independent in 1957), Nigeria (1960), Sierra Leone (1961), and The Gambia (1965), but Ghana, the first black African state to gain its independence, showed how swiftly socialism could wreck a relatively prosperous economy. Its leader Kwame Nkrumah (who ruled from 1957 to 1966, when he was overthrown in a coup while visiting Communist China) was widely admired by liberals and pan-Africanists even as he banned, jailed, and exiled his political opponents. All this was allegedly necessary to achieve Ghana's great leap forward, though it amounted to a great leap backward in terms of the economy, justice, and freedom. Nigeria, for its part, became a land of military coups. Sierra Leone started off decently but drifted into the swamp of African reprimitivisation; British troops had to return in 2000 to defeat a barbarous rebel movement, the Revolutionary United Front, infamous for its mutilations, use of child soldiers, and other atrocities. If the people of Sierra Leone had a choice, they would likely gladly return to being a Crown colony faster than you can say peace and justice. Plucky little Gambia, meanwhile, has done moderately well and not coincidentally has been keen on maintaining its ties to Britain and a free market economy. All in all, Lord Lugard would be unhappy, but not surprised, at the history of post-imperial British West Africa

Cry, the Beloved Country

It is a myth that the British seized South Africa from black Africans. If they seized it from anyone, it was the Dutch. The Dutch had been at the Cape since 1652 (they were preceded by the Portuguese, who arrived a century and a half earlier). The land was sparsely populated with cattle-herding

Hottentots and nomadic Bushmen. For centuries the Bantu peoples—who would later dominate South Africa, peoples like the Xhosa and the Zulu (who were not a separate tribe or clan until the eighteenth century)—had been migrating south, but they were still five hundred miles north of the early Dutch settlements.[7] It would be another century before the Dutch, reinforced by Germans and French Huguenots, and by then a fully established tribe of Southern Africa themselves, met the Bantu.

The Dutch—or Afrikaners or Boers (from the Dutch word for farmer)—were a sturdy, stubborn, independent-minded people; frontiersmen, deeply religious, devoted to family, self-reliant, and impatient of any government restraint; and there was not much of that from the Dutch East India Company, which had sponsored the settlement. The British began arriving in the eighteenth century and by 1806 had achieved paramount status, annexing the Cape. In the tribal history of Africa, the Hottentots had displaced the Bushmen, the Boers had displaced the Hottentots, and now the British were asserting their supremacy, while the Bantu tribes were migrating southwards staking their own claims. The Boers and the Bantu were cattlemen, and tough and hardy souls. The British, with their natural sense of superiority, saw themselves as the governing race, which would settle the claims between the Boers (whom they found unsympathetic) and the black Africans (whom they thought needed British protection from Boer rapacity, though constant border wars with the Xhosa were starting to bring some British officials to an almost Boer state of mind).

The Boers were immune to the charms of high-minded British liberalism and trekked to escape it. The Boers defeated the Zulus, made peace with them, and established the Natalia Republic on the southeastern coast in 1839, only to have it annexed by the British in 1843. So they pushed inland, establishing the settlements of the Transvaal (recognized as independent by the British in 1852 and established as the South African Republic in 1856) and the independent Orange Free State (which was recognized by the

British in 1854). At the same time, the British established local parliamentary institutions with voter rolls that included blacks and mixed-race voters if they had sufficient economic standing.

South Africa remained a colonial backwater until it was discovered to be rich in diamonds in the late 1860s (gold discoveries followed in the 1880s), leading to a rush of immigrants and pressure on the British to annex, bring order, and assert their rights over more of southern Africa. Sir Theophilus Shepstone, a longtime British diplomat and expert in native affairs in South Africa (his father had been a missionary) arranged for the annexation of the Transvaal in 1877. The governor of the Cape Colony, Sir Bartle Frere, took the next step. Bordering the British colony of Natal was Zululand. The entire civilization of the Zulus was based on war and killing, and though the British were at peace with the Zulu, Frere thought war inevitable with such neighbors; moreover, given the Zulus' fearsome reputation, if they were defeated by British arms, it would have a pacifying effect on every South African tribe. As James Morris noted in his book *Heaven's Command*, the Zulu nation "was like a vast black predator lurking in its downlands, now pouncing upon the Swazis or the Basutos, now threatening the British or the Boers. Everybody was scared of the Zulus, and the British in particular were nervous that some grand Zulu washing of the spears might trigger off a native rising throughout South Africa." Frere demanded the Zulus disband their armies and their belligerent way of life—and when they did not, the British pursued their own belligerent aims, marching into Zululand in what, in Morris's apposite words, "composed a pattern of action that was to become almost compulsory in the later campaigns of the British Empire— the opening tragedy, the heroic redemption, the final crushing victory."[8] In the Zulu War of 1879, Isandhlwana was the opening tragedy, Rorke's Drift the heroic redemption, and Ulundi the final crushing victory.

The British troops were under the command of Lord Chelmsford— generally considered the goat of the war, he was nonetheless a gentleman in every sense. His goal was simple: the Zulus must be brought to battle so they could be crushed. Marching boldly into Zululand—or as boldly as he could given his slow, lengthy wagon train of supplies—Chelmsford divided his invading force into three columns. Though well-informed about the Zulus' combat prowess and tactics, Chelmsford believed the bigger problem was luring them into battle: if that could be done, no Zulu army could possibly defeat the British, however small the British force.

That proved true at Rorke's Drift—a Zululand version of the Alamo, though with a happy ending for the defenders, with 150 Britons and colonials holding off a force of 4,000 Zulus—but it was preceded by the Battle of Isandhlwana, one of the greatest disasters in the annals of British imperial warfare. Chelmsford took 2,500 men, chasing a Zulu diversion, while leaving 1,700 men—British troops, South African volunteers, native levies—in an unlaagered, unentrenched camp on the plains of Isandlwhana, where they were overrun by 20,000 ferocious Zulus. The Zulus left behind them a field of carnage: more than 1,300 British dead; almost every corpse desecrated, slit open, guts stamped by Zulu feet, some beheaded, others degenitaled, some merely scalped or dejawed, two British drummer boys hung on meat hooks. Chelmsford returned to a burnt-out camp of stinking corpses, including more dead officers than had been lost at Waterloo; and more than a thousand rifles and hundreds of thousands of rounds of ammunition were now in Zulu hands.

The British government—which had not authorized the attack on Zululand—was shocked at the catastrophe and sent General Sir Garnet Wolseley to save the day; Chelmsford, however, was equally keen to save his reputation. As Wolseley arrived at Durban, Chelmsford pressed an attack on the Zulu king Cetshwayo's royal kraal at Ulundi. He was determined to crush the Zulus in open battle so that there could be no doubt they were well and truly beaten. Formed into the classic British square, Chelmsford's 4,000 troops met the attack of 15,000 Zulus and sent them reeling. Ulundi lay open for Chelmsford, who set it ablaze. Honor redeemed, he finally heeded Wolseley's orders and relinquished command. The Zulu kingdom was broken, but, as ever, it had been a close run thing.

More problematic was the white tribe of South Africa, the Boers. They had fought with the British against the Zulu, but they still yearned to be free from the British yoke, if yoke it was. There were only 3,000 British troops in the entire Transvaal, an area of roughly 110,000 square miles. It wasn't a matter of oppression so much as it was a matter of the incompatibility of two exceedingly different peoples—the imperial British, who believed they held Heaven's command, and the dour, leathery, Old Testament-thumping, stiff-necked Afrikaners whose entire imagination was suffused with the idea of the frontier, the independent farmer, and of being answerable to no one but God.

In 1880, led by Paul Kruger—the craggy, heavy-set former vice president of the South African Republic—they rebelled; their first action being a massacre of Connaught Rangers who thought they were marching through a peaceful Transvaal. No more: the Boer was in the saddle and a gun was in his hand, and in a matter of three months he had retaken the Transvaal for himself. The British had been bewildered and besieged, and the Gladstone government, with no stomach for a fight, agreed to a self-governing Transvaal still under the Crown and nominal British supervision, including authority over the blacks whom the British deemed in need of protection.

Zulu Dawn

"What a wonderful people! They beat our generals, they convert our bishops, and they write 'finis' to a French dynasty."

Prime Minister Benjamin Disraeli on the disaster of Isandhlwana, the pro-Zulu agitation of the liberal Anglican Bishop John William Colenso, and the death in battle of the only son and heir of Napoleon III, a commissioned lieutenant in the British army, quoted in Andre Maurois, *Disraeli: A Picture of the Victorian Age* (The Modern Library, 1955), p. 339

The Boer War

The patchwork peace lasted nearly two decades. When it was undone it was with far greater violence than anything that had happened before. It wasn't a campaign against a tribe; it was a full-scale war between two European armies. The war was sparked by the Boers' refusal to give voting rights to the British in the Transvaal (unless they were residents for increasing periods of time, reaching fourteen years in 1890) and other challenges to Britain's claim to be the paramount power in South Africa. It was the old issue revisited: the British believed in their divine right to rule, and the Boers wanted no part of it, preferring their own Boerish republic (which happened to be well-seeded with gold and diamonds that attracted *uitlanders*). Colonial Secretary Joseph Chamberlain and South African High Commissioner Alfred Milner pressed the case for war, and precipitated it by getting the government to renounce recognition of the Transvaal as an independent state. Paul Kruger responded by demanding that the British drop all claims on the Transvaal and setting a deadline for the British to agree. They did not, and on 11 October 1899, the Boers invaded Natal and the Cape Colony.

The commander in chief of the Cape Colony was General William Blunt, who had thought war against the Boers was unnecessary and imprudent—and as he had no orders to prepare for war, he had not. He was relieved of command, and the British troops were led by General Sir Redvers Buller. Buller appeared to have all the necessary bona fides—he had fought in China and Canada, and battled the Ashantis in West Africa, the Zulus in South Africa, and the Dervishes in the Sudan. But against the Boers he came a cropper. The British were besieged at Ladysmith, Kimberly, and Mafeking. In combat against the Boers, British commanders proved far too fond of frontal assaults. Boer tactics, on the contrary, counted on entrenching and blasting the gallant British infantry with powerful Mauser rifles. If the British ever got too close, the Boers simply mounted their ponies and galloped

Imperial Colossus

Cecil Rhodes (1853–1902) was a self-made multi-millionaire who lent his name to a country (Rhodesia), the Rhodes scholarship (perhaps the most famous in the world), and created the mighty De Beers mining company. Like so many empire-builders, he was the son of a clergyman. A sickly child—he was asthmatic—he was sent to South Africa in the hope that the climate would help him. It did well enough that he became a diamond miner and purchaser of mines—interrupting his burgeoning business dealings only to attend Oxford. He followed his business success with political ambitions, becoming governor of the Cape Colony, from which position he had to resign after attempting to overthrow the government of the Transvaal in 1895 in a misadventure known as the Jameson Raid. His goal was to paint East Africa British imperial red from Cape to Cairo. Leftists who make him out to be an imperialist monster need to come to grips with the fact that he was a political liberal (he even favored Irish nationalism as long as it was maintained under the big tent of empire); as a member of the Progressive Party he stood by the slogan of "equal rights to every civilized man south of the Zambesi" (however much he was prone to think of blacks in terms of a laboring class that needed paternal direction); was an early conservationist; and if not in favor of world government, favored an imperial federation and an imperial parliament that would bring together the English-speaking peoples in a united cause. And of course that's the problem—the left does not believe in "Anglo-Saxon" values and civilization and its mission to the world, as Rhodes did: God, he believed, "is manifestly fashioning the English-speaking race as the chosen instrument by which He will bring in a state of society based upon Justice, Liberty, and Peace." God, he said, would want him "to paint as much of the map of Africa British red as possible, and to do what I can elsewhere to promote the unity and extend the influence of the English-speaking race."* He is buried in the African hills he loved, in the country that was Rhodesia.

*Quoted in Robert I. Rotberg and Miles F. Shore, *The Founder: Cecil Rhodes and the Pursuit of Power* (Oxford University Press, 1988), p. 415

away. The result was a series of bloody British defeats and mounting British frustration, cheered on by much of the rest of the world, which sympathized with the Boers' defiance and their twisting of the lion's tail.

The British needed a new commander to rescue the day and found one in Field Marshal Lord Roberts, known as "Little Bobs," a five-foot-three bantam who had fought successfully in India, Abyssinia, and Afghanistan. Bobs turned the whole war around, relieving the besieged cities. The relief of Mafeking after 217 days (on 17 May 1900) was celebrated in England with more huzzahs and banners and streamers and parades and massed cheering than the wildest Hogmanay—though it was a town of only a little more than 8,000 people, 7,000 of them blacks. The defense had been led by Colonel Robert Baden-Powell—the Boy Scouts' founder who seemed to be an over-grown boy himself—he had kept up spirits with amateur theatricals (he liked that sort of thing).

Elsewhere, in swift strokes, Bobs captured the Boer towns, and on 5 June 1900 seized the Boer capital of Pretoria. Kruger scuttled off into exile, and by October it seemed peace was at hand. Bobs returned to England and left his second-in-command Lord Kitchener to do the mopping up, which proved to be an arduous and ugly business, involving the holding of Boer families in concentration camps, the burning of their farms, and the hunting down of Boer guerrillas. The final treaty ending the war—the Treaty of Vereeniging—was not reached until 31 May 1902.

South Africa was officially unified in 1910 as a British dominion (putting it on the same level of status and self-government as Canada, Australia, and New Zealand). The former Afrikaner republics retained a good deal of autonomy, proved resistant to British efforts to Anglicize them, and were politically powerful, though the Boers, as farmers, tended to be much poorer than the British who dominated industry. Largely black African areas—Basutoland, Bechuanaland, and Swaziland—were British protectorates. Rhodesia—then comprising Northern Rhodesia (Zambia) and Southern

Rhodesia (Zimbabwe)—was governed by Cecil Rhodes's British South African Company until 1923, when Northern Rhodesia became a protectorate and Southern Rhodesia became a largely self-governing colony.

South Africa fought at Britain's side in both world wars—though there was pro-German sentiment among a large number of Afrikaners. Jan Smuts—who had fought against the British in the Boer War—not only became a British field marshal and close confidant of British Prime Minister Winston Churchill in World War II, but was a leader in the creation of both the League of Nations and the United Nations. He was also a Zionist, and a supporter of South Africa's large Jewish minority. Twice prime minister of South Africa (latterly from 1939 to 1948), he lost the 1948 election largely because of his support for dismantling some of the segregationist laws that had been built up over the decades—a sign that Smuts was becoming too British for his own good, as the British, though complicit in racially discriminatory legislation, were generally more liberal on racial issues than the Afrikaners.

After the 1948 election, the victorious National Party began building the system known as apartheid, with its complexity of racial classifications and laws, which made South Africa an irritant to the British Commonwealth, from which it exiled itself in 1961, becoming a republic. From then until the collapse of the apartheid regime in 1994 and the introduction of one-man, one-vote elections, South Africa was an international pariah. It was also, however, an embarrassment to the rest of Africa in a different way. While other African nations were failing, South Africa was a regional superpower, an economic colossus (in African terms at least), and, despite its harsh racial laws, a recipient of large numbers of African illegal immigrants who preferred the racial discrimination of South Africa to the oppression, corruption, violence, and economic regression of independent sub-Saharan Africa. If nothing else, the British had provided a political and economic model—and the colonists to make it work—that gave South Africa an enormous leg up over the rest of the continent.

The Wind of Change

On 3 February 1960, British Prime Minister Harold Macmillan delivered a speech in Cape Town that reverberated the length of British Africa; it became known as "The Wind of Change" speech, from these lines: "The wind of change is blowing through this continent, and whether we like it or not, this growth of national consciousness is a political fact. We must all accept it as a fact, and our national policies must take account of it." The speech was largely a call for South Africa "to create a society which respects the rights of individuals, a society in which men are given the opportunity to grow to their full stature—and that must in our view include the opportunity to have an increasing share in political power and responsibility, a society in which individual merit and individual merit alone is the criterion for a man's advancement...."[9]

While the speech was greeted positively in South Africa at the time, it was immediately seen elsewhere as striking a blow for decolonization and majority rule—including in British East Africa. Macmillan's premiership coincided with the end of the Mau-Mau insurgency in Kenya, which had been a combination of Kikuyu tribal civil war, anti-colonial struggle, and—as it was seen in much of the Western press—an outbreak of savage barbarism against British settlers. With the Mau-Mau defeated, it appeared Kenya's colonial future might be at an end.

Britain's interest in East Africa was nominal at first. The Royal Navy might sail its coasts looking for slavers, missionaries and explorers might investigate it, but it was not until 1886 that Uganda and Kenya became Britain's responsibility, and even then the British government's chief interest was combating the slave trade, limiting German expansion in the area, and defending Egypt by controlling the source of the Nile. The Imperial British East Africa Company was established in 1888. In Uganda it had to navigate politics riven by Catholic, Protestant, and Arab-Muslim factions. In Kenya, things were simpler, but nevertheless the Company was dissolved, free trade imposed, and in 1895 the British government created the British East Africa Protectorate.

One of its first orders of business was building a railway from Mombasa into the interior, all the way to Uganda, a project that had to fight through tsetse country, lion attacks, and a sometimes arid landscape parched of water. Indian workers, who were considered far more reliable and skilled than the Africans, were imported to work on the railway construction. White settlers arrived too; for them, Kenya was an ideal land for enormous tea, coffee, and other plantations. The white farmers worked extraordinarily hard—the soil was good, but they were developing a country from scratch and had to defeat exotic tropical pests.

The British showed their usual facility for development, civilization, and self-rule. After the Great War—in which there were extensive, if small-scale, combat operations in East Africa—the British took over formerly German Tanganyika. By the end of the Second World War, the Kenyan Legislative Council, to which white voters had been electing members since 1919, had two black African representatives (one of them an Oxonian), a number that would slowly increase.

Of all Britain's possessions in East Africa—Uganda, Tanganyika, Zanzibar, Kenya—only Kenya was seen as "a white man's country." That

Jomo Kenyatta on the Mau-Mau

"We are determined to have independence in peace, and we shall not allow hooligans to rule Kenya. We must have no hatred towards one another. Mau-Mau was a disease which had been eradicated, and must never be remembered again."

Jomo Kenyatta 1962, quoted in Robert B. Edgerton, *Mau Mau: An African Crucible* (The Free Press, 1989), p. 216; Kenyatta was the "founding father" and first president (1964–78) of independent Kenya

complicated its politics and made it a focal point of international attention during the Mau-Mau rebellion. The state of emergency to deal with the Mau-Mau lasted from 1952 to 1960, though the movement was essentially defeated by 1956. The rebellion was limited almost entirely to the Kikuyu and the areas around Nairobi and the Aberdare mountain range, but the bestial nature of the Mau-Mau oath-taking ceremonies and the bloody nature of its terror and atrocities launched it into international headlines

Films about British Africa That Anti-Colonialists Don't Want You to See

The Four Feathers, 1939 (this version is by far the best), with John Clements, Ralph Richardson, and C. Aubrey Smith. Classic tale of heroism and redemption set during the Sudanese campaign to avenge the death of General Charles George Gordon.

Simba, 1955, with Dirk Bogarde and Virginia McKenna. Gripping drama of British settlers in Kenya trying to maintain their liberal values while under the threat of Mau-Mau terrorism.

Guns at Batasi, 1964, with Richard Attenborough and Jack Hawkins. Well-acted and well-scripted drama of British soldiers serving in post-colonial Africa.

Zulu, 1964, with Stanley Baker, Michael Caine, Jack Hawkins, and Nigel Green. Superb action adventure about the defense of Rorke's Drift. A few liberties, betraying a modern sensibility, have been taken with the history, but all in all a rousing film.

Khartoum, 1966, with Charlton Heston, Laurence Olivier, Richard Johnson, and Ralph Richardson. Memorable big-budget adventure that captures the spirit of General Gordon quite well.

even if the number of European civilians murdered (about 30) was relatively small (the Mau-Mau were estimated to have murdered another 2,000 black Africans). The war pitted the Mau-Mau terrorists not only against British rule, but against Kikuyu Christians, loyalists, and the more conservative-minded tribesmen. Mau-Mau atrocities incited the security forces to abuses themselves; and while there have been some hysterically exaggerated accounts of British-imposed torture, the fact is that the British government curbed these abuses and never authorized a campaign of terror.

The war became, in the end, not an attempt to maintain white rule (it should be noted that most of those fighting the Mau-Mau were black Africans), but a matter of restoring peace so that Kenya could make an orderly transition to independence, which came in 1964. Compared to its neighbors—Uganda gained independence in 1962; Tanganyika in 1961, becoming Tanzania in 1964 after its merger with Zanzibar—Kenya has done reasonably well, maintaining a moderately free market, a relatively free state, and avoiding the clownish barbarism of Idi Amin and the socialist flummeries of Julius Nyerere. Kenya's progress has been far from perfect, of course—but, as many Africans might tell you, the wind of change came much too fast for their continent.

Chapter 16

GENERAL CHARLES GEORGE GORDON (1833–1885)

"I have met but two men who realize my ideas of what a true hero should be: my friend [General] Charles Gordon was one, General [Robert E.] Lee was the other."

—*Field Marshal Viscount Wolseley*[1]

General Gordon is the epitome of a British imperial hero, the pre-eminent Christian soldier-martyr of the British Empire. But he is also important because Lytton Strachey turned his virtues into vices in his famous and influential book *Eminent Victorians*. Strachey, a wilting, effeminate socialist, wanted to discredit the patriotic muscular Christianity that lay at the center of the Victorian ideal of the British Empire, and Gordon was one of his targets.[2] Gordon was thus traduced by "liberals" (broadly speaking) after his death (though he was a Liberal himself), just as he was abandoned by the political leader of the Liberals, Prime Minister William Gladstone, during his life.

Gordon was born in London on 28 January 1833. His father, a Royal Artillery major, had a career not a quarter as colorful as his son's, but he retired as a lieutenant-general, a higher rank than "Charlie" Gordon ever reached. Young Charlie was full of rambunctious mischief and had a knack for martial arts—in the sense that he excelled at drawing maps and intimidating his peers. At the Royal Military Academy at Woolwich he polished his

Did you know?

♛ Though a serving British officer, Gordon spent much of his career as a mercenary—who didn't care about money

♛ An amateur Biblical archaeologist, he believed he had located the actual site of the Garden of Eden

♛ A doughty abolisher of the slave trade in the Sudan, he nevertheless allowed the Sudanese to employ slaves because the practice was too popular

map-drawing skills and proved himself a rebellious and quick-tempered lad (he once head-butted a cadet through a glass door). Nevertheless, he graduated and was commissioned in the Royal Engineers. After some specialized training and humdrum assignments repairing barracks, he was sent to Pembroke to build fortifications, and it was here that he met a couple who inspired him to become a firm Bible-based Christian.[3]

Gordon first saw action in the Crimean War (1853–56), arriving in Balaclava in January 1855. His first job was building huts for the troops exposed to the harsh Russian winter, but he soon found himself working on trenches, and exploring no-man's land. He befriended a young officer much like himself in high spirits, courage, and eagerness to reform the Army—Garnet Wolseley, who noted, as did many, that Gordon's "full, clear and bright blue eyes seemed to court scrutiny, whilst at the same time they searched into your inner soul."[4]

The Eyes Have It

"His clear blue eye seemed to possess a magic power over all who came within its influence. It read you through and through, it made it impossible for you to tell him anything but the truth, it invited your confidence, it kindled with compassion at every story of distress and it sparked with good humour at anything really witty or funny. From its glance you knew at once that at any risk he would keep his promise, that you might trust him with anything and everything, and that he would stand by you if all other friends deserted you."

W. G. Lilley, clerk of the Royal Engineers, on Gordon's much-remarked-upon piercing blue eyes, quoted in Charles Chenevix Trench, *The Road to Khartoum: A Life of General Charles Gordon* (Dorset Press, 1987), pp. 21–22

Gordon distinguished himself in the Crimea for his energy, readiness for action, and keen observation of enemy movements. He was awarded the Légion d'honneur by the French and assigned by his superiors to help survey the post-war border between the Ottoman Empire and Russia. It kept him abroad, which was what he wanted, because Charlie Gordon was eager to renew his acquaintance with the crack of musket balls and the roar of cannon.

The Ever Victorious Army

In 1860 he volunteered for the war in China, where the British and French were enforcing the Treaties of Tientsin (which had ended the Second Opium War, allowing for freer European trade with China and opening up the country to Christian missionaries), and was present for the sack of Peking. Though he bought some spoils for himself, he hated the wanton destruction of the emperor's summer palace (which he blamed on the French) and was appalled at how "everybody was wild for plunder."[5] Gordon built barracks and stables and anything else that needed building, pitching in with his own labor wherever he could, and helped manage a fund of donations for impoverished Chinese.

The Manchu dynasty was under threat not only from Europeans eager to open China to trade but by a massive domestic uprising, the Taiping Rebellion led by Hung-sen-Tsuen, a religious fanatic who propounded a new trinity of God the Father, God the Elder Son Jesus, and God the Younger Son Hung-sen-Tsuen. Hung proclaimed himself Tien Wang, the Heavenly King whose task was to create a Dynasty of Perpetual Peace—though of course the path to perpetual peace required massive slaughter of his opponents and also required that he marry thirty wives and keep a harem. Despite these rather heterodox beliefs and the movement's propensity for violence, some British evangelical Christians, flexible in doctrine themselves, based on each man's reading of the Bible, maintained a sympathy for what they viewed as a reformist Christian uprising against a cruel Manchu regime. A century later, the Taipings won praise from the Communist Chinese for their war against the Manchu monarchy and feudalism. Yet a better assessment came from the British vice-consul at Ningpo: "The Taipings have a fume of blood and a look of carnage about them. Their chief condition for success is to strike terror, first by numbers, and secondly by the tawdry harlequin garb worn by them.... Their long, shaggy black hair adds to the wildness of their look, and...this fantastic appearance is accompanied by a certain show of fury and madness."[6]

The Taipings captured Nanking and made it their capital in 1853. Aiding Hung were his chief lieutenants, his wangs (kings), who become warlords in their own right. One proclaimed himself the Holy Ghost and criticized Hung—and was executed for his impertinence. By 1860 the Taipings were threatening the international entrepôt of Shanghai. Though Shanghai was guarded by a small force of French and British troops, the city's merchants thought it prudent to raise an army of their own, the Shanghai Foreign Arms Corps, later and better known as the Ever Victorious Army, under the command of American soldier of fortune Frederick Townsend Ward. Ward, however, was killed in 1862, the year Captain Gordon arrived as chief officer of engineers for the British general Charles Stavely. Stavely had orders to clear the Taipings from a thirty-mile radius of Shanghai. He was impressed by Gordon and recommended he command the Ever Victorious Army, which had fallen into indiscipline and disarray since Ward's death.

In March 1863, Gordon, now a brevet-major, was given leave from the British Army, made a mandarin, and appointed commander of the Ever Victorious Army, a body of an estimated 4,000 Chinese and assorted rascally American and European mercenaries. Gordon brought with him five British officers and set to work whipping his new army into shape (and whipping the Taipings simultaneously). He uniformed his men, disciplined them, drilled them, barracked them, and let them know he cared for them, sick, wounded, or well; he banned hard liquor and looting; and he led them into battle calmly smoking a cigar and waving a bamboo cane (after having thoroughly scouted the enemy positions). The Ever Victorious Army now lived up to its name, and Gordon showed his tactical acumen in organizing its handful of small steamships for combined naval and land operations. The Taipings feared him and the Manchu authorities respected him, even if they disliked his insistent independence. He had told Li Hung Chang, the provincial governor and leader of the Manchu forces against the Taipings, that he would defeat the rebels in eighteen months. He did, though Gordon quarreled violently with Li whom he suspected of ordering the decapitation of several Taiping wangs who had surrendered on conditions of clemency. In protest, Gordon turned down the emoluments offered him by the Chinese emperor, though he did accept elevation to the highest rank of Chinese general and the award of a yellow jacket, which had been granted to only forty Mandarins and never before to a European.

In the British press, he earned the moniker "Chinese" Gordon. Yet whatever fame he gained—and he certainly did not seek it; he shunned social invitations and avoided and disparaged dinner parties—did not lead to fortune. Gordon made a habit of spurning financial rewards for himself; whatever money he had flowed through his fingers to others. Sir Frederick Bruce, the British minister at Peking, noted that "Not only has he [Gordon] refused any pecuniary reward but he has spent more than his pay in contributing to the comfort of the officers who served under him and in assuaging the distress of the starving population whom he relieved from the yoke of their oppressor [the Taipings]."[7]

The last thing Gordon wanted was to build forts in England, yet that was the next command he was given. He wanted postings abroad and he wanted action, but did his engineering chores with his usual impressive energy; he also spent hours every afternoon and evening working with the poor and

Gordon's Wangs

Early on, Gordon decided he would never marry. He recommended marriage to his bachelor friends, citing it as a cure for selfishness, but for himself—no woman, he thought, could ever sacrifice the comforts of home for his Spartan conception of his imperial duty. Gordon's celibacy became part of his mystique, especially impressive to the Arabs and Sudanese who could hardly fathom such a virtue. It was a sign—as with a priest—of his self-mastery and self-denial (another aspect of this was that he ate little, preferring to give food to the poor, though he was a champion smoker).

As part of his Christian life, Gordon, throughout his career, took in orphaned boys. Some became his servants during the Taiping campaigns; one he named "Quincey" and paid for his education (Quincey later became a Shanghai police officer). In England, he dubbed his collection of orphans or boys from poor or fatherless families his "wangs." He had his housekeeper scrub them clean, bought them clothes, gave them pocket money, and set them onto careers (often at sea). He was proud to chart their lives and fortunes, sticking pins in a map to mark their travels. Those who sense something untoward in this are apt to overlook that Gordon was equally devoted to comforting the aged and dying. His motivation was clearly charitable.

needy as part of his Christian commitment and kept his early mornings reserved for private Bible study and prayer. The great epiphany that motivated Gordon was the idea that God is within us, or within every believer in Jesus Christ—that was the lamplight of his Christian faith.[8]

Gordon of Khartoum

Gordon did not have another foreign posting until October 1871 when he was appointed to map out navigation rights on the Danube; it proved dull work, but he met Nubar Pasha, a powerful adviser to the khedive in Egypt who offered him a better posting: the khedive wished to make Gordon governor of Equatoria in the southern Sudan, replacing another Briton, the explorer Sir Samuel Baker. Gordon agreed, pending the approval of the British government, which granted its assent in September 1873.

Gordon, the former Chinese general, now became an Ottoman general, and took with relish to abolishing the slave trade. He crushed the slavers by force when he found them, won over previously hostile tribes, and built way stations along the Nile. In 1877, after a period of leave in England (which is what it amounted to, though he had officially resigned in protest at the khedive not expanding his governing powers), the khedive coaxed Gordon to return as governor-general of the entire Sudan, giving him the military rank of Egyptian field marshal. Gordon's program was the same—establishing peace, eliminating corruption (a never-ending task, he found), and most of all laboring to end the slave trade (if not slavery itself), which, along with ivory was the centerpiece of the Sudanese economy. He rode at speed everywhere on his camel, dropping unsuspecting among tribes and potential rebels demanding—and usually winning—their fealty. He was also something of a dealmaker, frequently trying to find ways to employ the slavers who were among the canniest and most powerful men in the country. He abolished whipping in Khartoum, cancelled projects the government could not afford (including a railway along the Nile), and defended "his" people (the Sudanese) against the khedive's French and British creditors. The arrival of a new khedive provided an exhausted Gordon with the opportunity to resign; he left Egypt in January 1880.

For the next four years he was an officer with, in essence, a roving independent

Gordon's Imperial Rule

"If you would rule over native peoples, you must love them."

General Gordon, quoted in John Pollock, *Gordon of Khartoum: An Extraordinary Soldier* (Christian Focus, 2005), p. 192

commission. He was offered a colonial military appointment in South Africa, work in the Congo by the king of Belgium, and the position of private secretary to Lord Ripon, governor-general of India, which he accepted but resigned almost as soon as he started. He launched his own diplomatic peace initiative in China, traveled in Ireland to study the Irish question (and was entirely sympathetic to the Irish peasants), was free with political and military advice in letters to *The Times* (he loathed Disraeli for supporting the Turks against the Greeks and because Gordon thought the Tories were more concerned with penny-pinching than empire-building; but the anti-imperialist Liberals were hardly better), was assigned as chief of engineers on Mauritius (where he developed some interesting theories on the Garden of Eden, which he located in the Seychelles), and saw diplomatic service in Basutoland. He spent a year on leave in the Holy Land where he mapped, to his own satisfaction, the actual sites of many Biblical events, and then finally accepted the Belgian king's renewed offer of governing the Congo. But the British government had other ideas.

In the Sudan, a religious visionary of fanatical aspect, Mohammed Ahmed, styling himself the Mahdi, had declared a jihad against all who stood against him. His dervishes swept across the country as the sword of Islam and slaughtered an Egyptian army led by a British officer, General (in Egyptian rank) William Hicks. The British government, which had taken responsibility for Egypt and the Sudan, had to do something, and that something, it was decided, was to withdraw from the Sudan as quickly as possible. The press, however, was clamoring for Gordon to be sent to the Sudan. Over the skepticism of Sir Evelyn Baring, British Consul-General in Cairo (who had experience of Gordon), Prime

St. Charlie

"Gordon was the nearest approach to a saint that I have met in a long life, in spite of his many mistakes."

Field Marshal Sir (Henry) Evelyn Wood, quoted in Bryon Farwell, *Eminent Victorian Soldiers: Seekers of Glory* (W. W. Norton & Company, 1985), p. 124

Minister William Gladstone, and even Lord Granville, the foreign secretary who had proposed the idea, it was decided to send Gordon to report on the military situation in the Sudan and how best to evacuate the Europeans and Egyptians. Though it was impossible to believe Gordon would merely file a report, he had proven a remarkable power over native peoples, and it was hoped he might achieve a face-saving exit.

Reappointed as governor-general, he entered Khartoum in February 1884 to the hosannas of the Sudanese; their miracle-worker had come. He had, however, let slip that the Egyptian government might abandon the Sudan, which cost him the support of wavering Sudanese leaders, who plumped for making their peace with the Mahdi. To regain some of their support, Gordon affirmed he would not abolish slavery. This brought cheers from influential Sudanese—and cries of disbelief from Gordon's anti-slavery supporters in Britain. In addition, he abolished taxes for two years and promised an end to the heavy-handed ways of the Egyptians, burning debt books and whips, and freeing prisoners. He came as a liberator, "without soldiers, but with God on my side, to redress the evils of the Sudan."[9]

Having failed to buy off the Mahdi with an offer of making him ruler of a Sudanese province, Gordon immediately set to planning how he could defend Khartoum and "smash up" the dervishes. Though his request for British troops was denied, he assured the people that a relief expedition would be on the way.[10] The Mahdi meanwhile was picking off Egyptian forts and setting a noose around Khartoum. By March he was shelling the city and by May he had cut off any hope for an evacuation along the Nile by capturing Berber.

Gordon used his considerable skills as a military engineer and tactician to strengthen Khartoum's defenses with ditches, mines, and gunboats. With his flair for drama and his taste for perpetual action, Gordon remained an inspiring figure to the Sudanese: facing an empty treasury, he designed and signed his own banknotes; he burst open the stores of grain merchants who had hid their wares to reap greater profits; he set up a system of relief for the starving poor; he sent troops sallying into the desert to smite the besiegers; and he worked endlessly to rally morale. He capitalized on his own famous lack of fear: "When God was portioning out fear to all the people in the world, at last it came to my turn, and there was no fear left to give me. Go, tell the people of Khartoum that Gordon fears nothing, for God has created him without fear."[11]

But even Gordon knew time was running out. On 14 December 1884, he wrote, "Now MARK THIS, if the Expeditionary Force, and I ask for no more than two hundred men,[12] does not come in ten days, *the town may fall*; and I have done my best for the honour of our country."[13] With Garnet Wolseley's relief force fighting its way up the Nile, the Mahdi almost gave up the siege, until he was informed of a weak point in the city's defenses—a point that Gordon had ordered repaired, but that the exhausted, starving Egyptian troops had left vulnerable. On 26 January 1885, the three hundred and twentieth day of the siege of Khartoum, the dervishes struck full force against the city. They burst through the weak point, slaughtering all in their path. When they finally reached the palace of Gordon Pasha he stood before them, armed with a sword and a revolver, at the top of a flight of stairs. There was a sudden silence as the horde looked at the calm figure who had kept them at bay so long. A dervish broke the silence shouting, "O cursèd one, your time has come!" and hurled a spear into Gordon's chest. "His only reply was a gesture of contempt. Another spear transfixed him; he fell, and the swords of three Dervishes…instantly hacked him to death."[14] Gordon's head was severed, presented to the Mahdi, and then made the sport of birds.

The relief expedition arrived two days too late. Gladstone was blamed—not just in popular opinion but by Queen Victoria: "To think that all this might have been prevented and many precious lives saved by earlier action is too frightful."[15] But Gordon would be avenged. Although it would come more than a decade later, the retaliatory sword would be wielded by another stalwart imperialist of piercing blue eye: the perfect recruiting poster, Major-General Sir Horatio Herbert (as he then was) Kitchener.

Chapter 17

HERBERT KITCHENER, 1st EARL KITCHENER (1850–1916)

"He is not a great man. He is a great poster."

—*Liberal Prime Minister Herbert Asquith on Kitchener*[1]

With the determined ice-blue set to his eyes, his walrus moustache, and his tall, stalwart, military bearing (as befits a field marshal), Kitchener strides out of old photographs as the very model of a modern (circa 1900) British general. His military career covered the Middle East, Africa from Cape to Cairo, India, and the First World War. He was ambitious, like many a British empire-builder, but it was always an ambition driven by a sense of duty—of doing all he could for the Empire. It made for an adventurous life.

Kitchener was born in Ireland[2]—a country with which he felt no later affiliation—the son of a retired colonel and a clergyman's daughter. He took his father's profession and his mother's religious convictions. Raised in Ireland and Switzerland (where they moved for his mother's health; she died in 1864), Kitchener attended the Royal Military Academy, Woolwich, where he trained to be a sapper (a military engineer), and was commissioned in 1871 (though not before he caused a diplomatic kerfuffle by crossing the Channel to get a firsthand glimpse of the Franco-Prussian War).

Did you know?

- The tall, fair-haired, blue-eyed Kitchener could, and did, pass for an Arab

- Kitchener collected porcelain and *objets d'art*

- He was one of the few who predicted that the First World War would be a long, bloody struggle

He received further training—and went on junkets to Austria and Germany—before gaining an assignment with the Palestine Exploration Fund, which bankrolled survey expeditions to locate and map Biblical sites in the Holy Land. Under royal patronage, and with the support of the War Office, which willingly lent its officers to scout territory of strategic interest, Kitchener spent three years (1874–77) on work that was ostensibly to prove the historical accuracy of the Bible. It also showed him as an imperial man of action at Galilee, where he faced down a violent mob that intended to "Kill the Christian dogs."[3] After completing the survey, he stopped on his way home to see the fighting in the Russo-Turkish War from the Turkish side.

As part of the settlement of that war, the British were made governors of Cyprus on behalf of the Ottoman Empire, and Kitchener was duly dispatched to make a survey of the island. While stationed there he became a collector of ceramics and founded the Cyprus museum. His time in Cyprus (1878–82) was interrupted briefly by an appointment as vice consul to Anatolia, where he was to oversee reforms of the Ottoman administration. But what he really wanted was action.

Secret Agent in the Sudan

In 1881, Colonel Arabi Pasha led a nationalist revolt against the authority of the Ottomans, which devolved into a revolt against all foreign influence in Egypt. In the summer of 1882, rioters in Alexandria, the center of Arabi's revolt, targeted foreign businesses, killing fifty Europeans. Something, of course, had to be done—especially given the potential threat to the Suez Canal—and the British did it (the French, though they had military and naval forces in the area, refused to join the punitive action). Kitchener wanted to be part of it too, claimed sick leave, jaunted off to Egypt, did reconnaissance work (he spoke fluent Arabic), and then avoided returning to Cyprus until he had a chance to watch the British naval bombardment of Alexandria.

The British squashed Arabi's revolt and set about creating a new—loyal—army for the Egyptian khedive. Kitchener, who had taken a temporary job surveying in Sinai, was tapped to help form and train the Egyptian cavalry. In 1883, he became a major (*bimbashi*) in the Egyptian army, wore a tarboosh—he took rather a fancy to Arabic habits and customs—and proved his mettle at making something out of unpromising material; Egyptians were not highly regarded as soldiers.

Yet something had to be made of them—and quickly—for the Mahdist revolt had begun in the Sudan. It arrested British attention after the destruction of a 9,000-strong Egyptian army led by a British colonel in Egyptian service, Hicks Pasha (William Hicks), at the Battle of El Obeid (5 November 1883). Word of the massacre reached Kitchener in Sinai, where he had taken leave to do some surveying work. Recalled by the British Consul-General Sir Evelyn Baring, Kitchener disguised himself as an Arab and raced across the desert (the sun and sand permanently damaging his eyes).

Starting in February 1884, Kitchener scouted possible lines of approach for an Anglo-Egyptian army to the Sudan; checked on the Egyptian garrisons in Sudanese cities; raised desert tribes against the Mahdi; gathered intelligence; and acted as a desert intermediary relaying messages from General Gordon, besieged in Khartoum, to Cairo.[4] In doing all this, he often traveled in disguise as an Arab, riding a camel, attended by a handful of Arab allies. It was daring, dangerous, and lonely work—and he thrived on it, even finding the loneliness of the desert a blessing.

After the fall of Khartoum, Kitchener advocated a swift advance against the Mahdi to recapture the city and crush the dervish revolt before it grew stronger. But it was not his place to make policy; the Liberal government wanted to rid itself of the Sudan and its troubles, which continued after the Mahdi died in June 1885. In July, Kitchener resigned his Egyptian commission—perhaps in part because his fiancée, Hermione Baker, the daughter of Kitchener's friend General Valentine Baker,[5] had died of typhoid in Cairo—and returned to England, a brevet-lieutenant-colonel.

He wasn't gone from Africa for long. In November 1885 he served on an international commission for the Sultan of Zanzibar and in August 1886 he became governor-general of the Eastern Sudan based at Suakin, where his chief responsibility was to guard the Red Sea coast from the depredations of the dervishes. He took a more aggressive policy than the government wanted, led men into battle (something he was supposed to avoid), and had to be invalided out after getting shot in the jaw. Rather than being punished, he was made a brevet-colonel. He returned to Suakin as adjutant-general of the Egyptian army and with its sirdar (commander in chief), Sir Francis Grenfell, he defeated the dervishes there in December 1888. In August 1889, Grenfell and Kitchener (commanding the cavalry) avenged Hicks Pasha by destroying the dervish army that had annihilated his—that of Emir Wad-el-Nejumi, who was killed.

Omdurman

More important than avenging Hicks was avenging Gordon. In 1892, Kitchener became sirdar of the Egyptian army, and shaped and prepared his force for what he felt certain must be the inevitable call: to finally and forever smash the dervishes of the Sudan. That call would never come from the Liberals, but in 1895 Lord Salisbury's Conservatives were returned to power, and the following year, Kitchener, a Conservative and a friend of Lord Salisbury's family, was ordered to recapture Dongola on the Nile in the upper Sudan. It was taken on 23 September 1896, but no one assumed that was to be the end of the campaign. It was a mere way station to Khartoum.

Kitchener ordered the building of a railway line from Wadi Halfa to Abu Hamed. Though it took a year to build, Kitchener thought the time well spent. It would make the army's advance much simpler, avoiding three treacherous cataracts of the Nile, and give it a sturdy line of supply. The dervishes fell back as he advanced. But gathering in massive numbers—at least 100,000 men—was a dervish army at Omdurman.

Before that confrontation, Kitchener was compelled to fight a dervish army of 20,000 men under the command of Mahmud Ahmed at the Battle of Atbara on 8 April 1898. Kitchener had 14,000 men. Unable to draw Mahmud out from his trenches and *zareba* (thorn-bush fortifications), he blasted them with a short artillery barrage and then sent his men charging into fierce hand-to-hand combat, in which the British—the Seaforths, the Camerons, the Lincolns, and the Warwicks, among others—bested the dervishes. Kitchener's casualties were 568 men—125 of them British, and of those only 26 were killed. The dervishes lost 3,000 dead and another 2,000 captured, including Mahmud, who was subjected to a Roman processional victory march in which loyal Sudanese could mock and revile him. Mahmud warned his British captors that they would be in for a nasty surprise at Omdurman. It would certainly be a nasty surprise for someone.

Against Khalifa Abdullah, the Mahdi's successor, Kitchener brought a force of some 25,000 men. His artillery—both land-based and mounted on gunboats on the Nile—outclassed that of the dervishes; he also had Maxim guns, which were extremely effective, when they didn't jam. He sent a messenger to the Khalifa asking him to evacuate the women and children from Omdurman, upon which he was about to open fire; and he promised that he was going to save the Sudan "from your devilish doings and iniquity."[6]

On 1 September 1898, a young lieutenant and war correspondent assigned to the 21st Lancers, one Winston Churchill, rode hell for leather to inform Kitchener that a dervish army of 60,000 men was on the move to attack him;

he estimated that Kitchener had an hour or perhaps an hour and a half before they would be upon him. Ascending a hill, Kitchener was able to confirm Churchill's report—it appeared the Khalifa's entire army was swarming towards him, perhaps surging with anger at the desecration of the great dome of the Mahdi's tomb by artillery shells fired from Kitchener's gunboats. He ordered his men into camp, established a defensive perimeter, and had the gunboats drawn up for support, their searchlights sweeping over the lines of a possible dervish approach. If the dervishes struck at night, all Kitchener's advantages in artillery, and from the Maxim guns, would disappear. It would be down to hand-to-hand combat. Kitchener arranged for some of his Sudanese camp followers to spread a rumor among the Khalifa's men that the British were planning a night attack. That feint seemed to work. The dervishes did not strike until dawn.

They charged with a fanatic frenzy, armed with rifles, swords, and spears. But British discipline and firepower—about 8,000 of Kitchener's men were British, the rest Sudanese and Egyptians (the former ranked better as soldiers than the latter)—took a devastating toll. With the exception

A Clean Sweep

"Well, we have given them a good dusting!"

Kitchener's comment on the battlefield of Omdurman, on which his armies killed more than 10,000 dervishes, while losing fewer than 50 dead. Quoted in John Pollock, *Kitchener: Architect of Victory, Artisan of Peace* (Carroll & Graf, 2001), p. 135

of the charge of the 21st Lancers into an unexpected, hidden mass of 2,500 dervishes and the rearguard action of Hector "Fighting Mac" Macdonald, whose mainly Sudanese forces, 3,000 strong, held off a massive two-pronged dervish counterattack of about 32,000 men, the Battle of Omdurman was a one-sided affair, with the dervishes losing nearly 30,000 men killed, wounded, or captured to fewer than 50 dead and some 400 wounded in the Anglo-Egyptian-Sudanese force.

Three days later, the victorious armies were drawn up in Khartoum for a memorial service in honor of the late General Gordon. The band played Gordon's favorite hymn, "Abide with Me," and the usually brusque, impassive Kitchener of the laser-blue eyes became a Kitchener with choking throat and eyes obscured by tears. With the expedition was William Staveley "Monkey" Gordon, Gordon's nephew and a fellow officer of engineers. He was given the task—or the honor, or the outrage—of blowing up the Mahdi's tomb.

Because Kitchener was openly contemptuous of the press, the war correspondents were quick to criticize. They alleged he had ordered the slaughter of the dervish wounded (untrue, though as dervish "dead" were famous for shamming and then striking with musket or rifle, sword or spear, there was plenty of after-combat firing, despite Kitchener's imprecations against fearful wastes of ammunition). They said he had desecrated the Mahdi's tomb (well, yes, though the Mahdi had not been too kind to Gordon either). Further, they reported that he had kept the Mahdi's skull as a souvenir, which was true. Kitchener had a famous—and some later asserted, effeminate—taste for collecting *objets d'art*, especially porcelain.[7] The skull might have made a smashing inkstand or even a coffee mug, but given the press controversy it was instead swiftly buried in an unmarked location.

Having dusted off the dervishes, Kitchener opened sealed orders that commanded him to head with all dispatch to the southern Sudan. There he was to head off an expedition by a gallant French officer, Jean-Baptiste Marchand, who had trekked overland, west to east, across the waist of Africa. He had reached Fashoda on the Nile and was claiming it for France. The area in question was, strictly speaking, Egyptian territory, which made

A Most Economical Soldier

"Lord Kitchener won his well-deserved peerage because he was an excellent man of business; he looked after every important detail, and enforced economy."

Lord Cromer, consul-general of Egypt, on a quality that perhaps made him more popular with mandarins than with his fellow officers, quoted in Byron Farwell, *Eminent Victorian Soldiers: Seekers of Glory* (Norton, 1988), p. 327

it, well, British, and it was Kitchener's task to get Marchand to withdraw without sparking a war. The Frenchman was plucky—a quality admired by every British officer—and as Kitchener spoke fluent French, they got on in rather gentlemanly fashion, preserving peace at Fashoda and referring the more important questions to their home governments who resolved the "Fashoda crisis" in Britain's favor.

Kitchener came to England a hero and was made a peer—Lord Kitchener of Khartoum and Aspall (or "K of K")—before returning to the Sudan in December 1898. He raised an endowment to create Gordon Memorial College (now the University of Khartoum), though he seems quickly to have lost interest in it (he was not the academic type).[8] He rebuilt Khartoum and the governor's palace. And as the first governor-general of the newly established Anglo-Egyptian "condominium" over the Sudan, he helped establish what many considered the finest civil service in the British Empire, one that leant heavily on recruiting Oxbridge and public school athletes.

Battling the Boers

In 1899, with the Boer invasion of the Natal, Kitchener was eager to wash his hands of Sudanese affairs and get on with smiting the Boers. He won an appointment as chief of staff to Field Marshal Lord Roberts or "Bobs" as he was called. Roberts took over as commander in chief of the British forces after a series of unnerving setbacks to British arms by the Boer commandos. But Bobs rapidly turned things to rights, relieved the besieged British cities and defeated the major Boer armies (though Kitchener was much criticized in the press for the heavy British casualties suffered under his command at the Battle of Paardeburg). The major operations apparently over, Roberts then left Kitchener in charge (in November 1900) to finish the job. It proved no easy task. The stubborn Boers refused to acknowledge they were beaten; so Kitchener methodically subdivided the country into blockhouse-guarded, barbed wire sectors, Boer farms were burnt, and the Boers themselves were locked into "concentration camps" where they could no longer provide sustenance for the Boer guerrillas, against whom British troops scoured the countryside. Again Kitchener was reviled in the press, this time for the horrors (eventually largely corrected) that developed in the camps, where disease cut a mortal swath through the poor Boer families.

Though he became tagged as a brute for his methods in crushing the Boer guerrillas, Kitchener wanted a negotiated peace on terms that would appease the Boers. It was his personal diplomacy with the Boer leaders that made the Treaty of Vereeniging (31 May 1902) possible. As General Sir Ian Hamilton observed, the treaty was a great testament to Kitchener:

> How is it that the Boer War put an end to feuds, race hatreds, bankruptcies, disorders, and bloodshed which had paralysed South African progress for a generation, whilst the Great War has on the contrary inflicted race hatred, bankruptcy and murder over the best part of the world from Ireland in the West to the Near East.... Lord Kitchener fought the politicians who wanted to make a vindictive peace...a peace which would above all things humiliate and wound the feelings of the conquered.... He beat them and made his own peace; a generous soldierly peace. He lent the Boers money; he rebuilt their farms; he rebuilt their dams; he re-stocked their farms.... The war lasted three years; South Africa was more completely ruined than Central Europe; hate was stronger than in Germany:—and yet within one year South Africa was smiling and so were we.[9]

Kitchener: The Great Recruiting Poster

Victorious in South Africa, Kitchener was made a viscount. He attempted but failed to get married, and as he seemed unlikely to have any direct heirs, he managed to arrange matters with King Edward VII that the title might pass through Kitchener's elder brother, Colonel Henry Elliott Chevallier Kitchener, the only brother who had in fact married, and who, luckily, had

The Trial of Breaker Morant

In one celebrated (at least in Australia) incident, Kitchener was alleged to have taken appeasement of the Boers too far—that was the trial of Harry "Breaker" Morant. Morant was a colorful character—a British emigrant to Australia where he gained a reputation as an expert horseman, poet, and rascal. He volunteered for service in the Boer War, starting as a corporal in the South Australian Mounted Rifles and ending as a lieutenant in the Bushveldt Carbineers. He was put on trial, along with two comrades, for shooting Boer prisoners (and a pro-Boer German missionary). He was ordered put to death by firing squad (Kitchener commuted the sentence of one of the other defendants). To his defenders, Morant was merely executing Kitchener's order to inflict summary justice on Boer commandos wearing British khaki, and, from a human point of view, was taking justifiable vengeance for the killing of his best friend, Captain Hunt, whose body was found mutilated (though, unknown to Morant, the mutilation was likely done by black witch doctors rather than Boer commandos). Morant's detractors denied that Kitchener ever gave an order to execute prisoners and maintained that Morant had committed a war crime. The case caused an uproar in Australia, where it became widely assumed that Morant had been sacrificed to appease the Boers, but Kitchener's position was a simple and straightforward one: Morant had ordered extra-judicial executions of prisoners and there were no legitimate extenuating circumstances. The trial proceedings are lost and there is no documentary evidence that can be conclusive either way. The film *Breaker Morant* is an outstanding dramatic account of the pro-Morant version.

produced a son. Alas, the son, a commander in the Royal Navy, died before he could inherit the title, which eventually went to Colonel Kitchener's grandson.

Kitchener's next post was commander in chief in India (1902–09). The viceroy, Lord Curzon, had requested him, but soon regretted the decision. The two men had very different ideas about military reform. Kitchener eventually won the bureaucratic battle, with Curzon's departure, and did good work in increasing the number of Gurkha battalions, but his time in India was marked chiefly by delegating his responsibilities, which he was not normally wont to do, and dedicating himself to his passion for interior decoration. Hard in so many matters, Kitchener was always vulnerable to the muezzin call of Eastern splendor. Passed over for appointment as viceroy and denied the opportunity to become ambassador to Turkey (he liked the Turks, and some speculate he could have prevented Turkey from becoming a German ally in World War I), he returned to Egypt as consul-general in 1911 and was de facto viceroy of the Anglo-Egyptian condominium over the Sudan.

Dog Quartet

Near the end of his life, Kitchener had four black cocker spaniels. Their names: Shot, Bang, Miss, and Damn.

With the guns of August 1914, he was called home and made secretary of state for war. Many politicians assumed the European war would be short and sharp. Kitchener knew better, predicting a three- or four-year-long campaign of hard slogging with massed armies enduring heavy casualties. Yet initially he was opposed to military conscription and lent his face to the most famous recruiting poster in the world: finger pointing, moustaches bristling, his eyes boring into the viewer, "Your Country Needs YOU."[10] The recruiting campaign was enormously successful, but as the war dragged on the advocates of conscription gained Kitchener's reluctant consent and achieved their goal with the Military Service Act of 1916.

When Kitchener entered the cabinet he enjoyed the intimidated respect of most of his colleagues, but his ways were not the ways of garrulous politicians. Lloyd George, who succeeded him as secretary of state for war (before becoming prime minister), said of Kitchener: "He was like a great revolving lighthouse. Sometimes the beam of his mind used to shoot out, showing one Europe and the assembled armies in a vast and illimitable perspective, till one felt that one was looking along it into the heart of reality—and then the shutter would turn and for weeks there would be nothing but a blank darkness."[11]

The light went out forever in June 1916 when he sailed on a diplomatic mission to Russia aboard HMS *Hampshire*. The ship struck a mine and went down with nearly all hands. Kitchener, according to the survivors, was resolute to the last.

Chapter 18

IAN DOUGLAS SMITH
(1919–2007)

"This man [Smith] has a certain mixture of characteristics of caution, obstinacy, dedication, vision, tenacity and toughness that have evoked rage in some, frustration in others, and admiration and loyalty in most. The plain truth is, I know of no other man who has the physical and mental toughness necessary to have led Rhodesia where it is to-day."

—*Ralph Nilson, party chairman of the Rhodesian Front, 1969*[1]

Ian Smith was in the perverse position of being a British patriot who led his country, Rhodesia, to independence from Britain. Under his leadership Rhodesia exported food, maintained a free press and judiciary, was anti-Communist, and yet was repudiated and boycotted by the rest of the free world. When all Smith's dire predictions about what one man, one vote would bring to Rhodesia came true, he was, bizarrely, blamed for making it so. Ian Smith lived a noble life, and that was its own reward. From the world at large he received no other.

He was born in Africa, in Selukwe, Rhodesia, to a Scotch immigrant father and an English mother. His father was a farmer and an entrepreneur who set up a small chain of bakeries and butcher's shops around the local mines (and tried a little mining himself), maintained the Selukwe auto garage, and bred race horses as an avocation (he even jockeyed a bit). As part of his civic duties, he judged cattle, led the local rugby and cricket

Did you know?

- Ian Smith was a World War II RAF fighter pilot whose face required plastic surgery after a fiery crash

- He predicted a dire future for Rhodesia under one man, one vote—and then was blamed by his critics when his predictions came true

- Though often condemned as a racist by outsiders, Smith stayed in Africa and gloried in his popularity among blacks as the great opponent of the dictator Robert Mugabe

clubs, and was a captain of the local defense force. He was awarded an MBE (Member of the Order of the British Empire) for his work raising money for Britain's defense during the Second World War. He was business-minded, hard-working, and, like the Scots of old, a man of stubborn moral convictions. Ian Smith's mother was equally active in local affairs—sporting, social, charitable, and educational (she founded the local branch of the Women's Institute). She too was awarded an MBE.

Smith was a boy's boy (as he would later be a man's man), preferring math and science to the liberal arts, but vastly preferring sports to either. He was proud of his own athletic prowess—and that of the rugby players and cricketers of independent Rhodesia (rugby and cricket were mandatory sports for boys in the secondary schools). He enrolled at Rhodes University in South Africa, where his focus was all sporting: he was a sprinter, a rugby player, and rowed crew as therapy for a knee he had banged up playing rugby.

Then came the war. Rhodesians rushed to enlist—and actually had to be held back, as those in essential industries, like mining, needed to have someone fill their jobs before they put on khaki. University students were encouraged to finish their studies, but Smith finagled an interview with the Air Force—not bothering to mention he was a university student—and was accepted as a recruit, joining Australians, Britons, and fellow Rhodesians training to fly in the clear blue skies of Rhodesia. Smith hoped to be assigned to a squadron in Britain, but instead was sent Egypt, Lebanon, Persia, and Mesopotamia before returning to the western desert of North Africa. On one flight in Egypt he crashed his plane and was lucky to survive—his face was smashed (requiring plastic surgery to repair); his jaw, a shoulder, and a leg were broken; and his back was badly injured. His recovery took five months. He was offered a chance to return home as a flight instructor, but was still hungry for action and rejoined his squadron in

Corsica. He had flown Hawker Hurricanes before—now he achieved his dream of flying Spitfires.

Smith saw heavy action in missions over Italy, and was eventually shot down. He evaded the Germans and was taken in by a rural Italian family, keeping fit with mountain climbing, wood chopping, and his RAF exercises. He tried to teach himself Italian, made contact with another RAF officer in the area, and then linked up with the partisans. The partisans wanted to keep him as one of their band, but Smith was determined to find his way back to the RAF. After several months he was smuggled into France, crossing the frozen Alps in summer clothes, and was eventually picked up by an American patrol.

He was sent to Naples where he again skirted the truth—about how long he had been behind enemy lines (the truth was: long enough that revealing it would have meant a posting back to Rhodesia), and about how England was essentially a second home to him—in order to see action on the Western Front, which he did. After a bit of training to knock off the rust, he flew from an Allied base in Germany; he wound down his service with a tour of the Nordic countries and a return to Blighty.

Smith resumed his studies, and sports, at Rhodes University, graduating with an economics degree. He had relatives in America who urged him to emigrate, but Rhodesia was home, and Smith was happy and determined to stay there. He became a farmer, married a young widow with two children (she was herself something of a sportswoman), and was cajoled into running for Parliament as a member of the free market Liberal Party. The Party was beaten badly, but Smith won his race. He remained a farmer—Parliament sat for only three months a year—but politics became his vocation. His strength was not his oratory or his deal-making; rather he seemed the epitome of what it meant to be a Rhodesian—a blunt, straightforward, principled farmer and war veteran, who was, as the Rhodesians thought of themselves, "more British than the British." Smith, like most Rhodesians, was stunned and disturbed when the British electorate gave Churchill the order of the boot in 1945; and he and they were even more disturbed when British politics followed an anti-colonial course over the next three decades.

UDI

Smith's other political strength was that he represented the views and ideals of most white Rhodesians. He was hated by the minority of white Rhodesian liberals who thought he stood athwart an harmonious multi-racial society; and he was disdained by the minority of white Rhodesians who saw apartheid South Africa as the model African state. Smith's view, and the majority white Rhodesian view, avoided extreme racialism, while denying the viability of one man, one vote in Africa—except perhaps as a distant goal—if a free and civilized society was to be maintained.

In 1953, Rhodesia (or Southern Rhodesia, as it was known at the time) joined Northern Rhodesia (Zambia) and Nyasaland (Malawi) in the Federation of Rhodesia and Nyasaland, which existed until 1 January 1964. Smith supported the Federation on economic grounds, and joined the new Federal Party, but his enthusiasm for the Federation was tepid. Southern Rhodesia was, de facto, practically self-governing, and while he and his fellow Rhodesians were extremely loyal to Britain, he also wanted to ensure that Rhodesia in no way jeopardized its future independence.

In 1961, Rhodesia enacted a new constitution, which broke the electorate into two voting rolls—divided not by race (though the vast majority of blacks would be on the secondary or "B Roll") but by education and class (based on income and property, and hence on the taxes one paid). The constitution was endorsed and partially drafted by representatives of the British government who estimated that it would lead to black majority rule in a ten to fifteen years time. But black nationalist politicians, who had originally signed on to the constitution, changed course and urged black Africans not to register to vote—a surely self-defeating strategy.

Matters came to a boil with the breakup of the Federation and Britain's granting of independence to Nyasaland and Northern Rhodesia in 1964. Independent Malawi and Zambia (as these nations became) were considered perfectly respectable members of the British Commonwealth even though both fulfilled Ian Smith's constant warning that in Africa one man, one vote meant one man, one vote, one time. Malawi immediately became a one-party totalitarian state looted for thirty years by its president-for-life Hastings Banda. Zambia became a one-party (de facto in 1968, de jure in 1972) socialist state and economic flop, governed by Kenneth Kaunda from independence until 1991. To Smith's dismay, Rhodesia, with its multi-party elections, free press and free judiciary, and economic success was considered unworthy of independence because it did not immediately grant equal voting rights to all black Africans.

Smith—who became the leader of a new party, the Rhodesian Front, in 1964—thought this was rank hypocrisy on the part of the British, who were more interested in appeasing liberal opinion than in doing what was right for the people in their African colonies. The British, in his view, ignored the practical problems—how to accurately register voters when most rural-born black Africans had no birth certificates—and the already clear evidence of the chaos, violence, dictatorship, and

Evolution or Revolution

"British policy for Africa led to one man one vote—once. Thereafter dictatorship ensued, with the resultant chaos and denial of freedom and justice.... We referred to [the Rhodesian system] as 'meritocracy', and tragically we will never know whether it would have succeeded and proved the exception to the rule—evolution in preference to revolution."

Ian Smith, *The Great Betrayal* (Blake Publishing, 1997), p. 108

economic collapse of most post-colonial African states, an experience white Rhodesians did not want to see repeated in their own country. While seeing white Rhodesia as an outpost of Western civilization, Smith accepted that black Africans did things differently, and supported the tribal chiefs who were the traditional authorities in black African politics. Smith was derided by liberal opinion outside of Rhodesia for upholding the chiefs as a barrier against Communism—which only highlights the blithe ignorance of liberal opinion, for this is precisely what they were and why they were targeted by the Communist-backed nationalist insurgents.

On 11 November 1965, Prime Minister Ian Smith announced Rhodesia's unilateral declaration of independence (UDI), a decision endorsed unanimously by the largest Indaba (political gathering) of chiefs (622) in Rhodesian history, representing, in their headman roles, ninety percent of the black African population. The declaration was consciously modeled, in part, on America's Declaration of Independence, though the United States government, with black civil rights controversies of its own, was in no position to accept a rebel white-dominated state in Africa—even an explicitly anti-Communist one that was willing to send troops to Vietnam.

For all the liberal angst over the horrors of white rule in Rhodesia, the country itself was peaceful; Smith had no security detail (his official residence had no staff either); the crime rate, Smith was told, was one of the lowest in the world; and in absolute comparisons of the educational, medical, and other facilities[2] available to the black population, black Africans in Rhodesia were far better off than their compatriots anywhere else in sub-Saharan Africa. Smith often said, "We have the happiest Africans in the world," and while that might sound patronizing, it was an honestly held opinion confirmed by the black Africans he met in his normal rounds and by the statistics his government provided him.[3]

The response of the British government, led by Labour Prime Minister Harold Wilson, was a mixture of the peevish, the preposterous, and the perverse: refusing to pay the pensions of Britons living in Rhodesia (the Rhodesian government made good the shortfall); sending British RAF units to Zambia (before independence, the superlative Rhodesian armed forces had been integrated with the British military; relations between the forces were extremely fraternal; and the British planes relied on Rhodesian air traffic control, which covered the entire area); and, most important of all, supporting international economic sanctions against what economically was one of the few success stories in Africa. While the British government backed punitive actions (short of violence[4]) to bring Rhodesia to heel, it also pursued a course of negotiations with Smith to end the embarrassment (to liberal and Commonwealth opinion) of its white-led rebel colony. Smith, however, was not inclined to accept that British embarrassment was sufficient reason to put Rhodesia's future as a prosperous, free society at risk.

In 1970, despite its loyalty to the old ideals of the British Empire, and hence the Crown, Rhodesia became a republic with a new constitution. That same year, a Conservative government was elected in Britain; and an

Blaming Colonialism

"The failures resorted to the parrot cry that they were in their current predicament because they were exploited by the colonial powers. But Canada, Australia, New Zealand, and Rhodesia had gone through the same history, and as a matter of interest, so did [the] USA and South Africa, and they are all glorious success stories. Those who have not made the grade must stop looking for a scapegoat, and look to themselves: their corruption, incompetence, nepotism, external bank accounts and high leisure preference."

Ian Smith, *The Great Betrayal* (Blake Publishing, 1997), p. 120

agreement was reached in 1971 between the British and Rhodesian governments establishing a gradual path to majority rule. But the agreement fell to pieces when a British commission judged that black African opinion did not support it, though the head of the African National Council, Bishop Abel Muzorewa, who had led opposition to the agreement, backtracked and announced, in 1973, that he now did indeed support it. That was too late for the British. The agreement was not resubmitted.

In the meantime, in 1972, a decade's worth of Communist-supported subversion had finally ignited what became the Rhodesian Bush War. The Rhodesian Army faced two main terrorist groups: the Soviet-inspired ZAPU (the Zimbabwean African People's Union) led by Joshua Nkomo, whose military forces (ZIPRA, the Zimbabwe People's Revolutionary Army) operated mostly from bases in Zambia, and the Maoist ZANU (the Zimbabwean African National Union), which was eventually led by Robert Mugabe, whose military forces (ZANLA, the Zimbabwean National Liberation Army) were concentrated in Mozambique, where they were sheltered by Communist forces fighting the Portuguese government. The two terrorist groups also occasionally fought each other, and were divided on tribal lines. The Rhodesian army and air force were extremely effective at counterinsurgency, but with the collapse of Portuguese Africa to the Communists, and South Africa's decision to try to appease its African neighbors by ending support for Rhodesia, Smith recognized that his country's isolation had become perilous.

Books the Anti-Colonialists Don't Want You to Read

Two by Peter Godwin: *Mukiwa: A White Boy in Africa* (Atlantic Monthly Press, 1996) and *When a Crocodile Eats the Sun: A Memoir of Africa* (Little, Brown & Co, 2006). Godwin is of liberal Rhodesian stock. (He even daydreamt of shooting Smith while guarding him as a member of the British South African Police, Rhodesia's anti-terrorist police force.) But he is nonetheless an honest reporter and an excellent writer. He offers a compelling portrait of Rhodesia as it was and Zimbabwe as it is.

Smith accepted the principle of majority rule and in 1978 reached an "internal settlement" with Bishop Muzorewa, Chief Chirau of Mashonaland, and the Reverend Ndabaningi Sithole, the former (and more moderate) head of ZANU who had been displaced by Robert Mugabe. Smith argued that these leaders, who had agreed to negotiate with him, represented the views of roughly 85 percent of black Rhodesians. Smith had agreed to a universal franchise, and as a necessary prerequisite to negotiations on the "internal settlement" these black leaders had agreed to an independent judiciary and civil service, a bill of rights to protect property and pension rights in particular, and a military immune from political pressures. The black leaders wanted majority rule, and Smith wanted to ensure that Rhodesia did not fall prey to the political disasters that were the African norm.

In April 1979, Rhodesia became Rhodesia-Zimbabwe, and Bishop Abel Muzorewa was elected prime minister (Smith remained in government as a minister without portfolio), but the two major parties supporting terrorism, Nkomo's ZAPU and Mugabe's ZANU, boycotted the election and continued their war. Appallingly, neither Britain (in deference to the Commonwealth) nor the United Nations recognized the new democratically elected government; Rhodesia-Zimbabwe would have no international standing until the Communist-backed terrorists participated in an election.

The British called all parties to negotiations conducted by Lord Carrington at Lancaster House in London. Muzorewa, Mugabe, and Nkomo agreed to a new constitution and new elections, with a British governor (Lord Soames) acting as interim leader of the country as it made its official transition from dependent colony (albeit in rebellion and enduring sanctions) to independent state. Smith attended the Lancaster House negotiations as part of Muzorewa's delegation, and though he was cast as a lone dissenter, he was the one man who accurately predicted events: that the radical Robert Mugabe would win the election on the basis of intimidation and the fact that he came from the Shona, the tribe of 80 percent of black

A Neo-Colonialist Movie the Anti-Colonialists Don't Want You to See

The Wild Geese, 1979. A group of mercenaries—led by Richard Burton, Richard Harris, Roger Moore, and Hardy Kruger—blow holy hell out of the Cuban-trained army of an African dictatorship, rescue an imprisoned African leader, and escape to Rhodesia. Highly recommended. Based on the novel by Rhodesian Daniel Carney.

Rhodesians. Lord Carrington—and most everyone else—assumed that the somewhat more moderate Joshua Nkomo would win or that a coalition government of Nkomo, Muzorewa, and Smith (because of twenty seats reserved for white Rhodesians) would emerge. Smith recognized that Lord Carrington was unable to imagine how African politics actually worked, and he was disgusted at what he saw as British politicians' appeasement of radical black nationalists who only despised them.

Après Smith le Déluge

In March 1980, Robert Mugabe became the leader of the new nation of Zimbabwe. The first man he consulted was Ian Smith. The black leader that all the other leaders had considered the most radical and dangerous had won, but he assured Smith that he had no intention of alienating the white Rhodesians who had given the country such a prosperous economy. Doctrinaire Marxism, he assured Smith, would not be the order of the day—and it wasn't, at first. Mugabe's public stance was one of conciliation, but the new Zimbabwean broadcast media churned out hours of pro-Communist propaganda. Then Mugabe himself began agitating for a one-party state and urged reprisals against whites who did not support him, threatening to imprison Smith. He also began a vicious war against the Ndebele (Nkomo's tribe). Mugabe's notorious North Korean-trained 5th Brigade ravaged Matabeleland. As a Catholic priest told reporter Peter Godwin, "I have lived through the Second World War in Austria and I have seen the terrible things the Gestapo could do. But let me tell you something, the Gestapo couldn't teach these Fifth Brigade fellows a damn thing!"[5]

The justice system became increasingly corrupted by the Mugabe government; political intimidation and repression became the norm; the economy was pillaged in socialist style and with socialist results; and white farmers were driven from their land by Mugabe-supported mobs. The breadbasket of central Africa became an economic basket case. Smith watched all this with sorrow. He remained a member of Parliament until 1987. Even in his retirement he was often threatened by the Mugabe regime, but he retained too much popularity—especially among black Zimbabweans opposed to the government—for Mugabe to take the political risk of imprisoning him or forcing him into exile. Smith lived to see all his worst predictions come true; had he been able to read his obituaries he would have seen that liberal opinion blamed him for being right.

Part VI

MIDDLE AND NEAR EAST

Chapter 19

THE LOVE OF DESOLATE PLACES

n the beginning it was all about India. It was India that made the acquisition of Aden on the Persian Gulf necessary in 1838. It was India that made Egypt and the Suez Canal vital British interests; by the end of the nineteenth century, three out of every four ships through the Canal were on the passage to or from India. British India administered Aden and Mesopotamia, and conducted its own Arabian policy. But there was something else, too. Britons became explorers of Arabia—attracted either by its dangers and religious mysteries (Sir Richard Francis Burton) or by the English love for desolate places (Charles Doughty).

Within imperial circles there was an entire class of English Arabists who made their careers in the desert and might better be called Anglo-Arabs. As was usual with British imperialists, they favored the "martial races," in this case, the Bedouin tribesman, who with his "patrician style," "picturesque appearance," and love of war (British officers lifted it above a love of booty), "seemed almost a kind of Englishman himself, translated into another idiom."[1] The Bedouins lacked British discipline, but theirs was a proper, conservative, hierarchical society that an Englishman could appreciate. City Arabs, the oily commercial classes, the jabbering nationalists, the vast Egyptian mob—these the Englishman often disdained. But the desert warrior was a worthy ally, and to some English women, a romantic foil.[2]

Passport to Suez

Britain's first foreign policy goal in Egypt was evicting the French. Napoleon entered the annals of Egypt's conquerors in 1798 and marched his armies up through Syria, posing as the liberator—as the British later would—of Egyptians and Arabs from Ottoman tyranny. But after Lord Nelson's smashing naval victory at the Battle of the Nile in 1799 and a resulting Anglo-Ottoman land campaign, Napoleon's conquests were rolled back in 1801.

More important was the British-French entanglement over the Suez Canal. The British had built a railway from Alexandria to Suez in the 1850s, but were skeptical of and hostile to the French Suez Canal Company (even fomenting a Bedouin-led revolt against the company's use of forced labor). But once the Canal was opened in 1869, British ships, eventually more than any others, made use of it. When the Egyptian khedive had to sell his shares

Imperial High Finance

When Prime Minister Benjamin Disraeli needed an immediate grant to buy the khedive's canal shares, he sent his private secretary Montagu Corry to find Lionel de Rothschild. As Andre Maurois recounts, Corry found Rothschild dining and "told him that Disraeli needed four millions on the following day.

"Rothschild was eating grapes. He took one, spat out the skin, and said: 'What is your security?'

"'The British government.'

"'You shall have it.'"

As told in Andre Maurois, *Disraeli: A Picture of the Victorian Age* (The Modern Library, 1955), p. 296

to pay off debts in 1875, British Prime Minister Benjamin Disraeli tapped his friend Lionel de Rothschild for a loan, and Britain became a major shareholder in the Canal, leading to joint British-French control.

Disraeli's financial coup was a boon for the national interest, but it was also—as Disraeli's Liberal opponent William Gladstone recognized and bemoaned—a looming imperial obligation. It came due on Gladstone's prime ministerial watch. In 1881, Colonel Ahmed Arabi led a nationalist rebellion against the khedive, who ruled Egypt on behalf of the decrepit Ottoman Empire. For the better part of a century the British had defended the Ottoman Empire as a barrier to Russian expansion (and fought the Crimean War of 1853 to 1856 at the Turks' side against the Russians). Gladstone, however, was never a friend of the Turks—seeing them as oppressors, if not slaughterers, of Eastern Christians—and Arabi's platform was attractive to a liberal frame of mind: not only nationalist, but appealing to British ideals of free government.

How to Be Posh

It is often said that "posh" comes from "port out, starboard home"—the preferred shady side of a ship traveling to and from India. Killjoys say there is no evidence to support this explanation, but they have yet to come up with a better one.

That was all very well, but when Arabi seized power it seemed as though the European population of Egypt—and Anglo-French management of the Canal and of Egyptian finances (to protect European holders of Egyptian debt)—might be at risk. A joint Anglo-French naval task force was sent to intimidate Arabi. The French arrived; mobs rioted; Egyptian batteries took aim at the flotilla; and the French turned tail. The British, however, knew what to do. They bombarded Alexandria (11 July 1882) and then, in September, landed an army under Sir Garnet Wolseley, who knocked Arabi and his rebellion into the desert wastes in what military historian Byron Farwell deemed "the most brilliantly devised and executed campaign of the century,"[3] the highlight of which was the Battle of Tel el-Kebir (13 September

1882). The British restored the khedive, exiled Arabi to Ceylon, and took as their responsibility the military protection and financial management of Egypt.

Her Majesty's consul-general in Egypt, Evelyn Baring, later Lord Cromer, acted as Egypt's de facto governor from 1883 to 1907. Even before that, as controller general of Egypt's finances, Baring had arranged for one khedive to be replaced by another. To common Egyptians he was known as *El Lord* and was thought to be behind everything that went on in the country—in reality, he was behind enough. A thoroughly efficient administrator, he installed a British shadow government behind the Egyptian ministries, completely reorganized the army, and with the creation of the Anglo-Egyptian Condominium over the Sudan (which lasted from 1899 to 1956) ran a little empire of his own.

Where Desert Rats Gathered for Cocktails

"Cairo in the 1940s was the last great assembly-point...where imperial legions mingled in their staggering variety. Every kind of imperial uniform was to be spotted in Cairo.... There were kilts and turbans and tarbooshes, slouch hats and jodhpurs. There were Kenyan pioneers, and Indian muleteers, and Australian tank crews, and English gunners, and New Zealand fighter pilots, and South African engineers. There were scholarly staff officers straight from their Oxford colleges, and swaggering extroverts back from secret missions in the Balkans.... The whole capital was now in effect a British military base."

James Morris, *Farewell the Trumpets: An Imperial Retreat* (The Folio Society, 1992), p. 366

When the Ottomans became a German ally in World War I, Egypt ceased to be an Ottoman territory administered by the British and became a British protectorate. It also became headquarters of the British Arab Bureau, which (as part of British Intelligence in Cairo) helped direct the Arab revolt against the Ottoman Empire. In 1922, Egypt was declared an independent kingdom, though the British kept their military bases in the country, which remained de facto a British protectorate. That proved awfully useful in the Second World War. While the Egyptian government remained officially neutral until February 1945—just in case—Egypt was home to Britain's Middle East Command, which was responsible for the war in Africa, the Middle East, and Greece.

Denouement at Suez

What had started at Suez ended there. In 1951, the Egyptian government revoked its treaty commitments to Britain[4] and demanded that all British troops leave Egypt. To prod the British out, the Egyptian government winked at terrorist attacks on the Canal Zone. The Egyptian mob went one better and burned down Shepheard's Hotel (the great World War II watering hole for Allied officers), the Turf club, and any British enterprise they could find. In 1952, a military coup advanced the nationalist cause further, with Egypt becoming a republic the following year. Facing an unsympathetic Eisenhower administration—with its stridently anti-imperial secretary of state John Foster Dulles—Britain negotiated with Egypt a gradual withdrawal of British troops from the Canal Zone, the last troops to depart in 1956.

In July 1956, Egyptian president Gamal Abdel Nasser nationalized the Canal. Dulles had naïvely supposed Nasser would be a pro-American nationalist, rather than a Communist-leaning one. He was peeved at Nasser's diplomatic dalliances with the Communist Chinese and the Soviets, and his arms purchases from the Eastern bloc, and in protest cut off American loans for the construction of the Aswan dam—which, ironically, Nasser used as part of his pretext for nationalizing the Canal. British Prime Minister Anthony Eden had a better read on Nasser, regarding him as a pharaonic Mussolini.

Eden believed the Suez Canal had to be placed safely under international control. To achieve this, the British and French governments resolved on a joint strike at Egypt; but inevitable calls for a diplomatic solution, led by the United States, delayed any action. The French, meanwhile, began cooking up an elaborate plot with the Israelis, who would attack Egypt across Sinai, giving the French and British an excuse to interpose themselves between the combatants and secure the Canal Zone.

The military portion of this Frankish legerdemain went off like a charm—the Israelis charged across Sinai on 29 October 1956; British and French troops occupied the Canal Zone on 5 November. Diplomatically, however, the operation came a cropper. World opinion—including that of the United States—was sharply hostile, and British domestic opinion, bullish immediately after the nationalization, weakened in the intervening months of futile diplomacy and became deeply divided. The supreme irony was that while Britain was calumniated by the rest of the world for protecting the Suez Canal from a petty dictator, the Soviet Union was crushing an Hungarian uprising against Communist tyranny. The Soviet Union and the United States actually allied themselves in condemning Britain, with the United States blocking an International Monetary Fund loan that Britain needed to stop a run on the pound, until the British government agreed to withdraw its troops from Suez. British imperial influence over Egypt was at an end. The myth that America is an anti-imperial power caused the Eisenhower administration to punish America's friends and reward her enemies.

Eisenhower later conceded that he had made a mistake at Suez; it weakened the West and strengthened the hand of radical Arab nationalists who would soon topple the pro-Western government of Iraq and stir up trouble throughout the Middle East. Among Nasser's targets was Lebanon, which he encircled by forming the United Arab Republic with Syria. In 1958, Eisenhower felt compelled to send 14,000 troops and 70 ships to Lebanon after Nasserite Muslims tried to overthrow the pro-Western President Camille Chamoun. Chamoun, unlike Ike, had not condemned the British and French at Suez.

The Kingdom of Iraq

British Prime Minister Anthony Eden was dining with Iraq's King Feisal II and Prime Minister Nuri es-Said when news came that Nasser had nationalized the Suez Canal. Nuri told Eden, "You must hit him. You must hit him hard, and you must hit him now."[5] He clearly understood that Nasser posed a threat to the pro-Western states of the Middle East, like British-created Iraq with its British-installed monarchy; but he was also a typical Arab statesman. When Britain finally acted against Nasser, he protested Franco-British aggression.

From the sixteenth century until it was taken by the British in the First World War, the territory of modern Iraq had been under Ottoman rule. The Turks had divided it into three provinces whose geographical boundaries were ethnic-religious ones, with a Kurdish north, a Shi'ite South, and a Sunni center. When the Ottoman Empire allied with Germany in World War I, the British seized Basra, beginning a Mesopotamia campaign that had its humiliations—especially the siege of Kut (December 1915 to April 1916), where the British lost 30,000 men as casualties, and another 13,000 were taken as prisoners, most of whom didn't survive the Turkish camps—but ended with British victory.

The British decided to govern Mesopotamia as a unitary state, and did so under a mandate from the League of Nations. After repressing an initial rebellion, the British ruled indirectly through local elites, mostly Sunnis who were thought to be better educated, more pro-British, and less prone to Islamic extremism than the Shi'ites. Prince Feisal—a political protégé of British officer T. E. Lawrence (of Arabia) and a Sunni—was put on the throne. In principle Feisal was acceptable to the Shi'ites because he belonged to the Hashemite family, which claimed descent from the Prophet Mohammed. He was, nevertheless, an obvious outsider with little reason, besides being favored by the British, to be named king of Iraq.

The British established Iraq as a constitutional monarchy with an elected parliament. In 1932, it became an independent state, though the British retained military bases in the country. During the Second World War, Iraq's Prime Minister Rashid Ali foisted a pro-Nazi military coup against Iraq's pro-British foreign minister (Nuri es-Said) and Prince Abd al-Ilah (regent for the young King Feisal II). The coup was short-lived. In a swift campaign, the British deposed the pro-Nazi regime and restored the rightful monarch. After the war, Iraq was the initial cornerstone of the Baghdad Pact (1955), which united Britain, Iraq, Iran, Pakistan, and Turkey in an anti-Soviet front in the Near East. In 1958, nationalist military officers launched a pro-Nasserite coup in Iraq. Feisal II, Abd al-Ilah, and Nuri were killed, and Iraq, like Egypt, became a republic (in 1959) and then a dictatorship, and it withdrew from the Baghdad Pact.

The Power behind the Peacock Throne

Though Iran was never formally part of the British Empire, the British Navy had patrolled the Persian Gulf since the eighteenth century. At first its mission was to suppress pirates and protect the trade routes to India; later it added the suppression of the slave trade; and as the presence of the Royal Navy grew so did the presence of British diplomatic "residents" who proved highly influential in Gulf ports. In Persia itself, the British dueled with the Russians for influence. In 1901, through superior finance and diplomacy, Britain gained the oil concessions for three-quarters of the country. That became all the more important as the Royal Navy started moving from coal to oil power.

After the First World War, the British no longer had to worry about the encroachments of czarist Russia. They did, however, confront the far more dangerous subversion of Russian Bolsheviks. British troops were dispatched to keep Persia free from the Bolshevik menace, as Red and White armies battled on Iran's borders, a Persian Communist Party was formed, and a northern Persian province was annexed by the Soviet Union. To alleviate the strain on the British army, whose troops were needed around the world for postwar policing operations, Major-General Sir Edmund "Tiny" (6'4", 275 pounds) Ironside came up with precisely the right solution, one suitable for most foreign policy jams: "A military dictatorship would solve all our troubles and let us out of the country without any trouble at all."[6]

To that end, Ironside found a likely lad in Colonel Reza Khan of the Persian Cossack Division. Ironside had no more than picked his man and the act was done. Reza Khan led his Cossacks into the capital and, presto change-o, became prime minister. The coup worked splendidly in terms of relieving British troops from defending Persia—it did rather less well in terms of perpetuating British influence, as Reza Khan saw British advisers as impediments to his absolute authority and dismissed them; the Persian people, nevertheless (like the Egyptians with El Lord), suspected a British hand behind everything.

In 1925, Reza Khan became king, inaugurating a new dynasty, setting Iran (the name he gave his country) on a modernizing course in the spirit of Kemal Ataturk. In the 1930s, as an anti-British, anti-Soviet autocrat, he sided with the Third Reich, which became Iran's major trading partner. Nevertheless, he kept Iran officially neutral during the war. That was not good enough for the British. In 1941, the British and the now Allied Soviets demanded the shah boot the Germans out of Iran. When the shah refused, the British and the Soviets booted Reza Shah out of the country. His son was crowned in his place.

After the war, Britain and the United States were both wary of Communist designs on Iran, but for the British the bigger problem became Iranian nationalism. In 1951, the Iranian Parliament voted to nationalize the Anglo-Iranian Oil Company, Britain's biggest foreign asset; the British withdrew in a huff, and Iranian oil production plummeted. The Truman administration was unsympathetic to British demands for action against Iran, but by 1953 the newly elected Eisenhower administration was alarmed by British reports that Iranian Prime Minister Mohammad Mossadeq—who was already governing under extended and dictatorial "emergency powers"— was leaning towards the Communists. The CIA agreed to cooperate with British Intelligence to remove him—and had plenty of allies in Iran, including the shah whom Prime Minister Winston Churchill advised had a duty as a constitutional monarch to act against Mossadeq's tyranny. The shah, after much nail-biting, issued a decree calling for Mossadeq's dismissal, and a royalist coup ensued, installing a new prime minister to apparent popular delight (though perhaps CIA "walking around money" helped in this regard). The shah told the American mastermind of the coup, Kermit Roosevelt (Theodore Roosevelt's grandson), "I owe my throne to God, my people, my army—and to you!" To which Roosevelt graciously noted, "He meant me *and* the two countries—Great Britain and the United States—I was representing. We were all heroes."[7] Thanks to him, Iran was a Western ally for the next quarter century.

Between Two Ancient Peoples: Arabia and Palestine

What is now Saudi Arabia was never a British colony, but it owes its existence to the British Empire—specifically to the contest between

T. E. Lawrence (of Arabia) and Harry St. John Philby (father of future spy and traitor Kim Philby). Both men were British officers involved in leading the Arab revolt against the Ottoman Turks in the First World War. Lawrence was the advocate of the guardians of Mecca, the Hashemites; Philby (and the British government in India) thought the virile Wahhabi tribesmen of Ibn Saud were the better bet. In that wager Philby was right, but Philby was also something of a traitor, as he helped Saudi Arabia's oil concessions go to America rather than Britain (Standard Oil of California paid him a retainer) and he converted to Islam, apparently not from any ardent religious belief but because of the doors it might open for him in Arabia.

The Hashemites—chased out of Arabia by Ibn Saud's raiders—became British-backed monarchs in Mesopotamia and (more successfully) Transjordan, to which Britain was tied purely by bonds of sentiment, because Transjordan had little strategic value at all. The British were also bound by conflicting loyalties—they had led the Arabs in a revolt against the

We Built It, We Pumped It, We Own It

"It was British enterprise, skill and effort which discovered oil under the soil of Persia, which has got the oil out, which has built the refinery, which has developed markets for Persian oil in 30 or 40 countries, with wharves, storage tanks and pumps, road and rail tanks and other distribution facilities, and also an immense fleet of tankers. This was done at a time when there was no easy outlet for Persian oil in competition with the vastly greater American oil industry. None of these things would or could have been done by the Persian government or the Persian people."

Sir Donald Ferguson, Permanent Undersecretary, Ministry of Fuel and Power, rejecting Iranian claims on the Anglo-Iranian Oil Company, quoted in William Roger Louis, *Ends of British Imperialism: The Scramble for Empire, Suez, and Decolonization* (I. B. Tauris, 2007), p. 731

Ottomans and they had pledged, with the Balfour Declaration of 1917, to support the creation of a Jewish homeland in Palestine. Palestine, like Jordan, had no natural resources—though it had the strategic advantage of fronting the Mediterranean—but to Britons raised on the Bible it was freighted with mystical associations (as was Greece to classically educated English gentlemen). David Lloyd George and Winston Churchill, neither one notably religious, supported the creation of a Zionist Palestine, which became the state of Israel.

It was, however, a thankless task, as it sparked enmity from the Arabs—who were moved to enmity rather easily, and who throughout the 1930s kept Palestine in a state of turbulent, low-grade guerrilla war. The British suppressed the rebellious Arabs with the de facto assistance of the Haganah, a Jewish self-defense force, and the more radical, underground Irgun, which was not overly scrupulous about its targets. In 1939 the British government pulled back from the Balfour Declaration—over the protests of Lloyd George and Churchill—with a White Paper that proposed slapping limits on Jewish immigration to Palestine. The desired outcome, according to the White Paper, was that within ten years Palestine would become an independent, non-confessional state shared between Arabs and Jews. The spirit of British compromise was not, however, widely appreciated in this part of the world—with both Zionists and Arabs, albeit for different reasons, rejecting the White Paper. During the Second World War, the Zionists joined the British in

The Balfour Declaration

"His Majesty's Government view with favour the establishment in Palestine of a national home for the Jewish people, and will use their best endeavours to facilitate the achievement of this object, it being clearly understood that nothing shall be done which may prejudice the civil and religious rights of existing non-Jewish communities in Palestine, or the rights and political status enjoyed by Jews in any other country."

British Foreign Secretary Arthur James Balfour in a letter to Lord Rothschild, 2 November 1917

the fight against Hitler, while the Arabs were rather more divided. If they were under British arms, they supported their British officers; but Arab sentiment, whipped up by the Grand Mufti of Jerusalem, trended naturally towards National Socialism.

After the War, Palestine was a hornet's nest for the British, who were only too happy to be rid of it. They were targeted by both Arab and Zionist terrorists; the former renewing their revolt, the latter angry at restrictions on Jewish immigration.[8] The day before the expiration of the British mandate[9] and the partition of the country into separate Jewish and Arab states (which the Zionists accepted and the Arabs did not), Israel declared independence, only to be almost immediately attacked by its Arab neighbors. British officers serving in the Arab Legion were put in the awkward position of securing the West Bank for Jordan. Jordan, the most moderate of the Arab states, gained ground in the 1948 Arab-Israeli war, and so did Israel, which won a decisive victory and secured more defensible borders. Britain officially recognized Israel as an independent state on 29 January 1949, four days after Israel's first general elections.

Adventures in Aden

The British Empire in Arabia lasted longest in the Gulf States of Kuwait, Bahrain, Qatar, the Trucial States, Oman, and Aden, all of which fell under the influence of the British East India Company by the late eighteenth century. Officially, Kuwait, Bahrain, and Qatar owed their allegiance to the Ottoman Empire (Bahrain was also claimed by Persia), but in reality they functioned more as British protectorates, where the British touch was light and the sheiks and emirs loyal.

Kuwait officially became a British protectorate after the First World War—its borders drawn by Britain—and was a valuable oil reservoir for the Allies during World War II (as was Bahrain, which declared war on

Germany as a British ally). Kuwait was granted independence in 1961, though British troops—at Kuwait's request—were swiftly dispatched to strengthen its borders against the aggressive intentions of Iraq (intentions that were repelled rather more vigorously after the Iraqi invasion that began the First Gulf War in 1990).

In 1853, a treaty between the British and nearly a dozen sheikdoms of the Gulf (including Abu Dhabi and Dubai) formed what became known as the Trucial States, which were placed under British protection. In 1968, after Britain declared it intended to relinquish its commitments east of Suez by 1971, the Trucial States tried to form the United Arab Emirates (the UAE) with Qatar and Bahrain. The UAE survived, but with Qatar and Bahrain opting for independence.

The Trucial States were sometimes known as Trucial Oman, as they fronted the coast of the Gulf of Oman, but Oman proper, to the south, had been an empire of its own, including Zanzibar, parts of the East African coast, and even a port on the Arabian Sea (Gwadar, which it held until 1958, is now part of Pakistan). Since the slave trade was a pillar of the Omani empire, it collapsed in the wake of the Royal Navy's anti-slavery mission. Zanzibar, the center of the trade, became a British protectorate and scene of the shortest war in history, the forty-minute Anglo-Zanzibar War of 1896, fought to make a British-favored candidate sultan and abolish slavery on the island. Zanzibar was granted independence in 1963 (which turned out to be a very bad thing for Arab and Indian Zanzibaris who were slaughtered by the majority African population); Zanzibar then merged with Tanganyika, now Tanzania. Oman was recognized as independent in 1951, though the sultan kept on British forces to help him put down a variety of insurgencies. Oman has remained a British ally and its army retains bagpipers.

The port of Aden was acquired by Britain in 1839, both for the protection of the route to India and as a naval base against the slave trade. British influence spread until the area that is now essentially Yemen came under the British Protectorate of Aden. By the 1950s Aden had become one of the world's leading ports, but Arab nationalism, stoked by Nasser, reached ignition point in 1963 when an Arab insurgency began against the British. The war ended with British withdrawal in 1967, and Aden, a linchpin of the Empire, an Arabian outpost where British law, not sharia law, held sway, was surrendered to what is today the much less attractive state of Yemen. But even here, in the final days, there was a touch of glory, as Lieutenant-Colonel Colin "Mad Mitch" Mitchell led his Argyll and Sutherland Highlanders, bagpipes skirling, to retake the terrorist-infested district of Aden known as "the Crater," which had been sealed off after mutinous Arab police had joined the insurgents and murdered British soldiers. Not a single man was lost in the operation, Mitchell recovered Aden's gold reserves, and he kept peace in what had been a dangerous and violent place by intimidating the terrorists with "Argyll Law"[10]: "They know that if they start trouble we'll blow their bloody heads off."[11] Even in the Empire's retreat, the British army still knew how to do things right.

Chapter 20

SIR RICHARD FRANCIS BURTON (1821–1890)

"Starting in a hollowed log of wood—some thousand miles up a river, with only an infinitesimal prospect of returning! I ask myself 'Why?' and the only echo is 'damned fool…the Devil drives!'"

—*Richard Francis Burton, Dahomey, 1863*[1]

If the Empire had a Byronic hero, it was Burton. As with Byron, many considered him mad, bad, and dangerous to know. But the dark, powerfully built adventurer and *soi-disant* scholar was an extraordinary man of many talents—and unlike Byron, conservative politics. He was a Crown-and-Empire man, socially conservative in the sense of sharing the class prejudices of a high Tory and believing in the English cult of the gentleman (especially its more aggressive, honor-bound aspects). He also had a bad boy's delight to shock; an anthropologist's interest in cataloguing native customs, beliefs, and practices, especially those that were outré to Victorian sensibilities; and an amazing ability to penetrate the inner mysteries of several religions while believing in none, preferring to take the Devil's (when not the Muslim's) part. As the Earl of Dunraven noted, Burton "prided himself on looking like Satan—as indeed, he did."[2]

He was born the son of an Anglo-Irish army officer and was educated—though that might be putting too formal a gloss on it—in France (where the

Did you know?

- Burton could pass for an Indian in India and an Arab in Arabia (he made the *haj* to Mecca in disguise), and acted as a British secret agent

- He was the first white man to see Lake Tanganyika (discovered during his search for the source of the Nile)

- Though happily married to an ardent Catholic, he preferred Islam to Christianity—in part because of Islam's support for slavery, polygamy, and not educating women

family sometimes lived, Burton's father had itinerant feet), Italy, and England. While already facile with languages, Burton's main interest as a boy was in settling *affaires d'honneur* with his fists. He fenced, boxed, and generally got in trouble of a precociously manly sort with cigars, dueling pistols, and cognac. Naturally, his father believed that Burton belonged at Oxford—and so he duly enrolled and set about frightening the undergraduates with his dark, brooding features and drooping black moustache; he was expelled for attending a forbidden (by the school authorities) horse race.

Soldier and Spy

Much more attractive to Burton was service in the army of the British East India Company, in which he was duly commissioned. He took up the study of Hindustani and every other Indian language for which he could find a teacher, as well as Persian and Arabic, which he had begun teaching himself at Oxford. In the course of his life he would become fluent in more than two dozen languages, and even—as a young officer in India—would keep monkeys hoping to make sense of their chattering (he also taught them to eat at table with him). He became an army translator, which gave him a boost in pay.

When Burton went to Oxford, he had known next to nothing of religion, but now it too became a passion. He learned so much about Hinduism that he was made an honorary Brahmin. On Sunday he attended a Catholic church, thinking Catholicism "a terrible religion for a man of the world to live in, but a good one to die in"[3] (his wife later made sure he did just that). Meanwhile, there were consolations to living in it—Burton once tried to pry a pretty nun out of her convent. He also began memorizing the Koran and investigating Sufism.

He joined the survey of Sind and began his hobby of passing as a native and taking notes on everything he could about native life—especially its vices, the detailed study of which, when his reports leaked from General Charles Napier to the Bombay government, caused a scandal. That put a black mark against his name, and with his health in tatters through cholera and eye trouble, Burton applied for sick leave. He did so in despair; it appeared that curiosity had killed his career. With nothing better to do he wrote the first three of the forty-odd books he was destined to write. The topics might have sounded dull—his reflections on Goa and Sind—but Burton's bluntly expressed prejudices, controversial in his day, would no doubt have him prosecuted for hate crimes today; pick a nationality, race, religion, or tribe, and Burton would have something shockingly bad (and verified by his experience) to say about it. Occasionally he turned his pen to manuals—on falconry, the use of the bayonet, and the art of the sword. Almost invariably his sales were minuscule, and the few readers he gained he offended.

His bad reputation—he was known as "Ruffian Dick"—inevitably made him attractive to women; and to one woman in particular: Isabel Arundell, ten years his junior, from one of the most aristocratic Catholic families in England. Burton was the fulfillment of her every romantic dream. Burton liked what he saw as well, but was too distracted by his other passions to do more than try out his hypnotic stare on her (he had studied hypnotism as he had studied alchemy and other mysterious arts). One of his ambitions at this time was to cross the Arabian Peninsula disguised as an Arab; he had practical and quasi-scientific reasons for his adventure, but the overriding desire was to see Mecca; the penalty for an infidel entering the holy city was death.

His pilgrimage took him from Alexandria to Cairo to Suez, down the Red Sea coast to Yenbo, then inland to Medina, circling down to Mecca through bandit country. One of his traveling companions—an unwanted one that Burton distrusted and tried to shake—suspected his imposture, especially after searching Burton's belongings and finding a sextant. But the other

Muslims who had joined Burton defended him, even if they could not explain away this odd appurtenance of infidel Western science. Lamed by a foot injury, Burton spent part of the journey in a litter, which made his covert note-taking a bit easier. In Medina, which he entered in July 1853, he noted, among other things, the price range for slave girls of different races. (European women should be proud that they fetched far the highest price.) In Mecca he even managed to secretly sketch the interior of the Kaaba, the holiest site in Islam. Burton, inevitably, wrote up his adventures, which were published as a book in 1855.

He returned briefly to his regiment in India, but knowing he had no future there, and his taste for exploration quickened, he solicited and gained permission from the Company to lead an expedition into the interior of Somalia. Burton's goal was Harar, a mysterious city closed to Europeans; he would be the first to enter it. Because of opposition from the British political resident at Aden, Colonel James Outram, Burton's expedition was to be limited to coastal exploration with Lieutenant John Hanning Speke—a man as sober and conventional as Burton was wild and extraordinary. But Speke was an adventurer too in his own careful, accountant-like way. He had explored the Himalayas, was a great hunter, and had carefully earned leave time so that he could spend three years in African exploration. They traveled separate ways to Somalia, because Burton had plans of his own.

Disguised as an Arab, he was determined to press on to Harar regardless of the wishes of Colonel Outram. Arriving in Somaliland on 31 October 1854, he impressed the natives with feats of strength and slowly assembled an expedition for the interior, though he was warned it would surely lead to his death, for strangers were not welcomed in Harar and fierce tribes haunted the way. As he approached the city he tore away his native disguise because, "my white face had converted me into a Turk, a nation more hated and suspected than any European, without our prestige."[4]

When he approached the city gates, he announced that he had a message for the emir from the British government in Aden. He was escorted into the presence of an unprepossessing young sultan whom Burton bombarded with compliments and who, surprisingly, did not order him killed. He instead ordered him to meet the wazir of Harar, to whom Burton spoke of Britain's desire for friendship and trade. The message appeared well received—all the more remarkable because the Harari believed their downfall would come from the first European to enter the city. Now, however, having boldly made his way in, Burton had to convince the emir and wazir to let him go, which they seemed in no haste to do. It was a relief when, after ten days, he was given a letter to take back with him to Aden.

There he planned his next expedition into Somalia. It literally scarred him for life. One night, camped on the Somali coast, Burton's party was attacked by hostile tribesmen. The natives fled, leaving Burton, Speke, and two other British officers to repel the attack with revolver and sword, which they did, though likely outnumbered by at least ten to one. At one point in the fighting Burton almost crashed his sabre into a native guide; when he paused, a Somali warrior drove a spear through Burton's face, knocking out several teeth. Burton staggered, the spear sticking through one cheek and protruding from the other. Somehow he survived and was discovered the next morning by the crew of the ship that had left him on the coast; one of the crew members had to yank the spear from his face. Of the four attacked officers, one was killed; two made miraculous escapes (though Speke was badly wounded); and Burton gained a most fitting scar.

Feelings, Whoa, Whoa, Whoa, Feelings

Dr. George Bird: "Now, Burton, tell me, how do you feel when you have killed a man?" Burton: "Oh quite jolly, doctor! how do you?"

Quoted in Edward Rice, *Captain Sir Richard Francis Burton: The Secret Agent Who Made the Pilgrimage to Mecca, Discovered the Kama Sutra, and Brought the Arabian Nights to the West* (Scribners, 1990), p. 352

Though needing a little time to recuperate, Burton volunteered for active service in the Crimean War, only to find that hostilities were winding down by the time he arrived. He was, however, eventually sent to Turkey to help raise a unit of Turkish irregular cavalry (bashi-bazouks) that would be under British command. The cavalry, alas, terrorized its allies more than the enemy—Burton thought they were misunderstood—and Burton resigned his post, putting another black mark on his army career. Thinking entrepreneurially, he envisioned creating a business that would help Muslims on their way to Mecca—The Pilgrimage to Mecca Syndicate, Limited—though this plan too was abandoned; and one has to wonder how Muslims would have taken to doing business with an infidel who had tricked his way into the holiest site in Islam. A better plan, and one that would make him famous, was to search for the source of the Nile.

The Great Adventure

In 1857, Burton, joined by Speke, led an expedition sponsored by the Royal Geographical Society to find the great lakes of Africa, from which the Nile presumably sprang. It was an epic journey of calamities—Speke went temporarily blind; had a beetle penetrate into his ear; and was inevitably beset by fever—but Burton, though he had to be carried part of the way, kept on. Burton saw Lake Tanganyika, which Speke could not because of his blindness, but when Burton was the sick one, Speke discovered Lake Victoria, which is indeed the chief source of the Nile, though Burton doubted it and Speke couldn't prove it. Their separate discoveries and separate accounts of the expedition led to an unbecoming rivalry and rift between the two men. In modern accounts of this affair, Burton generally comes off better, because he is, well, Burton; and perhaps this is just. Speke, though undoubtedly courageous, comes through in his letters as insecure and boastful. As Burton's best biographer, Byron Farwell, concludes, while Speke had a reputation for modesty, "It is difficult to escape the conclusion that the discoverer of the major source of the Nile and the largest lake in Africa was a cad."[5]

Burton was no less an imperialist than the conventional Speke and no less contemptuous of the natives. This is the man, after all, who called East Africans "an undeveloped and not to be developed race."[6] Still, liberals like to claim Burton because of his scholarly interest in erotica (fulfilling the great liberal desire to "break down taboos"), his weakness for shocking Victorian Christian moral sensibilities (there is nothing liberals like to do more), and a misreading of his worldly adventures to qualify Burton as an early multicultural citizen of the world. But to know anything of Burton is to know that he was a political and social Tory, that he would view modern liberals as weak and decadent (for all his unflinching interest in men's vices, he knew decadent civilizations when he saw them), and that he believed absolutely in Western superiority (even given his predilection for Sufism) and in advancing the British Empire.

The Burton-Speke rivalry did not end until 16 September 1864 when Speke, who was supposed to debate Burton at the British Association for the Advancement of Science, instead went hunting and died in an apparent accident, shooting himself in the chest while crossing a stone wall. Some, including Burton, thought Speke had committed suicide; he had been openly distraught at having to debate Burton again, and had left the Association the day before saying, "I cannot stand this any

The Perils of Being a Consul in West Africa

"…the British Consulate, like that at Fernando Po, a corrugated iron coffin or plank-lined morgue, containing a dead consul once a year…."

Burton, describing the buildings in Lagos, in his own *Wanderings in West Africa from Liverpool to Fernando Po* (Cambridge University Press, 2011), vol. II, p. 213

Burton on America's Mormons

"I would not willingly make light in others of certain finer sentiments—veneration and conscientiousness—which Nature has perhaps debarred me from ever enjoying...."

Quoted in Byron Farwell, *Burton: A Biography of Sir Richard Francis Burton* (Penguin Books, 1990), p. 189

longer."[7] Whatever the animosities between the two men, Speke's death shook Burton; in the public eye, it left Burton looking all the worse.

Cannibals and a Knighthood

Between his return from Africa (1859) and Speke's death, Burton had not been idle. He had written his book on *The Lake Regions of Central Africa*, traveled to America where he hoped to do a little Indian fighting (which never happened) and study the Mormons (which he did; he was impressed by and liked Brigham Young, whom he interviewed), and in 1861 married Isabel Arundell to whom he had become unofficially engaged before his African safari. He pledged that he would allow her to practice her religion (he made occasional bows in its direction as well, dipping his fingers in holy water and making the sign of the cross at their wedding), saying later: "Practice her religion indeed! I should rather think she *shall*. A man without a religion may be excused, but a woman without a religion is not the woman for me."[8]

Burton joined the diplomatic corps. He was dispatched to be the British representative at Fernando Po—an assignment that brought no prestige but a high risk of deadly fevers. Burton felt ill-used; all the more so after John Company's[9] army was absorbed into the British army and Burton lost his commission. "They want me to die, but I intend to live, to spite the devils."[10] He prudently left Isabel behind in England.

He hated the Africans, whom he regarded as bloodthirsty, cruel, and uppity; but he had kind words for the Muslims whose religion he continued to admire even if he flouted its prohibition on alcohol. In Africa he drank heavily to protect himself from the innumerable tropical diseases, just as in America liquor was a useful precaution against snake bite. Burton didn't need an excuse, but it was nice to have one. He also consoled himself with travel to the West African coast where there were mountains to be climbed and named, gorillas to be sought after (for scientific purposes), as well as the usual research into circumcision and polygamy, in addition to West African cannibalism and Amazons (who were, as a rule, large and ugly). He also wrote nine books and became the British ambassador to Dahomey where his principal duties were to discourage slavery and human sacrifice (the sacrifices being made from criminals or captured enemies); the Dahomey king toasted Burton drinking from a cup made from a human skull.

Through Isabel's machinations Burton was transferred to where she thought she could join him, Brazil (1864), though it proved less salubrious than she imagined. She was ravaged by tropical fevers and disease. When she became delirious, Burton used hypnosis to cure her; when she wasn't bedridden, she tried converting black slaves to Catholicism (though Burton told her not to bother); and often when she needed him Burton had gone galumphing off on another adventure (including a search for a sea serpent). Burton almost died from tropical disease and misadventures and was gratified to be granted medical leave in 1869. Isabel sailed for England; Burton deferred his departure

Burton the Patriot on the Amazons of Dahomey

"They were mostly elderly and all of them hideous. The officers were decidedly chosen for the size of their bottoms.... They manoeuvre with the precision of a flock of sheep.... An equal number of British charwomen, armed with the British broomstick would...clear them off in a very few hours."

Quoted in Edward Rice, *Captain Sir Richard Francis Burton: The Secret Agent Who Made the Pilgrimage to Mecca, Discovered the Kama Sutra, and Brought the Arabian Nights to the West* (Scribners, 1990), p. 378

to investigate Paraguay and Argentina and drink himself well. As Wilfred Blunt wrote of this low point in Burton's life, he looked like "a released convict" or a "black leopard, caged but unforgiving" and would talk of "all things in Heaven and on Earth...till he grew dangerous in his cups, and revolver in hand would stagger home to bed."[11]

Isabel saved Burton. She won him the job he had coveted, British Consul in Damascus. The Foreign Office warned Burton to be on his best behavior—and he was, relishing the opportunity. He had his moments, staring down rock-throwing Greek Orthodox Christians; criticizing Jewish money-lenders (which aroused accusations of anti-Semitism); and trying to help a sect of Muslims who wanted to convert to Catholicism (though apostasy and conversion were capital offenses to the Islamic authorities). This last act ended Burton's diplomatic career in the Middle East, though after his departure he was celebrated as someone who had opposed Ottoman oppression and defended honesty and fair play; Muslims in particular prayed that he would be sent back.

As a sop, he was offered the position of British consul in Trieste. This, surely, was a post that would keep him out of trouble, though it was here that he wrote his translation of the *Kama Sutra*, which would only add to his notoriety. Burton still had his adventures—always titillated by stories of lost fortunes and mining millions to be made, he plunged into the Arabian desert searching for the riches of Solomon—but age was beginning to tell, and he increasingly devoted his hours to his scholarly pursuits, including an unexpurgated translation of the *Arabian Nights*.

In 1886, Burton was stunned to discover that he had been knighted—he was now Sir Richard Francis Burton, and though he never knew it, the honor was the result of Isabel's incessant lobbying on his behalf. Burton died in October 1890 and even his death was controversial. Isabel insisted her husband was a Catholic and browbeat a priest to give the already dead Burton the last rites. Many of Burton's friends and relations scoffed at this, though Isabel had in her possession a signed letter from Burton, dating from the last year of his life, affirming his adherence to the Catholic Church. To her critics, Isabel compounded her sins by burning vast quantities of Burton's papers—presumably those she thought would do his reputation harm, though the harm fell chiefly on *her* reputation. Still, she did, as she always had done, what she thought was best for him. They are buried together (Isabel died in 1896) in Mortlake Catholic Cemetery, London, in a tomb fashioned in the shape of an Arabian tent with a crucifix atop its faux entry.

Chapter 21

T. E. LAWRENCE
(1888–1935)

"Is this man God, to know everything?"

—*Abdullah ibn Hussein, future king of Jordan, after his first meeting with T. E. Lawrence in October 1916*[1]

T. E. Lawrence was a crusader. As a boy he aspired to chivalric ideals (he later confessed that since boyhood he had always wanted to be a hero); at Oxford his thesis was on crusader castles; as an officer he tried to lead Arabs (of all people) on a crusade against the Ottoman Empire; and he is perhaps the only crusader after whom Arabs still name their sons (Aurens). After World War I, he immured himself, under an assumed name, in the ranks of the RAF, which was, for him, the rough equivalent of a monastic life: if lacking prayer (save for church parades), it provided anonymity, a sort of poverty, work (he was mechanically minded), and time for literary pursuits (including translating *The Odyssey*). Modern views of Lawrence are colored by the myth that he was an Arab nationalist, but he was in fact a British imperialist; Winston Churchill was his political patron.

His father was an Anglo-Irish gentleman, Sir Thomas Chapman. But after having sired four daughters with his wife, Chapman ran away with the nursemaid and had five sons (Lawrence was the second), adopting the nursemaid's last name as his own but never marrying her. He also never divorced his first wife, who became Lady Chapman when he inherited the baronetcy. Lawrence knew nothing of this until he was a teenager; before that, he grew up in an apparently conventional, even pious, Protestant Christian household of evangelical stripe.[2] His father, far from being a rogue, appeared a mild-mannered man dominated by his wife.

"Ned" (as the young T. E. Lawrence was known) was simultaneously practical (he liked knowing how things worked), literary (especially in an historical and aesthetic way), and imaginative (including embellishing the truth to make a better story—such as claiming Napoleon's birthday as his own, though he was born a day earlier). With his schoolmates he was cheerfully aloof. He relished friendship, but only on terms where he felt he could maintain his independence and integrity. He was impudent and flippant, but sensitive to his own amour-propre. Though not a sportsman, he developed a wiry, muscular physique. He consciously trained himself to be capable of performing knightly deeds, in part by pushing his body to its limits with marathon bike rides, often taken to visit castles or churches (to make brass rubbings). He was thoroughly immersed in medieval tales of chivalry and martial valor. A tad rebellious, Lawrence ran away at age seventeen and enlisted in the Royal Artillery before his father found him and got him out. A life in the ranks was no life for the son of Sir Thomas Chapman; he must go to Oxford.

So he did, but he was no collegiate roisterer. He lived alone in a cottage in his parents' garden; he neither drank nor smoked; he ate sparingly and was, as he was to remain, chaste.[3] He studied medieval armaments and fortifications and chivalric literature; he joined the Oxford University Officer Training Corps as well as a rifle club and became an expert marksman with a pistol; he also became a protégé of the archaeologist (and future intelligence officer) David Hogarth, who was himself a dedicated British imperialist. Hogarth encouraged Lawrence to read books on modern military

Wild Nights, Wild Knights

"He came one evening into my rooms…and began to fire a revolver, blank cartridges fortunately, out of the windows…one glance at his eyes left no doubt at all that he told the truth when he said he had been working for forty-five hours at a stretch without food, to test his powers of endurance."

E. F. Hall writing of his experience of Lawrence at Jesus College, Oxford University, quoted in Jeremy Wilson, *Lawrence of Arabia: The Authorized Biography of T. E. Lawrence* (Atheneum, 1990), p. 44

strategy and study Arabia, and helped him arrange a trip to Syria, which Lawrence undertook for his thesis on crusader castles.

Lawrence graduated with a first-class degree in 1910. Hogarth then hired him for an archeological dig in Carchemish, Syria, which had a military intelligence purpose: to observe progress on the construction of a German-Ottoman (Berlin to Baghdad) railway. Lawrence worked on the site until the First World War.[4] During this time he perfected his knowledge of Arabic, learned to pass for an Arab (dressing as one when he went exploring), and was regarded as a good manager of the Arab workmen. These talents came in handy when, in 1914, he became a British intelligence officer, an enthusiastic player of "the Great Game"—albeit in a different theatre from the Northwest Frontier, and with a different enemy.

Revolt in the Desert

It was a game of jihads. Through its Turkish ally, Germany tried to instigate a jihad against the British Empire, which counted millions of Muslim subjects. The British, however, had already made diplomatic overtures to

Ibn Ali Hussein, the Sherif of Mecca, who not only refused to announce a jihad against the British, but was eager to gain their support for an Arab revolt against the Turks.

He had an ally in T. E. Lawrence. Lawrence's aim, at least initially, was not to serve Arab nationalism (which didn't exist outside the minds of theoreticians) but to bring the Arabs under British influence. If in doing so he betrayed the interests of the Arabs he helped lead, Lawrence replied, "I risked the fraud, on the conviction that Arab help was necessary to our cheap and speedy victory in the East, and that better we break our word and win than lose."[5]

In 1916, Lawrence was sent briefly to Mesopotamia, where, among other tasks, he was charged with assessing the prospects of an Iraqi Arab revolt

Divide et Impera

"The Arabs are even less stable than the Turks. If properly handled they would remain in a state of political mosaic, a tissue of small jealous principalities, incapable of cohesion and yet always ready to combine against an outside force. The alternative to this seems to be the control and colonization by a European power other than ourselves, which would inevitably come into conflict with the interests we already possess in the Near East.... If we can only arrange that this political change shall be a violent one, we will have abolished the threat of Islam, by dividing it against itself, in its very heart. There will then be a Khalifa in Turkey and a Khalifa in Arabia, in theological warfare, and Islam will be as little formidable as the Papacy when Popes lived in Avignon."

Intelligence report from Lieutenant T. E. Lawrence on "The Politics of Mecca," quoted in Michael Yardley, *T. E. Lawrence: A Biography* (Stein and Day, 1987), p. 72

against the Turks. The Indian Foreign Office thought Mesopotamia did not have the makings of an independent state. Lawrence was inclined to agree: "I have been looking…for Pan-Arab party at Basra. It is about 12 strong," he reported.[6] He was glad to return to Cairo because for him the real action was in the Hejaz, the coastal strip of Arabia that faces the Red Sea and encloses Mecca and Medina. This was the base of Sherif Hussein, who by June 1916 was in open rebellion against the Turks.

Lawrence of Arabia

In October 1916, the bumptious but brilliant Captain Lawrence—who could both charm and appall with his flippancy, his sense of superiority, and his disdain for military protocol and uniform (he was invariably dressed in the wrong kit, even before he took on Arabian robes)—left for the Hejaz. Abdullah ibn Hussein, one of Sherif Hussein's sons, was taken by the elfin Englishman. Lawrence was less impressed, thinking Abdullah too fleshy and lazy and untrustworthy, and too eager to rely on British troops, to be the hero he wanted to lead the Arab revolt. He met two other sons of Sherif Hussein, Ali (the eldest, dismissed by Lawrence as a physically feeble religious fanatic) and Zeid (the youngest: callow, unsuitable, raised in a Turkish harem), before he met Feisal whom he knew "at first glance…was the man I had come to Arabia to seek—the leader who would bring the Arab revolt to full glory."[7] Feisal also had the advantage of knowing English, though he was not fluent; and Feisal's family, the Hashemites, had the advantage of descent from Mohammed. Lawrence became the British liaison officer to Feisal.

The glue that held the Arab revolt together was English bribery. Some, like Feisal, were devoted; the British officers were dutiful; but many of the Arabs came for English gold and fought for no cause more elevated than pleasure and plunder. Their morale was boosted by the Royal Navy, which could support them from the Red Sea, and when the Arabs were on the march, Lawrence recorded, it "was rather splendid and barbaric."[8] Lawrence was, by now—and at Feisal's request—dressed in Arabian clothes, and it is easy to imagine how this medievalist "romantic Tory" (as one of his biographers described him)[9] could feel he had drawn the "tides of men into my hands / and wrote my will across the sky in stars / To earn you Freedom, the seven-pillared worthy house."[10]

Dear Mum

"The revolt of the Sherif of Mecca I hope interested you. It has taken a year and a half to do, but now is going very well. It is so good to have helped a bit in making a new nation—and I hate the Turks so much that to see their own people turning on them is very grateful."

T. E. Lawrence to his mother, 1 July 1916, quoted in John E. Mack, *A Prince of Our Disorder: The Life of T. E. Lawrence* (Little, Brown and Company, 1976), p. 140

Maker of the Middle East

Cardinal Newman described Toryism as loyalty to individuals and institutions—and that was the defining drama of Lawrence's life as an officer. He was loyal to his country and its empire, but he was also Feisal's political and military adviser. Feisal recognized Lawrence's devotion to him and his cause, admiring "his patience, discretion, zeal and his putting the common good before his own personal interest." "Such honesty, such faithfulness," thought Feisal, "are found in but few individuals."[11] Lawrence did not see an inherent conflict between British and Arabian interests, and neither did Feisal, who believed in British protection. Both were resolute against French ambitions in Syria and Lebanon[12]—yet the indulgence of such ambitions was precisely what had been secretly agreed to in the Sykes-Picot Agreement of 1916. When Lawrence became aware of Sykes-Picot is uncertain; what is certain is that it put him in a difficult position with Feisal. He was not, however, alone in his opposition to Sykes-Picot. Lord Curzon, for one, became an open opponent of the agreement after it was revealed by the Bolsheviks; and whether and how it might be fulfilled would become a matter of contention at the postwar peace conference at Versailles, where Lawrence continued to act as Feisal's adviser and advocate.

Of course, the war had to be won first, and it was the forces of the British Empire (Australians in the forefront) led by British General Edmund Allenby, a Lawrence ally, who routed the Ottoman Turks. The British, however, were eager, for political reasons, to give much of the credit to the Arabs, among whom Lawrence had become renowned for his wisdom, courage, and skill at train-wrecking (it helped his reputation that the Turks put a pretty price on his head). It was Lawrence and Allenby who kept the Arab revolt together when it looked as though it might collapse in 1918 because of a contretemps between Feisal and his father.

Indeed, putting aside Sykes-Picot, the British had every imperial interest to advance the Arab cause on Lawrence's well-founded grounds that the Arabs preferred British oversight to French colonial control. In June 1918, the British government made this manifest, announcing that His Majesty's Government would recognize the independence of all areas "liberated from Turkish rule by the Arabs themselves."[13] Lawrence pretended the Arabs had liberated Damascus when in fact it had been done by Australian General Sir Henry Chauvel; the pretence was politically expedient because it put the French on the diplomatic defensive against Hashemite claims on Syria.

When the war ended, Lawrence lobbied for scrapping Sykes-Picot. In its place he proposed his own plan, which limited French claims to Lebanon, carved out a larger sphere for the British, and gave Syria to Feisal and Mesopotamia to Abdullah and Zeid under British protection. In Palestine, Lawrence believed there was no inevitable conflict between Zionist and Arab aspirations—indeed, he supported both—and he won Feisal's support for the Balfour Declaration. Feisal agreed to Jewish emigration into Palestine provided that Palestine remain under British control and that the Zionists offer financial support to his Arab state in Syria.

Lawrence turned down decorations from King George V, because of what he felt Britain owed the Arabs. The Arabs, however, were less certain of this than Lawrence was, because there was no unified Arab front; in fact, the Hashemites were fighting the forces of Ibn Saud, the founder of Saudi Arabia, another Arab loyal to Britain, and one with his own extraordinary British adviser, Harry St. John Philby. Philby and the British India Office believed Ibn Saud was the great power on the Arabian Peninsula, not the Hashemites—and in due course they would be proved right.

It was finally resolved, in 1920, that the French should indeed have Syria and Lebanon, and the British Palestine and Mesopotamia. Winston Churchill (secretary of state for war and soon to become colonial secretary) persuaded Lawrence to join him as a special adviser to help clean up the postwar mess. Part of this was done by air power, as Lawrence and Churchill

An American in Damascus

Rudyard Kipling and T. E. Lawrence came up with idea—as a compromise given that the Arabs did not want the French, and the French did not want the British—of the United States accepting a mandate over Syria. The American King-Crane Commission (after Oberlin College president Henry Churchill King and Charles R. Crane, a businessman, diplomat, and financial supporter of President Woodrow Wilson who appointed King and Crane to the commission) thought this a proper outcome, but there was little popular or congressional desire to make democrats of Arabs (at least those that couldn't vote in the United States).

were enthusiasts for using the RAF to police and tame the turbulent tribes of Iraq (Lawrence had warned about a "Wahhabi-like Moslem form of Bolshevism"[14] developing there). Part of it was political, as Churchill and Lawrence pushed to have Feisal installed as the monarch of Mesopotamia, his consolation prize for having lost Syria, and to carve out a new state, Transjordan, as a consolation prize for his brother Abdullah. Lawrence and Churchill managed to pull this off, with Lawrence shoring up Abdullah's regime when it looked like it might collapse (today's King Abdullah II of Jordan owes his position to Lawrence of Arabia). They could not, however, reach an accord with Sherif Hussein, who was too stubborn, greedy, and mercurial. Without Britain's protection he was ousted from the Hejaz by the forces of Ibn Saud in 1924 and became an exile in Transjordan. Lawrence left the Colonial Office in 1922, reasonably pleased with what he and Churchill had achieved, writing how he "must put on record my conviction that England is out of the Arab affair with clean hands."[15] He predicted, "There'll be no more serious trouble for at least seven years," which, in those territories for which Britain was responsible, proved broadly true.[16] In 1935 he wrote to Robert Graves, "How well the Middle East has done: it, more than any part of the world, has gained from the war."[17]

Despite his satisfaction with this apparent achievement, Lawrence had a strong penitential streak. He served as an enlisted man, under assumed names, in the Tank Corps and the RAF. About his fame—the floodlights hit him fully when American newsman Lowell Thomas's touring film of Lawrence's exploits appeared shortly after the war—he took a famously Garbo of Arabia line. As Lowell Thomas said, "He had a genius for backing into the limelight."[18] Celebrity was, in a way, the fulfillment of his boyhood dreams of being a hero, and he traded on it when he wanted to—but he also hated himself for such pride, wanted to be left alone and free, and was so guilt-ridden that he actually ordered regular beatings for himself. He left the RAF in February 1935. In May he was dead. A motorcycle enthusiast, he was riding near his cottage when he had to swerve to avoid two young boys on bicycles. His injuries were fatal.

His massive memoir of the war, *Seven Pillars of Wisdom*, is regarded as a classic, if also an oddity and unreliable as history. It was intended as a work of literature—and has been employed as a textbook on guerrilla warfare. He was an extraordinary man, torn between a brilliant intelligence, a chivalric imagination, a weakness for posturing, a Christian conscience without Christian faith, and a strong adolescent streak. But most of all he was a British patriot who, though he had served a foreign race, knew that ultimately what mattered was the green, soggy ground of Old Blighty: "I went up the Tigris with one hundred Devon Territorials, young, clean, delightful fellows, full of the power of happiness and of making women and children glad. By them one saw vividly how great it was to be their kin, and English.... All our subject provinces to me were not worth one dead Englishman."[19] Yet it can rightly be said that Lawrence gave his own life for those very provinces. At Wareham Church in Dorset there is a carved memorial, a faux catafalque, of Lawrence recumbent in death, dressed in his Arab robes and headdress, hand clutching a dagger, an imitation, by the artist Eric Kennington, of the medieval effigies that so attracted Lawrence as a boy.

Chapter 22

LIEUTENANT-GENERAL SIR JOHN BAGOT GLUBB (1897–1986)

"He dealt as an Arab with the King's palace, as a Bedouin with the tribes, as a British officer with London. No one except Glubb knew everything that was going on."

—*A British officer of the Arab Legion on John Glubb*[1]

He was universally known as Glubb Pasha: a short, soft-spoken man of gentle demeanor (if occasional fiery temper), deep Christian faith, quiet courage, and adamant will. He, like Lawrence of Arabia, dedicated his life to the Arabs and to the British Empire. As commander of the Arab Legion, he led his Bedouin troops to the only decisive Arab victory ever inflicted on an Israeli army—putting him in the odd position of defending one British ally (Jordan) by fighting a British creation (Israel).

His mother, Frances Letitia Bagot, was witty, pious, and Anglo-Irish, while his father, Major-General Sir Frederic Manley Glubb (then a major and not yet knighted) was a stalwart, charming, gentlemanly fellow who in the Great War was chief engineer of the Second British Army. Their household had that typical British imperial flavor—they were all terribly well-mannered, with lips as stiff as starched shirts, but loving as well, and beneath their apparent conventionality, adventurous individualists to the core. Their daughter Gwenda became a race car driver and their son not

Did you know?

- Glubb's sister became a race car driver

- He led the only militarily successful Arab army against the Israelis (leading a British ally, Jordan, against a British creation, Israel)

- Glubb's son, named after a crusader, took an Arab name, converted to Islam, and became a Palestinian activist

only led Arab armies—frequently dressed in Arab garb—but was the chief adviser to an Arabian king.

Glubb spent most of his boyhood in England, with some time abroad in Mauritius (which he loved, and where he learned French) and Switzerland. His education was at Cheltenham College (a typical public school of the time, full of muscular Christianity) and the Royal Military Academy at Woolwich. His goal was to become an officer of engineers like his father, but he almost enlisted in the Rifle Brigade instead, because his entrance exams coincided with the outbreak of the First World War. His father, however, convinced him that the army needed officers, so Glubb dutifully went to Woolwich. He would see war soon enough.

The two-year course at Woolwich was crammed into six months in order to get new officers to the front. It was an early lesson in hurry up and wait—Glubb graduated and then had to fidget for six months because he was too young for active service. In November 1915, he finally made it to France, where he was three times wounded and had to be evacuated—the worst injury coming on 21 August 1917 as he was riding a horse amidst shellfire (he didn't believe in taking cover, thinking it bad form in front of the men), and was blown from his saddle, shrapnel hitting him in the face so that

A Father's Advice

"Don't chase after women, old boy. If you do so, you will regret it bitterly when you ultimately meet the woman you want to marry. Some men can think of nothing else, but I have not been tempted in that way and I hope you will not be."

Major-General Frederic Manley Glubb's counsel to his son, the future Glubb Pasha; he followed it. Sir John Glubb, *The Changing Scenes of Life: An Autobiography* (Quartet, 1983), p. 108

"half my jaw, which had broken off, teeth and all...was floating around in my mouth."[2] It was a gruesome wound, and in the days before antibiotics a potentially fatal one. The surgery and the recovery (including from infection) was unpleasant, to say the least. When it healed, his shortened jaw led to his eventual Bedouin nickname: *Abu Hunaik*, Father of the Little Jaw. Glubb recovered in time to rejoin the war. His father wanted to arrange a staff job for him, but Glubb insisted on returning to the front.

Glubb of Mesopotamia

Like the fictional hero Bulldog Drummond—who found peace after the Great War "incredibly tedious"—Glubb blanched at the prospect of dull peacetime assignments. His salvation came when the War Office asked for volunteer officers to fight an insurgency in Mesopotamia. Glubb applied and was accepted. It was the decision that made his career.

What a Piece of Work Is a Man

"One cannot see these ragged and putrid bundles of what were once men without thinking of what they were—their cheerfulness, their courage, their idealism, their love for their dear ones at home. Man is such a marvelous, incredible mixture of soul and nerves and intellect, of bravery, heroism and love—it cannot be that it all ends in a bundle of rags covered with flies. These parcels of matter seem to me proof of immortality. This cannot be the end of so much."

Captain John Glubb, 7th Field Company, Royal Engineers, September 1916, at the Battle of the Somme, taken from John Glubb, *Into Battle: A Soldier's Diary of the Great War* (Cassell, 1978), pp. 67–68

He was employed on engineering assignments in the Mesopotamian hinterlands. Encouraged by Arab hospitality, he did reconnaissance among the Iraqi tribes, taught himself Arabic, and developed a lasting affection for the life of nomadic Arabs. His developing knowledge of the country attracted the attention of the RAF, which was charged with keeping the peace, because air power was the most economical way to do so. But air power, to be effective, required land-based scouts to provide intelligence on potential targets. Glubb happily took this role, which kept him mounted on a stallion, riding through the desert, meeting with tribesmen: "Although these people were, in some ways, addicted to violence and bloodshed, although there were lice in their clothes and they ate with their hands, there was something about them which attracted me."[3] That was the typical British attitude: up with warrior tribes and races, peoples grounded in courage and honor; down with pushy, calculating merchants, disputatious lawyers, and babbling, aspiring clerks. British standards were classical standards, because the British imperial ruling class was classically educated.

Glubb furthered his own education by reading classic Western accounts of the Arab world; like Lawrence he adopted Arab dress (though only in the field); and he provided invaluable topographical and human intelligence to the RAF. He also came directly to the aid of the Mesopotamian Arabs against the Ikhwan, fanatical Wahhabi warriors loyal to Ibn Saud. Ibn Saud tried to use the Ikhwan to further his ends in central Arabia, but even he couldn't control them. The 60,000-strong Ikhwan army mercilessly put to slaughter every male, from newborn to old man, of any village they attacked. Their goal was to convert the world to their brand of Islam by killing all dissenters. They had targeted Mesopotamia for conversion, and Glubb, witness to their terror and destruction, vowed to stop them. He did—in large part because Ibn Saud diverted his wild warriors to conquering the Hejaz and deposing Sherif Hussein. In 1925, Ibn Saud signed the Basra Agreement, pledging to uphold the border between Arabia and Iraq.

In 1926, Glubb received orders to return to engineering duties in England—which he was loath to do. Instead, he resigned his commission and became a civil servant of the government of Iraq. Though now a civilian, he was back in the saddle fighting the Ikhwan, whose Islamist fervor would not be bound by Ibn Saud's agreements with infidels. An Iraqi nationalist newspaper testified to Glubb's standing among the Arab tribes: Glubb, though undoubtedly an agent of British imperialism, "is the refuge to which the nomads fly; he is the shield behind which they seek safety and he is commander and the prohibitor. It is sufficient to pronounce his name when all will fall down to their knees and to tell them that here comes Abu Hunaik and they will begin to tremble and then freeze as if thunder struck."[4]

Glubb formed a new unit, the Southern Desert Camel Corps, made up of Iraqi border Arabs—each one chosen by Glubb himself—to provide better intelligence to the RAF and help sheep-herding tribesmen fend off Ikhwan raids. Supplementing the camels were a smattering of cars and trucks mounted with machine guns. The Corps stung the Ikhwan and despite its small size—it started with only 70 men—it played an important role in another peace agreement (in 1930) between Ibn Saud (who pledged to restrain the Ikhwan) and King Feisal of Iraq.

With Iraq set to become independent in 1932, the number of British advisors was dramatically reduced—even Abu Hunaik was made redundant. But he was not long removed from his camels. Feisal's brother Abdullah, the emir (and eventual king) of Transjordan, had his own troubles with tribal raiders (and later with Syrian gangs and terrorists spilling over from Jewish-Arab fighting in Palestine), and invited Glubb to recreate his camel-borne constabulary. He did this by forming a Desert Patrol within the existing Arab Legion, to which he was appointed deputy to Frederick Gerard Peake (a former colleague of T. E. Lawrence's)—without Peake's knowledge or consent while Peake was on leave. Peake never quite got over his irritation at Glubb's appointment, yet the two men proved an able pair—especially as Glubb was never happier than when far away from Peake, patrolling the desert and enjoying the company of the Bedouin whom he made the dominant force within the Arab Legion.

Glubb frequently rhapsodized about the desert stars, the Bedouin gift for hospitality with dinner set out before an aromatic fire, coffee served in little cups, and manly conversation into the evening. The journalist (and later Labour member of Parliament) Tom Driberg profiled Glubb in 1938:

Glubb spends few days in the year at his house in Amman; goes there only to have the occasional bath and do a bit of office work. He is never seen at social functions in Amman or Jerusalem.... This is not Lawrence coyness. It's simply that Glubb has to be constantly in touch with all the corners of his territory. He goes by car (reading a good deal of history on the way). He does not affect Arab dress; when I met him he was in khaki uniform. "The trouble all over the east," he told me in a clear, imperial rather school-masterish voice, "is that with improved communications and so on, the British people [in the outposts of empire] lead an increasingly Western life. They go to each others' parties. They never mix with the people of the country. They might as well not be here."[5]

Perhaps not surprisingly, Glubb was suspicious of Western oilmen, urban Arabs, Jewish immigrants ("In Palestine the influx of Jews and foreigners, and seventeen years of direct British administration, have made the country Levantine or Mediterranean"[6]), and modernizing capitalism ("I do not wish to state that the importation of foreign capital into Transjordan might not be for the benefit of the capitalists. It would probably increase the total revenue of Transjordan. It might be for the general benefit of the human race. But let us be quite clear and honest—it would not be for the benefit of the tribesmen"[7]).

Glubb relished life in the desert with the Bedouin. He said as much time and again; it was his tonic. As a romantic conservative, he wanted that honorable, free, martial life preserved forever; and he was a perpetual, ardent advocate for Bedouin interests to a degree that sometimes made British officials wonder if he hadn't gone native. He had, in fact, dual loyalties. When, in 1939, he became commander of the Arab Legion (and a lieutenant-colonel in Jordanian rank) he gave his word to Abdullah that on

No Peace, Please, We're Arabs

"The abstract European worship of peace is absolutely unknown to them. They believe it to be the natural state of all rulers, princes and governments to be continually toiling to gain some advantage over their neighbouring rulers. A prince content to sit down and merely enjoy his natural dominion is regarded by them as hopelessly poor-spirited and effeminate. Moreover, it is not only the prince who conquers his enemies whom they admire. In high politics, successful lying, deceit and subtlety evoke exclamations of admiration."

Glubb in a July 1933 memo to the Colonial Office, quoted in Trevor Royle, *Glubb Pasha: The Life and Times of Sir John Bagot Glubb, Commander of the Arab Legion* (Little, Brown and Company, 1992), p. 185

all occasions, save a conflict between Britain and Jordan, he would serve as an Arab soldier.

The End of Glubb Pasha

But 1939 was a time when Britain needed her own soldiers, as she would soon be at war with Nazi Germany, Fascist Italy, imperial Japan, Soviet Russia, and their allies, which would include Vichy France and its imperial appendages, Syria among them. There were also fears of growing Nazi influence in the Middle East. Rumors had it that Ibn Saud was flirting with the Nazis. Growing Arab hostility to Jewish settlers—and occasionally to the British troops who protected them—in Palestine left Arab public opinion dangerously inclined to Nazi propaganda. Glubb rapidly expanded the Legion, acquired improved equipment for it, and continued his magnificent training regimen, which would make the Legion the premier pro-British Arab fighting force.

In 1941, a military coup in Iraq made the country a Nazi ally. As the British prepared a counterstrike, Glubb organized Iraqi resistance to the new regime. He also pressed into service detachments from the Arab Legion, who proved loyal when other Arab units did not. In thirty days, the British reconquered Iraq, denying the Nazis its airbases, and recovering its oil supplies. Glubb characteristically blamed Iraq's near Nazi-defection to Britain's having vouchsafed the country a Western democratic government, when what was wanted was a federal state, united by the monarchy, which dispersed power from the cities to the more conservative rural areas.

In Glubb's view, the best method of British imperial administration was one that maintained order, but leant heavily on the local authorities themselves. He credited British success in Jordan to the fact that the British made a point of rarely intervening. "The British attitude to the Arabs," Glubb said, "was 'This is your country! You can have a rebellion if you like. We shall not mind!' This was not strictly true, but it was highly effective. The Trans-Jordan Government was obliged to exert itself to maintain order."[8] It was the British imperial version of: That government is best which governs least.

In the 1941 Allied invasion of Syria, of which Glubb's Arab Legion was a part, many British officers came to believe that Syria independent of France would be a natural ally of Britain. The Syrian Arabs themselves appeared to take a pro-British line, feeling they were back in the heady days of T. E. Lawrence. British officers were not only anti-Vichy—that was their duty—but unimpressed by de Gaulle's Free French, who wanted to reclaim Syria for the French republic.

Churchill had pledged his support for de Gaulle's ambitions, but the Free French were naturally suspicious of their British allies. The British, they knew, were imperialists of a different sort from themselves. As the French General Philibert Collet noted: "Wherever the British have penetrated we meet British officers who believe the Bedouins, the Kurds, the Ghurkhas, the Sikhs or the Sudanese (whichever they happen to command) to be the most splendid fellows on earth. The French do not share this passionate interest in other races—they only praise individuals or communities insofar as they have become Gallicized."[9] At the request of the Free French, Glubb and the Arab Legion were expelled from Syria.

The success of the Arab Legion raised Abdullah's prestige, and it was essential that the Legion was maintained, with a British subsidy, when Transjordan gained independence and Abdullah became king in 1946. Glubb, as the Legion's commander, became the de facto power behind the Jordanian throne, and as such he was the target of both Zionist and Arab nationalist terrorists. Larry Collins and Dominique Lapierre capture perfectly the Glubb Pasha ("an unlikely Lawrence") of this period:

> Their commander was a complex and complicated man. His face was anything but fierce: a small, unmilitary moustache, plump cheeks, pale blue eyes and graying hair parted neatly in the middle of his head. He had soft, almost feminine hands and a shy, reserved manner. Yet he had a ferocious temper. Once, in a fit of fury, he had beaten a sheik so badly with a camel stick that he had to send him twenty camels the next day to make amends. More than one of his officers had fled his office with an inkwell or paperweight flying past their ears. He was a hard-driving ascetic man who insisted on meddling in every aspect of the Legion's affairs.[10]

As the British mandate in Palestine expired in 1948, the Arab Legion was in an extremely difficult position. Zionists and Arab nationalists were already in a state of undeclared war. The Legion was uneasily in the middle, charged with maintaining order between the contending factions. When the British left Palestine in May 1948, the Arab Legion—by agreement between King Abdullah and the Zionists, approved by the British—was ordered to occupy, as peacekeepers, the western half of the West Bank on a line from Nablus through Ramallah and Jerusalem to Hebron.

Israel, however, was immediately invaded by Egypt, Syria, Iraq, and Lebanon, and in the resulting war, the Israeli Defense Forces not only repelled the attacking Arab armies but occupied lands partitioned to the Palestinian Arabs. The Israelis also advanced into Jerusalem, which was supposed to be administered by the United Nations as an international city; Abdullah ordered Glubb to retake it; and the Legion captured East Jerusalem after stiff street-by-street combat. Glubb carefully kept the Legion's actions purely defensive, avoiding any attacks on areas the United Nations had designated Israeli territory; Abdullah, however, could claim he had joined his fellow Arabs in attacking the hated Israelis.

In 1949, the war ended with an armistice that divided Palestine between an enlarged Israel, Jordan (which took the West Bank), and Egypt (which gained the Gaza Strip). Glubb bemoaned the exodus of Arab Palestinians into Jordan, where he thought they would be a destabilizing influence. He was right: in 1951 an aggrieved Palestinian, in a plot organized by a former Arab Legion officer and the Grand Mufti of Jerusalem, assassinated Abdullah.

An Officer and a Gentleman

"An officer should never swear, tell vulgar jokes or behave in an undignified manner."

Lieutenant-General Sir John Glubb, taken from Sir John Glubb, *The Changing Scenes of Life: An Autobiography* (Quartet, 1983), p. 35

King Hussein, Abdullah's grandson, who ascended to the throne in 1952, was far less tied to Glubb than his grandfather was and made a point of ignoring his advice. He abruptly dismissed him in 1956, ending Glubb Pasha's career in the Middle East, though Glubb spent the rest of his life writing books and lecturing about the Arabs. His devotion could never have been in doubt. He wrote, "I originally went to Iraq in 1920 as a regular officer of the British Army, seeking fresh fields of adventure.... But when I had spent five years among the Arabs, I decided to change the basis of my whole career: I made up my mind to resign my commission in the British Army and devote my life to the Arabs. My decision was largely emotional. I loved them."[11] It was clear that many of them loved him too, as countless Arabs left him as ward to their children. His wife helped create and support a school for Bedouin orphans and Palestinian refugees. His son, christened with the crusading name of Godfrey, took on the Arab name he had been given by Abdullah, Faris. He converted to Islam and became an activist for the Palestinians. Like his father he fell in love with the Arabs. His father's image of them had been perpetuated in the Arab Legion—of bandoliered, red-and-white keffiyehed Arab warriors who sang gaily in action. For a certain sort of Englishman, there was little in that image not to like.

Part VII

AUSTRALIA AND
THE FAR EAST

Chapter 23

AUSSIE RULES

For a country that started out as a penal colony, without much in the way of natural resources—indeed, most of the harsh Australian landmass is unsuited to agriculture and sparsely populated—one would have to say Australia has done remarkably well. It is prosperous (one of the top fifteen economies in the world, with a population of fewer than 23 million people), free (a parliamentary democracy under the British Crown), and a responsible power on the world stage (since World War II, Australia has deployed troops in the Korean War, Malaya, the Vietnam War, the Gulf War, the Afghan War, the Iraq War, East Timor, and elsewhere). And few peoples have a better public image in the United States than the Australians—regarded as a friendly, hardy, sporting, down-to-earth, sort-of-Cockney-accented, surf-friendly cross between H. Rider Haggard's Allan Quatermain and Owen Wister's Virginian.

The British claim on Australia came with Captain Cook in 1770, who christened eastern Australia New South Wales. The idea of Australia as a penal colony developed after Britain lost the thirteen North American colonies. The land seemed of little use for anything else, and the Empire needed a new dumping ground. Nevertheless, most Australians were *not* sent to Australia as prisoners; they came as settlers; and even those who were transported as prisoners were generally treated tolerably well on the transport ships (known as "hulks" and judged otherwise unseaworthy), despite sensationalist contemporary reports making them out to be seaborne hells.

Imperial Australia

As ever, the British were in competition with the French—both possibly eyeing Australia merely to foil the other. But the British, as usually proved the case, won out.[1] The first settlement was made by the high-minded Captain Arthur Phillip who hoped to make something of the convicts in his charge, landing first at Botany Bay, then at Port Jackson (Sydney Harbor), and finally at Norfolk Island. Phillip, the first governor of New South Wales

Hurray for Captain Bligh!

The real heroes of the mutiny on the HMS *Bounty* (28 April 1789) were not Fletcher Christian and his colleagues, who were too intoxicated by the favors of the Polynesian women of Tahiti to do their duty, but dear old Captain William Bligh (1754–1815) and his eighteen loyalists who were set adrift in a longboat with a small amount of food and water. Bligh, with a keen sense of fair play (and Royal Naval tradition), divided these rations and anything they caught absolutely equally. He led his men in an open boat over 3,600 miles of water to safety and later became governor of New South Wales, where he again faced a mutiny from corrupt uniformed men. Christian, meanwhile, and eight of his colleagues and their wahines figured the Navy would look for them on Tahiti and so set sail for an uninhabited island. They found Pitcairn Island (today a British Overseas Territory), where a goodly number of folk are named Christian (descendants of Fletcher) and are Seventh Day Adventists (thanks to some persuasive missionaries).

(1788–95), quickly set about establishing a functioning settlement, even as it was reinforced by new convicts who proved to be an unmotivated work force. The convicts brought in smallpox and other diseases that had the inadvertent effect of knocking dead great heaps of aborigine warriors who might otherwise have attacked the settlement. Phillip, it should be noted, took a forbearing and protective attitude towards the aborigines, and also ensured that slavery was never part of the settlement of Australia. As for reformed convicts, they became free men.

Non-convict settler society was naturally always a bit worried about the convict class, especially when it was reinforced with Irishmen. Irish prisoners were more than a trifle rebellious, rising in arms and having to be put down by force. The military units of Australia were themselves not altogether reliable. Sickness forced Governor Phillip to leave New South Wales in 1792. In his absence, the New South Wales Corps took charge. The Corps was made up, in the words of Australian historian Marjorie Barnard, "of the riff-raff of the [British] Army, men who had been in trouble, even mutineers, who were misfits or so useless that their regiments wanted to be rid of them, the officers were either as unsuccessful as those they commanded, or were anxious to leave England for some personal reason, like debt."[2] The convicts were thus overseen by men who but for the grace of God might have been in their place. The Corps

Australian Idle (the Convict Version)

"Experience, sir, has taught me how difficult it is to make men industrious who have passed their lives in habits of vice and indolence. In some cases it has been found impossible; neither kindness nor severity have had any effect; and tho' I can say that the convicts in general behave well, there are many who dread punishment less than they fear labour; and those who have not been brought up to hard work, which are by far the greatest part, bear it badly. They shrink from it the moment the eye of the overseer is turned from them."

Arthur Phillip, governor of New South Wales, writing to Lord Grenville, 17 July 1790, quoted in Frank G. Clarke, *The History of Australia* (Greenwood Press, 2002), p. 27

expanded the land-holdings of the colony (in order to enrich themselves), were such active importers of rum they became known as the Rum Corps, and even deposed Governor William Bligh (of *Mutiny on the Bounty* fame) in the Rum Rebellion in 1808. The Corps was disbanded and legitimate rule restored by the British with the arrival of Lachlan Macquarie, governor of New South Wales from 1810 to 1821.

It was Macquarie who transformed Australia from a ruffian's reform school into a reputable colony. He made a point of giving appointments to former prisoners, in order to show that all Australians were equal under the law whether they came originally as settlers or as convicts; in return he required that former prisoners lead upright Christian lives, which meant church attendance on Sunday. He laid out the street design of Sydney, was the first governor to call the colony Australia, and in general so improved the place that he was recalled to England for his spendthrift ways. He is nevertheless generally regarded as "the Father of Australia," a phrase engraved on his tombstone in Scotland.

As proof of its growing muscle, Australia began to add territory. It spread across the continent; South Australia became a free colony—free, that is, of convict labor. Australians crossed the sea to settle New Zealand, which became a separate colony in 1841. Van Diemen's Land, established originally as another penal colony, became the colony of Tasmania in 1856. But what really got things moving was a gold rush, or rushes, starting in 1851. Gold seemed a quicker way to wealth than Australia's economic standby of sheep-herding, and immigrants popped up everywhere eager to stake their claim. In 1851, there were 437,665 people in Australia. In 1860 that number had nearly tripled to 1,145,585.

These were boom times for Australia, lasting until 1890; they were also Australia's version of the Wild West, including the usual cast of characters from Chinese immigrants (though these were miners rather than laundry-men) to outlaws—the most famous being Ned Kelly, an Irishman needless to say, who wore a homemade suit of armor; but he was no knight, and was hanged. Because Australia had been a penal colony, it was chock full of Irishmen, who did not, as a rule, share the exuberant pro-British imperial sentiment of their fellow Australians. The Catholic Church proved invaluable in keeping Celtic high spirits from spilling over into riot and sedition (though many Australian administrators failed to appreciate this) and was a great anti-statist institution. Unlike Protestant denominations, it refused to shutter its own schools in favor of universal state-provided education in the latter half of the nineteenth century.

Politically, the Australian colonies were organized on democratic lines—complicated at first by the proportion of convicts in the population—and innovated voting by secret ballot, which was adopted by several of the colonies in 1856. By the end of the nineteenth century (Tasmania being the last Australian colony to sign on), every man who was a British subject could cast a ballot. Perhaps because they wanted to attract more sheilas, New Zealand and Australia were leaders in granting women the right to vote. In Australia, a woman's right to vote varied by colony and was sometimes limited by qualifications (such as owning property).[3] When it came to granting universal suffrage to women, New Zealand struck first—not just in the British Empire in the South Pacific, but in the world—in 1893.

In 1901, the Australian colonies confederated as the Australian Commonwealth. Australians felt a growing sense of nationhood and recognized—especially because of Chinese immigration during the Gold Rush—that Australia was a British island in an Asian sea. Even with the massive influx of gold-fevered immigrants, Australia remained overwhelmingly British, and was determined to remain so, enacting the "White Australia" policy to discourage non-whites from entering Australia. Because the British would not allow a starkly racial policy, Australian immigration law was based on passing a literacy test in a European language of the Australian immigration officials' choosing, the choice almost invariably being a language that might stump any non-white would-be immigrant. The restrictions were gradually relaxed, in piecemeal fashion, after World War II, rapidly in the 1960s, and were fully repealed by 1973.

Australia eagerly took up imperial responsibilities, contributing troops to the Boer War in South Africa (16,000 of them), taking over as a colonial power itself in Papua New Guinea in 1902 (a British protectorate since 1884), and most of all joining the fighting in the First World War—with the Gallipoli campaign becoming part of Australia's national myth. Out of a total population of 5 million, some 330,000 Australian men served overseas in the Great War and suffered the highest casualty rate of any Western force (65 percent),[4] earning Australia its own place at the Versailles Peace Conference, represented by its prime minister, William Morris "Billy" "Little Digger" Hughes, and his deputy and former prime minister Joseph Cook.

The Gripe of Gallipoli

Chippy republicans eager to sever Australia's ties to Britain have tried to turn the heroic service of Australian and New Zealand servicemen at Gallipoli—marked every 25 April, the date of the Gallipoli landings in 1915, as ANZAC day, the memorial day of the Australian New Zealand Army Corps—into one great national whine rather than a day of remembrance. Their mythical gripe is that stupid British officers callously threw Australians into Turkish fire and slaughter. In fact, casualty rates were far higher (more than twice as high) on the Western Front than at Gallipoli, most of the troops involved (and most of the casualties) were British rather than ANZACs, and Australian officers commanded the Australian troops. The Australians earned the nickname of "diggers" from their trench work at Gallipoli. It is time for the diggers to bury the myths propagated by anti-British malcontents.

Hughes was a nationalist, a socialist, and an Empire loyalist: "Without the Empire we should be tossed like a cork in the cross currents of world politics. It is at once our sword and our shield."[5] He helped ensure that German New Guinea, Nauru, and the Bismarck islands (including the Admiralty Islands, New Ireland, and New Britain) went to Australia and German Samoa went to New Zealand as mandated territories. Australia also gained its own seat at the League of Nations, though Hughes rightly thought the League was a crock.

Great Movies of the British Empire

The Lighthorsemen (1987), an Australian film—much better than the wildly overrated and axe-grinding movie *Gallipoli*—trumpets the heroism of the Australian troops at the Battle of Bersheeba (1917) in the Middle East campaign of World War I. Rousing throughout.

In 1931 Britain gave Australia (as well as Canada, Ireland, South Africa, New Zealand, and Newfoundland) dominion status as an equal and self-governing part of the British Empire. The Australians themselves, however, were so little interested in this change of status that their legislature did not approve the measure until 1942—because of the Second World War—and New Zealand did not approve it until after the war, in 1947.

Australia at War

The keystone of British defenses in the Pacific was allegedly impregnable Singapore—except for the fact that Singapore fell to the Japanese on 15 February 1942. With British Malaya overrun, Singapore lost (Churchill called it "the worst disaster and largest capitulation in British history"[6]), and Britain's two great Pacific battleships, HMS *Repulse* and HMS *Prince of Wales*,[7] sunk by the Japanese (on 10 December 1941), Australia had to look to the United States as its chief effective ally in the Pacific to stave off a Japanese invasion. On 27 December 1941, Australian Prime Minister John Curtin announced in the pages of *The Melbourne Herald,* "The Australian Government regards the Pacific struggle as primarily one in which the United States and Australia must have the fullest say in the direction of the Democracies' fighting plan. Without any inhibitions of any kind, I must make it quite clear that Australia looks to America, free of any pangs as to our traditional links of kinship with the United Kingdom."[8] To that end, Curtin put Australia's Pacific force under the command of American General Douglas MacArthur.

Nevertheless, as part of the British Empire, Australia itself acted as a world power, with its troops deployed against Axis forces in Europe, Africa, the Middle East, and Asia. Sixty thousand Australians had been killed in World War I. Despite sending 200,000 more men overseas than it had in the First World War, Australia lost just under 40,000 dead in World War II—8,000 of them perishing in Japanese prison camps.

After the war, the Australian government felt more acutely than ever that demography is destiny and made an aggressive play to attract European immigrants in general and British immigrants in particular; from 1946 to 1949, 700,000 aspiring Australians arrived. What they found was a country that, despite its notoriously Bolshie unions, was profoundly conservative. Robert Menzies of the Liberal Party (Australia's leading conservative party) governed as prime minister from 1949 to 1966 in coalition with the rural conservative Country Party (now the National Party). The economy boomed, Australian foreign policy was resolutely pro-British, pro-American, and anti-Communist, and in 1951 Australia and New Zealand cemented their wartime alliance with the United States in the ANZUS Security Treaty. Australia was also a member of SEATO, the Southeast Asian Treaty Organization (1954–77), an Asian version of NATO—its original members consisted of the United States, Britain, Australia, New Zealand, France, Pakistan, and Thailand—that dissolved with France's declining power,

Britain's decision to curtail its commitments east of Suez, and Pakistan's withdrawal after the secession of Bangladesh. It nevertheless provided part of the rationale for America, Australia, and New Zealand's defense of South Vietnam against Communist aggression (as did ANZUS).

Britain's residual authority over Australia was demonstrated in 1975 when Governor-General John Kerr, representing Her Majesty the Queen (though actually appointed by Australia's then-Prime Minister Gough Whitlam), dismissed Whitlam, leader of the Labour Party, as prime minister (he had been in office since December 1972) because his spendthrift ways had forced an apparently insoluble government budget crisis. Kerr appointed an interim government under the Liberal Party's Malcolm Fraser and ordered an election, which Fraser won in a landslide. An attempt to turn Australia into a republic—removed from the queen's authority—was defeated in a national referendum in 1999. The only change, occurring in 1974 during Gough Whitlam's Labour government, was that *Advance Australia Fair* replaced *God Save the Queen* as the national anthem—not the best choice, but a forgivable one.

The Kiwi Connection

For the British in Australia, New Zealand started as a whaling and seal-hunting station. Then came missionaries who saw the cannibal Maoris and their white ruffian friends as souls to be saved. The Maoris gained the essentials of civilization—potatoes (introduced by Captain Cook) and muskets—and proceeded to feast on the one and prey on their tribal neighbors with the other in the so-called Musket Wars (1807–42). Fun-with-muskets reduced Maori numbers by possibly a third.

New Zealand in the first half of the nineteenth century was a pretty rough place. The Christian missionaries helped change that. The Christians taught, shockingly, that cannibalism was bad, that treating women as items of sexual barter was improper, and that selfishness was wrong. The missionaries also gave the Maori a written language, medical care, and an example of peaceful service.

The other saving grace for New Zealand was its incorporation into the British Empire with the Treaty of Waitangi in 1840. Signed by more than 500 Maori tribal chiefs, the treaty provided New Zealand with a British governor and gave Maoris the rights of Englishmen (only up to a point, in practice). Under the protection of the Union Jack, New Zealand became an attractive prospect for immigrants from the British Isles and elsewhere. Just as the Maoris had enjoyed the company of the jolly jack tars with whom they first traded, they found more respectable settlers fine trading partners, and early New Zealand prospered.

But lurking beneath the Maori farmer was the warrior, and as white immigrants showed a voracious hunger for land (though they still only inhabited twenty percent of it), some Maoris began to show their teeth. The Maori Wars were limited to the North Island of New Zealand, where the vast majority of the Maori lived. They ranged from early skirmishes in the 1840s, to battles involving British regulars in the early 1860s, to minor émeutes that lasted until around 1872. The hostile Maoris were a hard and challenging foe, though most Maoris supported the British and were willing to fight for them. Given their experience in the "Musket Wars," they were useful allies.

Once the wars were over, New Zealand's settlers turned the country into a most prosperous democratic colony. Miners struck gold on the South Island while on the North the land was dominated by farmers and sheep. In the 1880s, with the advent of refrigerated shipping, New Zealand became a large-scale exporter of meat and dairy products. It also happily shipped soldiers—including warrior Maoris—to serve the Empire whenever required. New Zealand sent as many troops, in proportion to population, to the Boer War in South Africa as Britain did. In the First World War about a third of New Zealand's total male population between the ages of twenty and forty were casualties (killed or wounded). When Britain declared war on Germany in 1939, there was no doubt that New Zealand would be at Britannia's side. Michael Joseph Savage, New Zealand's first Labour Party prime minister, elected in 1935 and serving until his death in 1940, said, "Both with gratitude for the past, and with confidence in the future, we range ourselves without fear beside Britain. Where she goes, we go, where she stands, we stand."[9] After the war, the Kiwis proved equally as martial as the Aussies, sending troops to Korea, Malaya, Borneo, and Vietnam.

After the Vietnam War, New Zealand's political climate, always liberal, turned decidedly leftish (while maintaining a market-oriented economy). In 1984, New Zealand's Labour government declared the country a "nuclear-free zone" and tried to pretend it was a trendy, fashionable non-aligned nation. Later, though, Kiwi troops were sent to the war in Afghanistan and

For He Is an Englishman (Even If He Happens to Live in New Zealand)

"The New Zealander among John Bulls is the most John-Bullish. He admits the supremacy of England to every place in the world, only he is more English than any Englishman at home. He tells you he has the same climate,—only somewhat improved; that he grows the same produce,—only with somewhat heavier crops,—that he has the same beautiful scenery at his doors, only somewhat grander in its nature and diversified in its details; that he follows the same pursuits and after the same fashion—but with less of misery, less of want, and a more general participation in the gifts which God has given to the country."

Anthony Trollope, *New Zealand, Being a Portion of 'Australia and New Zealand'* (an abridgment of the original work) (Chapman and Hall, 1874), p. 128

Kiwi medical and engineering units were sent to join Allied forces in the Iraq War. The New Zealand Labour Party goes turn and turnabout with the conservative National Party, and the country remains an important member of the British Commonwealth, whose Far Eastern membership includes: Brunei, Kiribati, Malaysia, Nauru, Papua New Guinea, Samoa, Singapore, the Solomon Islands, Tonga, Tuvalu, Vanuatu, and occasionally Fiji.

Poms, Diggers, and Kiwis United in World War II

"I was called over and so met the famous [German Field Marshal Erwin] Rommel for the first time.... He asked 'Why are you New Zealanders fighting? This is a European war, not yours. Are you here for the sport?'... I held up my hands with fingers closed and said, 'The British Commonwealth fights together. If you attack England you attack New Zealand and Australia too.'"

Kiwi Brigadier George Clifton, quoted in Desmond Young, *Rommel: The Desert Fox* (William Morrow, 1978), pp. 134–35

Hong Kong

Missing from that list of course is Hong Kong, an unlikely Chinese pearl of the British Empire, which was relinquished to mainland China in 1997. Hong Kong had been acquired after one of Britain's most gloriously high-minded little wars, the First Opium War (1839–42), fought to establish the important libertarian principle of free trade. As John Quincy Adams said: "Which has the righteous cause?... Britain has the righteous cause." Opium, he pointed out was "a mere incident to the dispute; but no more the cause of the war than the throwing overboard the Tea in Boston harbor was the cause of the North American revolution.... The cause of the war is the Kow-tow! the arrogant and insupportable pretensions of China, that she will hold commercial intercourse with the rest of mankind, not upon terms of equal reciprocity, but upon the insulting and degrading forms of relation between lord and vassal."[10] Of course in any battle over arrogance, Britain was sure to win, and did; in this case gaining among other prizes an unremarkable, rocky, and barely inhabited island named Hong Kong. Britain would make it remarkable; British law and honest-dealing made it an entrepôt for enterprising immigrants.

The Arrow War (or Second Opium War, 1856–60) expanded Britain's holdings to include the Kowloon Peninsula, and they were expanded again with the so-called "New Territories" in 1898. Hong Kong was the British Gibraltar of the East, but far wealthier, as British tai-pans turned it into a hub of imperial trade. As James Morris noted, "Everywhere the symptoms of empire showed: the ships always steaming in from India, Australia or Britain itself, the Indian soldiers who often formed its garrison, the Sikh policemen and hotel doormen, the Australian jockeys who won all the races at Happy Valley, above all the British mesh of the place, the webs of money, style, and sovereignty which bound the colony so unmistakably to the imperial capital far away."[11]

Even so, the population was overwhelmingly Chinese, the government undemocratic (on the paternal-authoritarian model), and the British, as Morris notes, "thought of the Chinese as foreigners in the colony, and themselves as true natives."[12] While there was color prejudice, there was also an exhilarating air of freedom, which is why Chinese thronged to it. If they were not admitted to certain clubs or granted the democratic rights of Englishmen, they were utterly free to practice commerce, which they did with gusto.

Occupied by the Japanese during World War II, then a haven for refugees fleeing Communist China, Hong Kong was a beacon of freedom (without democracy) in the Far East. Its reigning genius in the 1960s was Sir John James Cowperthwaite, who as Hong Kong's financial secretary from 1961 to 1971 kept the island blissfully free of regulations and government intervention, preferring to keep taxes low and let people get on with their commercial affairs. When the British surrendered Hong Kong to mainland China, they handed the Communist Chinese a capitalist dynamo (and guarded it by what paper accords they could) that the People's Republic has so far refrained from dismantling.

An Empire of Capitalists, Rajahs, and Planters

Another capitalist powerhouse created by Britain was Singapore; founded as a British trading post by Stamford Raffles in 1819, it is now a global financial center and port, one of the busiest in the world. In addition, the British were in Borneo—where they planted a line of "white Rajahs" in the province of Sarawak—and Malaya. The East India Company had been active in Malaya since the late eighteenth century. As generally happened, the Company proved a dab hand at government and took responsibility for administering Malaya, until British colonial administrators—ruling sometimes directly, sometimes through local sultans—took over for them.

In Malaya, the British fought pirates, encouraged trade, and tried to keep the peace between the variegated peoples—whom they made even more diverse. British merchants arriving with the East India Company were followed by rubber planters, engineers to run the tin mines, businessmen, policemen, and administrators. Chinese traders came to the coast and then expanded vastly in numbers. Indians, specifically Tamils, were imported as laborers.

A Book the Anti-Colonialists Don't Want You to Read

SAS: Secret War in South-East Asia, 22 Special Air Service Regiment in the Borneo Campaign, 1963–1966, by Peter Dickens, not only for its lessons in how to defeat anti-colonialist subversion but also for its proof that Britain's former colonies often gladly relied on British help to defend themselves. Dickens, incidentally, was the great-grandson of Charles Dickens and a captain in the Royal Navy.

British expatriates loved Malaya for its tropical beauty, its gracious people, and its pleasantly ordered outdoor life. The British, of course, also kept the peace—and keeping the peace meant defeating a Communist insurgency in Malaya that lasted from 1948 to 1960, the British succeeding with tremendous courage and political and military skill, most especially under British General Sir Gerald Templer, whom Winston Churchill appointed High Commissioner of Malaya (1952–54). They succeeded again, defending Brunei, Borneo, and independent Malaysia from Indonesian aggression in a "confrontation" (or undeclared border war) that lasted from 1962 to 1966.

Britain did rather well by her Far Eastern colonies: from Singapore to New Zealand, from Australia to Hong Kong. In 1960, at celebrations marking the end of the Malayan Emergency—celebrations that included a victory parade with "everyone from Aborigines with blowpipes to men in armoured vehicles" while overhead "Canberra jets roared"—a pro-British American businessman, Norman Cleaveland, "looked at the placards of the Tunku [Tunku Abdul Rahman, first prime minister of Malaysia] smiling down from every corner, and turning to [British Field Marshal Sir Gerald] Templer said simply, in his direct American way, 'Pity no one thought of putting up a photo of Churchill. This country owes him a hell of a lot.'"[13]

Chapter 24

SIR THOMAS STAMFORD RAFFLES (1781–1826)

"One of the greatest and best servants our Empire ever possessed. He was perhaps the first European who successfully brought modern humanitarian and scientific methods to bear on the improvement of the natives and their lot."

and
SIR JAMES BROOKE (1803–1868)

"An equally remarkable man, 'Rajah' Brooke of Sarawak, without official aid, won northern Borneo by sheer force of personality and by the best British methods of treating native races."

—*G. M. Trevelyan*[1]

tamford Raffles not only had a great name for a dashing empire-builder, he was the example *par excellence* of an enlightened, energetic, entrepreneurial English imperialist. In fact, Raffles, "the Father of Singapore," was the model for the aspiring James Brooke who became the White Rajah of Sarawak, a title we would no doubt all long to hold.

Raffles was born on a ship bound for England from Jamaica, the very year that Cornwallis surrendered at Yorktown. By the time he was fourteen his spendthrift father could no long afford Raffles' school fees, so he was sent to work as a clerk for the East India Company in its London headquarters of East India House. Whatever formal schooling he lacked he more than compensated for by becoming a dedicated lifelong autodidact. His employers noted his industry, his keen intelligence, and his steady nature, and in 1805—the same year he married a striking and vivacious widow ten years his senior—he was sent to Penang (or Prince of Wales Island, as they called it) as an assistant to the governor. Typically, he taught himself Malay on the voyage to his new post.

Raffles, throughout his career in Southeast Asia, was flush with enthusiasm to learn everything he could about the peoples and the land he served: language, art, religion, history, botany, zoology—whatever there was to learn, Raffles wanted to learn it, even if his commercial duties meant he had to do so on his own time. During normal working hours, he pored over accounts and mastered all the commercial skills necessary to running a Company outpost—so much so that in 1807 he became chief secretary to the governor.

He gained a patron in Lord Minto, the admirably liberal governor-general of India, who recognized Raffles' talent and looked for a way to deploy it against the French, who were the recipients, under Napoleon, of the Dutch Southeast Asian empire. Minto made Raffles his special agent in Malacca, charged with gauging whether the Javanese would support a British invasion against their Franco-Dutch rulers. As a Malay noted of Raffles, he was "most courteous in his intercourse with all men. He had a sweet expression on his face, was extremely affable and liberal, and listened with attention when people spoke to him."[2] In other words, Raffles was a perfect diplomatic agent.

With stout English confidence, Raffles advised Minto that Java could be taken with fewer than 10,000 men (3,000 Europeans, the rest sepoys), though the Franco-Dutch forces numbered a good 14,000. He thought the Javanese nobles would back the British. In 1811, in a swift summer campaign, Java was added to the East India Company's empire, and Raffles was made lieutenant governor of Java.

Raffles ruled the island from September 1811 to March 1816. He put down rebellious sultans, kept the peace, abolished slavery, reformed the administration of the island, dismantled the Dutch mercantilist system, and established a freer market system that guaranteed property rights (including the rights of small Javanese farmers). The only reform he could not achieve was making Java profitable to the Company— and the Company, while happy to be rid of the French, was not so very happy being saddled with responsibility for the island. With the restoration of Java to the Dutch after the defeat of Napoleon at Waterloo, Raffles was out of a job. He returned home a hero, though facing minor, trumped-up charges (insinuated by a disgruntled and dishonest subordinate) of corruption, of which he was later entirely cleared.

Imperial Advice

"Let us do all the good we can while we are here."

Lord Minto to Raffles after the conquest of Java, quoted in Maurice Collins, *Raffles* (The John Day Company, 1968) p. 70

He also came home a widower. He remarried in 1817, the same year he published his *History of Java* and was appointed governor-general of Bencoolen. Favored by the prince regent (the future George IV) and his daughter Princess Charlotte, he left for Sumatra as *Sir* Stamford Raffles. Bencoolen, however, was less welcoming. The settlement was a wreck, his official residence badly damaged by an earthquake, the government house abandoned and derelict, the roads choked with vegetation; it was, he wrote, "without exception the most wretched place I ever beheld. I cannot convey to you an adequate idea of the ruin and dilapidation which surrounds me."[3] While rebuilding he followed his usual path of free market reforms, freeing slaves, and exploring the interior, where he discovered a giant flowering plant now known as the Rafflesia Arnoldi. His wife, meanwhile, the first white woman many of the natives had ever seen, was regarded as something of a goddess (even though, to English eyes, she was nowhere near as good-looking as his first wife; she was, however, six years his junior).

His wife's presumed divinity aside, it was not the backwaters of Bencoolen where Raffles would make his mark—that would be in Singapore, an island city-state he founded in 1819 in order to give the British a foothold, and a free trade entrepôt, on the Straits of Malacca. Raffles wrote to William Wilberforce that Singapore had given the British "command of the Archipelago as well as in peace as in war: our commerce will extend to every part, and British principles will be known and felt throughout."[4] By British principles he meant free trade, fair play, and honest administration of just laws.

Raffles' usual sunny spirits were clouded by the loss of his eldest three children—victims of the tropics—and his own health began to falter as he was beset by blistering headaches. It became evident that he would have to return to England. Before he left, however, he drew up Singapore's constitution, established a Malay College, and had the pleasure of seeing Singapore develop as a successful, rapidly growing, port city. He also endured the tragedy of his youngest daughter dying (another daughter in England survived) and having the ship carrying all his notes, his animal specimens, his maps—virtually all his belongings—burst into flames and sink to the bottom of the sea. The great entrepreneurial statesman, the great amateur anthropologist, zoologist, and botanist, the great scholar of the Malay people—their history, religion, language, and culture—returned to England empty-handed. There was only this consolation: in 1824, a sweeping Anglo-Dutch treaty accepted Singapore as British (though Bencoolen and the whole of Sumatra went to the Dutch), drawing an equatorial line, giving the British the northern territories of Malaya and the Dutch the southern territories of Indonesia.

In England, still in bad health, Raffles again successfully rebuffed accusations from a disgruntled subordinate, this time over the administration of Singapore. In addition, he was harried by an ungrateful East India Company, which not only denied him a pension but demanded he reimburse the Company for a variety of charges, including those he had incurred to found Singapore. Still, he maintained an active social and intellectual life, including establishing the London Zoo. He died of a stroke in 1826, one day before his forty-fifth birthday. His parish priest—who had investments in plantations dependent on slave labor—refused to commemorate the anti-slaver Raffles with a memorial in his church; Westminster Abbey made good the difference, erecting a statue in Raffles' honor. Raffles has other memorials, too, most of them in Singapore, ranging from colleges and schools, to a horse racing cup, to the celebrated Raffles Hotel. In the words of one of his biographers, "He taught Malays, Chinese and Javanese to think of the Englishman as just, liberal and sympathetic."[5] Raffles was all that.

The White Rajah

When Raffles died, James Brooke was twenty-three, an army officer with the British East India Company. His father had served the Company too, and James had been born in India. He was a child of some privilege, doted on by his parents who didn't ship him home to England to be educated until he was twelve years old; and then it appears he was less interested in hitting the books than hitting the decks and sailing. His formal education didn't last long: by sixteen he was an ensign in John Company's Indian army. He much enjoyed the frat house side of a young officer's life—sports and pranks—but was rather less keen on serious desk duties (which he acquired on rising to sub-assistant commissary general). Far more to his taste was raising a troop of native cavalry scouts to fight for the Company in the First Anglo-Burmese War (1824–26). In that war, Brooke suffered a grievous wound—perhaps, it has been surmised, shot in the genitals; others say the lungs—which put him on the invalid list for five years. To fill the empty hours, he daydreamt about adventure and fantasized that he was meant to do something big, if only circumstances would allow.

The first thing circumstances did was prevent his return to duty within the designated five-year limit.[6] So Brooke resigned his commission, decided that his life's work was to plough the sea and set foot on a far eastern island where no white man had trodden before, and to that end badgered his reluctant father into buying him "a rakish slaver-brig."[7] Better that, his father thought, than having young James moping about like an adolescent—though his schemes sounded impractical to the old man.

His father was right. James's schemes were impractical, and commercial failures—but profit-making was never really Brooke's goal. Brooke's real interest was in unexplored territory. When his father died, he used his inheritance to acquire a bigger boat, a schooner, and set himself to studying nautical books and the works of Sir Stamford Raffles, after whose adventures he hoped to model his own. He decided, as a young Englishman might in the nineteenth century, to annex a goodly portion of Borneo for the British Empire and in the process "relieve the darkness of Paganism, and the horrors of the eastern slave-trade."[8]

Brooke's schooner, *The Royalist*, was fitted out with guns, gave its master a reason to wear a dashing uniform, and, as a listed vessel with the Royal Yacht Squadron, could fly the white ensign of the Royal Navy. It had in short everything required to impress the natives of Sarawak, northern Borneo, where Brooke landed in 1839. He helped the Sultan of Brunei put down a rebellion in the province; and in consequence of that—as well as a martial show of force by Brooke, who was rather better at the art of war (and diplomacy) than the locals—the Sultan thought it wise to make the enterprising Englishman his governor. In 1841, Brooke assumed the title—to be affirmed later—of Rajah of Sarawak.

Like Raffles, he set about an administration of reform—in particular, trying to protect the Hill Dayaks ("one of the most interesting and easily to be improved races in the world"[9]) from the piratical, headhunting Sea Dayaks and imperious Malays. As the Lycurgus of Sarawak, he gave the province a legal code. Typically, while he boasted of Sarawak's natural resources, it actually had little to offer, and Brooke kept his government afloat by writing checks on his own account or by offering protection to business-savvy Chinese who were harassed by the Malays.

He also began building a navy. Granted, it was mostly made up of large canoes with small mounted guns, but in his Dudley Do-Right way he was determined to sink Sarawak's pirates; though in typical British imperial fashion he rather liked the ruffians, just as he found headhunters had their good points too. But most of all, he relished the role of liberating peaceful Sarawakians from fear and injustice. In that cause he enlisted a Royal Navy captain, charged with protecting British shipping, to expand his portfolio and lend him a hand. Brooke became quite the swashbuckling nemesis of the pirates of Sarawak.

As he extended his authority, so too did he expand British interest and influence. In 1845, he was given the title of Her Majesty's Confidential Agent to the government in Borneo. With that title, he and the Royal Navy became the kingmakers of Brunei and took ownership of the island of Labuan.[10] In 1847, Brooke, the conquering hero, paid a trip back home to England and was lionized—not to mention knighted as Sir James.

When he returned to Sarawak, he buckled down to further wars against pirates. While he focused on the sword and the cannon, he welcomed Christian missionaries to win converts to peace through good works and schools (the Americans, he thought were better at this approach). Proselytizing Muslims was discouraged, but the Dayaks were fair game. What stunned Brooke was that his recent fights, reported in the British press, brought him not more of the fame he desired but attacks from liberals (ironically, he was himself a Liberal) who questioned why Britain was cooperating with a man who left a trail of dead Sarawakians behind him (even if they were pirates and headhunters). He was rather more popular with the Dayaks and the Malays and Chinese, who prayed for his recovery when he was laid low by smallpox. He survived—both the smallpox and a British inquiry into his affairs, which exonerated him from the highly colored charges thrown against him, though the British government distanced itself from Brooke. To his dismay, he was no longer an official British imperial agent; he was a mere rajah subordinate to the sultan of Brunei.

The smallpox aged him—perhaps Britain's ingratitude did as well—and the pirate-hunter turned again to the example of Raffles and became a man of study. Not much interested in female companionship—he always preferred the company of young men, though he was once engaged and had fathered an illegitimate son—he became an avid chess player and liked nothing better than sitting up nights convivially talking about religion, politics, and philosophy. Nevertheless, in 1857 Brooke again buckled on pistol and sabre to put down an insurrection by rebellious Chinese angry over high taxes on their opium and ambitious to seize control of Sarawak now that Brooke was stripped of British support. The Chinese, allegedly more civilized than the Dayaks, proved as barbarous as any—even beheading children or tossing them alive into flames. But as they slaughtered Christians, looted and torched European homes, and burned Malay villages, they were surprised to find an avenging army coming behind them. Brooke was joined by his nephew and eventual successor Charles Johnson (who later took the last name Brooke), already an experienced naval officer. With them were Dayak and Malay warriors who chased the Chinese rebels over the border of Dutch Borneo. There the Chinese fought bloodily amongst themselves; the Dutch finally disarmed them; and the rebels' booty was returned to Sarawak.

Brooke—exhausted, his pockets emptied on behalf of Sarawak—came to England again a hero and used his status to raise money for his province. He did that, but also suffered a stroke, in 1858. Malaria and smallpox had taken their toll; the stroke, it seemed to his friends, clouded his mind and judgment. The governance of Sarawak rightly belonged to a younger man who could take the field against pirates, rebels, and barbarous ruffians, who were never in short supply. Brooke toyed with the idea of retiring to an

Sir James Brooke, in Memoriam

"The Rajah Sir James Brooke…was one of the really great men of his time.…He came to a disorganized crowd of savages, and left them a compact nation. He gave peace in their borders and taught them for the first time the meaning of Justice, Mercy and Truth."

From an article by P. F. Tidman (who had worked for the Borneo Company and seen Brooke in action) in *The Monthly Packet*, 14 September 1874, quoted in Nigel Barley, *White Rajah: A Biography of Sir James Brooke* (Abacus, 2009), p. 229

English cottage, but in the end could not leave his life's work, even if he conducted it from England. He suffered another stroke in 1866 and a third in 1868, which finished him off.

The White Rajahs, however, carried on, Brooke's nephew Charles assuming the title in 1868, followed by his son Charles Vyner Brooke (who governed as rajah from 1917 to 1946). After the Second World War, the British made Sarawak a crown colony—which proved unpopular; the Sarawakians preferred the personal paternalism of the White Rajahs. Brooke's "model for Sarawak was," says one of his biographers, "one blatantly transplanted from the English shires—small is good, valorization of face-to-face relationships, the local over the metropolitan, tradition and emotion over rationality," giving Sarawak an "agreeable Torytown façade." It was certainly agreeable to the Sarawakians, for whom the memory of the White Rajahs is a fond one.

Chapter 25

FIELD MARSHAL SIR THOMAS BLAMEY (1884–1951)

"In receiving your surrender I do not recognize you as an honorable and gallant foe...."

—General Blamey, to Japanese Lieutenant-General Fusataro Teshima, 9 September 1945[1]

ad there never been a British Empire, there would never have been an Australia as we know it today, which would have been an incalculable loss, especially for those who like eating at Australian steak houses, watching Aussie Rules football, and drinking Foster's Lager. There would also have been no Sir Thomas Blamey of Australia, the Aussies' only field marshal to date, and one who earned his field marshal's baton for service to the Empire in two world wars.

Blamey was born near picturesque Wagga Wagga in New South Wales. WAG did not stand for "wives and girlfriends" in those days, and Blamey was about as far removed from football celebrity, bikini waxes, and paparazzi as one can imagine. He was the seventh of ten children, his antecedents were Scotch and Cornish, and his upbringing was as a farmer's and drover's son near the banks of Lake Albert.

Australia was a long way from the Sudan, but a year after Blamey was born, Australia made its first overseas military contribution to the British Empire by sending troops, guns, and horses for the "too late" campaign to

Did you know?

♛ Blamey is the only Australian to attain the rank of field marshal

♛ He was MacArthur's commander of land forces in the Southwest Pacific

♛ He dreamt of importing elephants to help develop Papua New Guinea

save General Gordon. Growing up in a patriotic home, Blamey breathed British imperial air, scented with the aromatic dust of Australia.

He was a small, tough, religious boy, a good student and a reliable horseman, who liked nothing better than setting himself tactical problems with toy soldiers. In school he was in the cadet corps, and tried to enlist, at fifteen, to fight in the Boer War but was sent home by the recruiting sergeant. He did, however, help train fellow cadets as a pupil-teacher, and then as full-time teacher starting in 1903. He did the job remarkably well, with a natural air of command and authority—so much so that in 1906, after passing a rigorous examination (in which he placed third in the country), he became a cadet instructor for the Australian military, an appointment that made him a lieutenant. He trained the teachers of the cadet corps in Victoria, and made sure the cadets were up to snuff.[2]

When the Staff College in Quetta, India, set aside a slot for an Australian officer, Blamey determined to win it. He did, placing first in the qualifying examination, and enrolled for the 1912–13 term. He was a captain now, a married man, and a father (of a son who would die at twenty-two in a plane crash while serving in the Royal Australian Air Force). When he finished the course, he was briefly posted to some Indian units, and then sent for staff training in England. The year was 1914. He wouldn't return home for six years; and then he would be a brigadier general.

Australia Will Be There

At the start of the First World War, Blamey was a major in British military intelligence, but with the raising of the Australian Imperial Force he was transferred to become its intelligence chief and sent to Egypt in December 1914. In April 1915 he embarked with his fellow Australians for the Gallipoli Campaign. In the trenches, he spotted a lance corporal with a mocked-up periscope rifle; impressed by its design, Blamey refined it and had periscope rifles issued to frontline Australians. When the frustration of Gallipoli ended, in December 1915, Blamey was sent to experience the frustration of the Western Front in France, including the Battle of the Somme. Adding to that frustration was that he spent almost all his time as a staff officer—including chief of staff to the commander of the Australian Corps—rather than in a field command. But he was considered an outstanding, hard-driving staff officer, with a gift for precise and detailed battle orders. He took credit for initiating the Battle of Amiens, the August 1918 offensive that spurred the Allied march to victory, so it wasn't time altogether wasted. The commander of the Australian Corps, Lieutenant-General Sir John Monash, thought highly of Blamey, saying he "possessed a mind cultured far above the average, widely informed, alert and prehensile. He had an infinite capacity for taking pains."[3] Blamey's service won him a knighthood.

Back home in Australia after the war, he became deputy chief of the General Staff and helped establish the Royal Australian Air Force. In 1922, he returned to London as the Australian representative to the Imperial General Staff. He was expected to become chief of Australia's General Staff in 1923, but jealous senior officers made that politically impossible, so he was instead made "Second" Chief of the General Staff. Everyone recognized his merit, but Blamey was not the sort who sought to ingratiate himself. As General Sir William

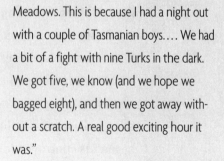

Olive Garden

"The two large olive trees in the middle of the fields are known as Blamey's Meadows. This is because I had a night out with a couple of Tasmanian boys.... We had a bit of a fight with nine Turks in the dark. We got five, we know (and we hope we bagged eight), and then we got away without a scratch. A real good exciting hour it was."

Blamey at Gallipoli in a letter to his parents, quoted in John Heatherington, *Blamey: The Biography of Field Marshal Sir Thomas Blamey* (F. W. Cheshire, Melbourne, 1954), pp. 40–41

Imperial Loyalty

"General [Douglas] Haig [Commander of the British Expeditionary Force] asked General Monash a few days later to bring the Australian leaders to meet him.... He uttered a few words of thanks and said, 'You do not know what the Australians and the Canadians have done for the British Empire in these days.' He opened his mouth to continue, and halted. The tears rolled down his cheeks. A dramatic pause, and we all quietly filed out."

Blamey writing on the aftermath of the Battle of Amiens, quoted in John Heatherington, *Blamey: The Biography of Field Marshal Sir Thomas Blamey* (F. W. Cheshire, Melbourne, 1954), p. 49

Birdwood, the English commander of the Australian Imperial Force during the Great War, had said of Blamey, he was "an exceedingly able little man, though by no means a pleasing personality."[4]

His boss, Lieutenant-General Sir Henry Chauvel, recommended Blamey for another position entirely—Chief Commissioner of Police for the state of Victoria, which had recently suffered a mutiny of a third of its officers and needed a strong hand to knock the force back into shape and knock emboldened bully boys off the streets. Blamey accepted the job in 1925, and so began his controversial career as a copper.

As a young man, Blamey had been a teetotaler and so successful a lay preacher that he had considered a career as a Methodist minister. But as a police chief, there were accusations that he was no longer a choir boy. In India he had acquired a taste for drink—the norm among British officers—and some said he drank too much. During a police raid on a suspected brothel, a small, stocky man flashed a police badge bearing the number 80, saying everything was all right because he was an undercover constable. Badge 80 was Blamey's. In a later investigation, the police officers who made the raid testified that the man was not Blamey, Blamey could account for his whereabouts, and his badge was not in his possession at the time of the raid. Though he was conclusively cleared, Blamey's political enemies on the Left made the "Badge 80" affair a bit of baggage he had to carry for the rest of his life; as they did another minor affair where he had misrepresented a constable's wounds in a misguided effort to guard the policeman's reputation (which, as the investigating judge pointed out, was clear in any event). Blamey was a political target for the Labour Party because he was known to have strong right-wing views. He was forced to resign in 1936.

For a while he filled his time commanding a militia division. Then he found work as a radio commentator, where he warned that Australia's future was menaced by an aggressive Japan and National Socialist Germany. He toyed with the idea of a political career but was rejected as a candidate. He had little money, and apparently no future. But in 1938, his rehabilitation began. He was appointed chairman of a national manpower committee to prepare for the possibility of war; in 1939 he was appointed commander of the 6th Division of the Australian Imperial Force; by 1940 he was commanding officer of the 1st Australian Corps. He and his fellow Australians were sent to the Middle East.

As a commander, his goal was to raise and maintain an Australian army that would remain under Australian command and not be parceled out as replacement units for the British. As a strategist, he believed—especially after the Hitler-Stalin pact—that American intervention was necessary for the Allies to win. As a soldier, he impressed his staff officers as tough, demanding, unyielding to physical pain, deeply and widely read, interested in the cultures of the areas to which he was posted (while serving in the Middle East he taught himself basic Arabic), appreciative of the arts (he commissioned war artists for the Australian army), and stubbornly loyal.

Field Marshal Sir Archibald Wavell gave Blamey extraordinarily high praise, calling him "probably the best soldier we had in the Middle East. Not an easy man to deal with, but a very satisfactory man to deal with. His military knowledge was unexampled, and he was a positive, firm, and very satisfactory commander."[5]

Blamey's military knowledge was good enough to tell him that the decision to send Australian troops to Greece in 1941 was a bad one. He quietly spent much of his time in Greece reconnoitering the beaches for an inevitable evacuation from a doomed campaign. Helping to direct the eventual retreat, he was ordered to Cairo where he was appointed Deputy Commander in Chief, Middle East.

MacArthur's General

Everything changed for Blamey, however, after Australia declared war on Japan, one hour after the Japanese struck Pearl Harbor on 7 December 1941. As the Australians prepared for a fight closer to home, Blamey was appointed Commander in Chief, Australian Military Forces.

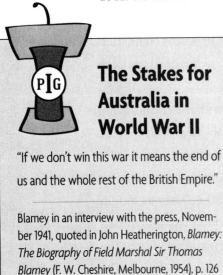

The Stakes for Australia in World War II

"If we don't win this war it means the end of us and the whole rest of the British Empire."

Blamey in an interview with the press, November 1941, quoted in John Heatherington, *Blamey: The Biography of Field Marshal Sir Thomas Blamey* (F. W. Cheshire, Melbourne, 1954), p. 126

On 19 February 1942, Australia came under direct, sustained attack for the first time in its history with the massive bombing of Darwin, along with the towns of Broome and Wyndham. It was the first of what would be nearly one hundred Japanese air strikes on Australia. Blamey had to organize a new army quickly—an army prepared not only to defend the Australian mainland but take the battle to the enemy in the jungles of the South Pacific. He was made Commander of Allied Land Forces under the Supreme Allied Commander of the Southwest Pacific Area, General Douglas MacArthur, whom he—mostly—admired, saying, "The best and the worst things you hear about him are both true."[6]

Blamey had been appalled by Australian complacency on the home front before the Japanese raid on Darwin. Now he found himself the voice of calm amidst the fall of Singapore and the advance of Japanese troops to New Guinea. He was not, however, any more diplomatic. On 9 November 1942, Blamey delivered a speech to Australian troops who had driven back the Japanese on the Kokoda Trail Campaign. Blamey was in a dour mood because MacArthur had expected a speedier victory, and in his speech Blamey invoked a garbled metaphor about running rabbits, which the men took as an accusation of cowardice (an imputation Blamey later said he didn't mean to imply). The speech made him bitterly resented. Stung, Blamey belatedly stood up for his Aussies against the criticisms of MacArthur and his staff. He demanded he be given Australian troops in the battle for Buna "because he knew they would fight."[7] The belittling of each other's troops—the Americans dubious about the slouch hats, the slouch hats carping about the Yanks—became a running sideshow in the New Guinea campaign.

Calumny from an ex-Colonial

"[The] Australian is not a bushman, he is not a field soldier, he is nothing but a city slum dweller. The Massachusetts soldiers knew more about the New Guinea jungle in two days than the Australians in two years."

American General "Hap" Arnold in his diary entry for 28 September 1942, cited in Major-General John W. Huston, ed., *American Air Power Comes of Age: General Henry H. "Hap" Arnold's World War II Diaries* (University Press of the Pacific, 2004), vol. I, pp. 396–97

Another sideshow was Blamey's imperial interest in developing New Guinea with tea, coffee, and quinine plantations (he was a self-taught expert on preventing malaria). He even wondered about importing elephants to help work the land. While most of his troops considered New Guinea a green, steaming, miasmic hell, Blamey liked it, and liked sleeping out under the jungle stars, dreaming of how Australia could fulfill its colonial mission to the Papua New Guineans after the war.

They put him in much better mind than the Japanese, whom he despised. When he accepted the Japanese surrender at Morotai, Indonesia, one week after the general Japanese surrender to Douglas MacArthur aboard the USS *Missouri*, he said,

> In receiving your surrender I do not recognize you as an honorable and gallant foe, but you will be treated with due but severe courtesy in all matters.
>
> I recall the treacherous attack on our ally, China. I recall the treacherous attack upon the British Empire and upon the United States of America in December 1941, at a time when your authorities were making the pretense of ensuring peace between us. I recall the atrocities inflicted upon the person of Australian nationals as prisoners of war and internees, designed to reduce them by punishment and starvation to slavery. In the light of these evils I will enforce most rigorously all orders issued to you, so let there be no delay or hesitation in their fulfillment at your peril.[8]

If the Allies—and his fellow Australians—found Blamey a hard man, the Japanese found him no softer.

On 14 November 1945, after working hard to return temporary wartime soldiers to Civvy Street, he was dismissed as commander in chief. Angered that the Labour government of Australia, as a matter of policy, would not nominate senior officers he recommended for knighthoods, Blamey spurned any talk of rewards for himself, saying, "I don't want anything. All I want to do after I leave the barracks is attack your Government. I'll do it at every opportunity,"[9] which he did as a conservative newspaper columnist. His final reward for his wartime service was his old Buick staff car; Blamey had wanted to buy it, but the government insisted, over his protests, that he accept it as a gift. He retired from the army on 31 January 1946, though he was reappointed after the conservative Liberal Party defeated Labour in the 1949 elections. Prime Minister Robert Menzies wanted to promote him to field marshal, a rank that required approval of the British War Office and the Crown, and which could only be granted if Blamey was on the active service list. He became a field marshal in the King's Birthday Honours list for 1950.

Blamey's end followed swiftly. Previously in robust good health, he was bedridden when he received his field marshal's baton. He was a determined patient, convinced he would recover, and fought to that end longer than his doctors thought possible, before dying of a stroke on 27 May 1951.

Blamey was an imperial servant, patriotically and jealously devoted to his native land of Australia, but equally loyal to the British Empire and the king. Even if his experience of field command was slight, he was a gifted strategist, and a polymath with a curiosity and knowledge that was catholic in its scope. Regarded as a cold-hearted administrator, he did what he thought politically and militarily necessary, and those who knew him well sometimes saw the tears that cracked the severe visage. He felt deeply the losses his men incurred, and was utterly devoted to helping wartime veterans. Only in the British Empire could a drover's son from dusty Wagga Wagga rise to become a general jousting with the likes of Wavell and Auchinleck and MacArthur—not to mention the enemy—and win a field marshal's baton from the king.

Chapter 26

FIELD MARSHAL SIR GERALD TEMPLER (1898–1979)

"He looked rather like Charles II…fairly short, wiry, and he had a little penciled moustache…and the moment he talked his eyes lit up.… You felt the whole time you were under his gaze.… He was one of those leaders who attracted younger officers who later most of them became generals in turn.… You gave him all you could, partly out of loyalty to him. He was a very, very great man.… He was legendary."

—*John Loch, who served under Templer in Malaya*[1]

ir Gerald Templer was a tough, terse soldier—the least likely person, some might think, to argue for defeating the Communist insurgency in Malaya by winning over "hearts and minds." But it was indeed Templer, a veteran of two world wars won by overwhelming military force, who gave us that phrase and a model of successful counterinsurgency warfare.

For all his formidable reputation, he could be a puckish sort—particularly when discussing his origins. Sometimes he would insist he was Devonshire English (which was true). At others, he would claim to be Irish, or at least Anglo-Irish (which was also true), and certainly he always took an especial interest in Irish regiments. Templer once told Nikita Krushchev that while the Irish were Catholics who hated Protestant Englishmen, he

Did you know?

- ♕ Templer was a hurdler on the 1924 British Olympic team (as well as an army shooting and bayoneting champion)

- ♕ He was the youngest lieutenant-general in the British Army at the start of World War II

- ♕ He developed the "hearts and minds" strategy of counterinsurgency that helped defeat the Communists in Malaya

was a Protestant Irishman who was chief of the British Imperial General Staff. In truth he was the English-born son of an Anglo-Irish father who served in the Royal Irish Fusiliers. Both sides of his family had Anglo-Irish blood and military traditions.

He was dispatched to boarding school at ten, was an enthusiastic boy scout (he would later try to win the hearts and minds of young Malays with scouting), and was in the Officer Training Corps in Wellington College. He loved OTC but loathed the school—he later refused to become its governor—and in comparison a life in the trenches seemed a jolly prospect. He took an appointment at Sandhurst, which had dramatically shortened its training program to six months; "nobody failed at that stage of the First World War [1916] because we were so badly needed as cannon fodder."[2] A month before he was eighteen, he was a second lieutenant with the Royal Irish Fusiliers, though he wouldn't be posted to France until he was nineteen.

> ### An Anglo-Irishman's Lament
>
> "At heart he loved Ireland, but he was hurt by it—he felt that it had behaved badly."
>
> Jane Templer on her father's attitude to the old sod, quoted in John Cloake, *Templer: Tiger of Malaya* (Harrap, 1985), p. 3

He survived the war, had his share of modest adventures, including retrieving a drunken Irishman from no man's land, and when he was stricken with diphtheria in March 1918, he cleverly switched the tag on his toe so that he was sent to "American Ladies Hospital" rather than a dreary old field hospital. Templer liked telling such stories against himself (including how he lasted only ten days as an intelligence officer) and treated his First World War experiences with grim humor. But one image in particular—of panicked, pitifully whinnying, "wounded horses...tripping over barbed wire, and treading on their own guts"[3]—gave him nightmares until the day he died.

After the war he was sent on anti-Bolshevik duty with the Royal Irish Fusiliers in Persia, where he had a mostly merry time except for an altercation with a hot-headed Persian that left him with a broken collar bone (badly set by a drunken doctor). Then it was on to Mesopotamia for a bit of counterinsurgency, which, he recalled later, had all the excitement of war with little of the danger. His tour of the Middle East ended with rather unpleasant constabulary duties—he had to witness hangings—in Egypt.

His regiment survived the creation of the Irish Free State, and back in England he became an accomplished sportsman—not just with horse and gun (he was a champion shooter and bayonet fighter), but as a hurdler for the army track team, which in due course led to his winning a spot on the 1924 British Olympic team, though he ended up as a reserve hurdler and did not run. He enjoyed an active social life (the Irishman in him liked having a good time) though he was a stickler about regimental history, traditions, form and uniform (he was that sort too), until his battalion of Fusiliers was reposted to Egypt. Here too, his duties were rather leisurely; so leisurely that he took leave to get married in 1926, before returning to his rounds of polo, shooting, and drinks (and, to be fair, maneuvers and courses, including one in aerial reconnaissance). A polo injury immobilized him long enough to pass the exams for Staff College.

He entered the college in 1928. It was a two-year course and he was the youngest in his class. Among his instructors was future field marshal Bernard Montgomery. When he graduated he joined a new regiment, the Loyals, as it was the only way for him to be promoted to captain. He performed the usual rounds of a young officer—including encountering a bête noir commanding officer who wanted him retired for chronic ill health (for all his athleticism, Templer was accident- and sickness-prone)—until in 1935 he was posted to Palestine. He thought it an unfortunate, filthy, overtaxed wasteland. He was unimpressed by the Jewish settlers, though the Zionists were rather more impressed with him, hoping at one point to convince him to become Chief of Staff of a Jewish army. Still, he found patrolling against Arab terrorists quite fun, even if he only spent about six months doing it before being ordered back to Old Blighty.

Setting Europe Ablaze—and Sacking Konrad Adenauer

Templer's most important posting in the years leading up to the Second World War was as an intelligence officer in the War Office. It was a job that mixed cocktail diplomacy with the building of an intelligence network—duties he carried into France with the British Expeditionary Force in September 1939, where he proved equally adept at confusing the Germans about

Templer vs. JFK's Father

"I did not mince my words about Britain's terrible unpreparedness, about the cowardly attitude of the French army on the right of the BEF [British Expeditionary Force] which I had observed with my own eyes at close range, or about the uncivilized behavior of the [German] Stuka pilots herding the Belgian, Dutch and French refugees up and down the roads.... [American ambassador to the Court of St. James, Joseph] Kennedy said to me, 'Young man, England will be invaded in a few weeks' time and your country will have its neck wrung by Hitler like a chicken.' I got up and told him exactly what I thought of him in most undiplomatic language.... I have no doubt it was relayed on to 10 Downing Street quickly. I have often wondered whether it was from this incident that Churchill coined his famous phrase 'some chicken...some neck.'"

Templer quoted in John Cloake, *Templer: Tiger of Malaya* (Harrap, 1985), pp. 81–82

British troop movements and helping British agents—who might be exposed after the German blitzkrieg through Belgium, Holland, and France—to escape. In 1940, he was evacuated at Dunkirk and set the task of raising the 9th Battalion of the Royal Sussex Regiment.

Templer spent much of 1940–43 organizing England's defenses against a German invasion and rising to become the youngest lieutenant-general in the army. All that was very well, but he wanted a field command where he could see action. In the summer of 1943, he got it with command of the First Division of the British Army, then in North Africa, soon to be transferred to Italy. Italy was a slogging campaign, and Templer—who was highly regarded for his informative, lively, to-the-point briefings—saw plenty of fighting at Monte Camino and Anzio. The fighting men knew he was there, as he made a point of lightning visits to the units under his command. He might have inspired his men, but he was less inspired by them, concluding that the British soldier of the First World War was made of sterner stuff than the British soldier of the Second. He was a demanding officer, took an interest in everything—from church parades to tactics—kept up the standards of an officer and a gentleman by never talking shop in the mess, and got things done through his combination of bon vivant diplomacy and iron-hard character. He proved the last quality when his back was broken: On 5 August 1944, he was driving a jeep (he usually insisted on driving himself), when a truck carrying a piano swerved off the road and into a land mine, shooting a wheel (and chunks of piano) into Templer's back, smashing him against the steering wheel. He was invalided to England and didn't emerge from his plaster until November.

Though not yet cleared for anything more taxing than administrative duties, he managed to land a job with the SOE, Special Operations Executive, which had the remit to, in Churchill's famous words, "set Europe ablaze"[4] through its saboteurs. But whatever its excitements—Templer expanded its operations into Germany—he wanted a return to the field.

Bulldog Drummond at War

Among Templer's staff officers with the Royal Sussex was Lieutenant-Colonel Gerard Fairlie, former officer of the Scots Guards (1918–24), former British army heavyweight boxing champion, fellow member of the 1924 Olympic team (bobsled), and the model for the character Bulldog Drummond. Fairlie was a journalist, screenwriter, and author in his own right, and in fact occasionally collaborated with Drummond's creator, "Sapper"—Herman Cyril McNeile—and as his officially designated successor took over writing the Drummond books after Sapper's death. During the war he trained commandos, himself parachuted into France to fight beside the Maquis, and won the Croix de Guerre and a Bronze Star.

Instead, he was posted to Montgomery's headquarters as director of civil affairs and military government. Rather than leading troops into battle, he was charged with governing the British-occupied zone of Germany, which, if anything, was a more daunting responsibility: requiring him to create order out of chaos, an economy out of ruins, and a ready supply of food to stave off famine. Templer managed it, and later confessed it "was more exciting than commanding a division in battle."[5] He also gained notoriety as the man in charge when the British sacked future German chancellor Konrad Adenauer as mayor of Cologne.

Templer's reward for a job well done in Germany was to be appointed, in succession: director of Military Intelligence; vice chief of the Imperial General Staff (first under Montgomery, then under General Sir William Slim, hero of the Burma Campaign); and general officer commanding Eastern Command. Churchill, however, gave him the appointment that made his name: in 1952 Templer became High Commissioner of Malaya. The previous high commissioner had been assassinated, and the colony was in the throes of a Communist insurrection. Templer's job was to defeat the Communists and guide Malaya to a pro-Western (especially pro-British, given British economic interests in the rubber plantations and tin mines) independence. "If you pull it off," Churchill told him, "it will be a great feat."[6]

The Tiger of Malaya

In his two years in the Malayan Federation Templer laid the groundwork for victory. His method was to make surprise inspections and send a rocket up dozy performers. He was direct, energetic, and—to his enemies—rude, ready not only to ask the awkward question but to demand an immediate righting of obvious shortcomings. He liked going out and seeing things himself and even accompanied a platoon of Gurkhas on a jungle patrol. If he ever found troops at target practice, he joined in (he was a crack shot).

On the military side, he was an innovator in the use of helicopters for jungle warfare. On the political side, he believed his service in Palestine and his Anglo-Irish background helped, giving him insight into the difficulties of uniting a country divided by race and religion—though the Malay, Chinese, Indian Tamil, aboriginal, British, Eurasian, and Iban headhunter populations offered rather more exotic contrasts (Templer used the Ibans as military scouts and later formed them into a ranger regiment to "out-bandit the bandits"[7]).

Such diversity sometimes impinged on his ability to chew out the natives effectively; as when he chastised villagers whose home guard had collapsed, telling them they were a weak lot of bastards and that they would find he was an even bigger bastard—which in the words of his translator came out that Templer's father, like the villagers' fathers, had not been married to his mother when he was born.

Templer worked on trying to integrate the police and military forces, and he informed the British residents of Malaya that they had an especial duty to do volunteer work and demonstrate their long-term stakes in the country. His background in intelligence—crucial to penetrating and disrupting the Communist cadres—was useful as well.

Templer was a hard man and knew that hard military measures had to be taken: the Communists had to be hammered. But he also knew that

Hearts and Minds (the Original Malayan Version)

"The shooting side of this business is only 25 percent of the trouble; the other 75 percent is getting the people of this country behind us.... The answer lies not in pouring more troops into the jungle, but in the hearts and minds of the people."

General Sir Gerald Templer, High Commissioner and Director of Operations, Malaya, 1952, quoted in David Kilcullen, *Counterinsurgency* (Oxford University Press, 2010), p. 212

winning Malayan "hearts and minds"—not just among waverers, but with propaganda directed at the insurgents themselves—was essential if the insurgency was to be well and truly doused. His "hearts and minds" campaign had the usual ambitious and plentiful programs of public uplift and good works in schools, "new villages," and many other ventures. It included his wife's work setting up Women's Institutes (she even taught herself Malay) and writing a collection of Malayan fables after Templer complained that Malayan children had no fairy stories. Then there was his own leadership of the Malayan scouting movement. But his hearts and minds campaign was no namby-pamby affair—it couldn't be with Templer in charge, as witnessed when he tore into the residents of a town where a district officer, an engineer, and several policemen had been ambushed and killed while trying to repair the town's water supply:

You want everything done for you, but you are not prepared to assume the responsibility of citizenship. I want law and order, so that I can get on with many things which are good for this country. Why should it be impossible to do these good things? Because people like you are cowards? Do you think that under a communist regime you will be able to live a happy family life?... I shall have to take extremely unpleasant steps.... It does not amuse me to punish innocent people, but many of you are not innocent. You have information which you are too cowardly to give.[8]

Ever wary of overconfidence, Templer was nevertheless sure by 1953 that the Communists—who had retreated deep into the jungle—were in dire straits. In 1954, just before he left Malaya, he characteristically warned that the fight was not yet over: "In fact, I'll shoot the bastard who says this emergency is over."[9] But he was confident enough to promise the country its first national elections; and though the emergency was not officially ended until 1960, Templer had put the country well on the road to independence (1957) and victory over the Communists.

He came home to become chief of the Imperial General Staff (1955–58), field marshal (1956), and a roving military diplomat. After his retirement Templer devoted himself to establishing the excellent National Army Museum in London, serving as a trustee for other worthy ventures (such as preserving historic churches), doing business as chairman of the British Metal Corporation (among other company work), and indulging his interests in art (his views were soundly traditionalist) and wine. He became Constable of the Tower of London in 1965, Her Majesty's Lieutenant for Greater London in 1966, and in 1970 made the newspapers for, in his dressing gown and waving a sword stick, helping the police capture a burglar. Templer's honors, duties, colonelcies, and exploits (with a sword stick and without) stacked up until his death in 1979. He died of lung cancer, but went out the Templer way—after drinking a pink gin.

And from the Heavens Spoke Templer

"The first day the whole thing put the fear of God into the inhabitants of Kuala Lumpur, who heard a voice repeating over and over again the words 'World Communism is doomed' from thousands of feet up in the air above the clouds. And as they couldn't see where the voice was coming from, they thought it was all very spooky."

Templer on his strategy of aerial propaganda—broadcast from planes—quoted in John Cloake, *Templer: Tiger of Malaya* (Harrap, 1985), p. 239

Part VIII

RECESSIONAL

Chapter 27

WINSTON CHURCHILL'S LAMENT

"'I have worked very hard all my life, and I have achieved a great deal—in the end to achieve NOTHING,' the last word falling with somber emphasis. And since his greatest aspirations were for a powerful British Empire and Commonwealth in a peaceful world, what he said was, by his own definition, also historically correct."

—Winston Churchill to Anthony Montague Brown, his private secretary from 1952 to 1965[1]

O n 10 November 1942, Prime Minister Winston Churchill gave a speech marking the victory at the Battle of El Alamein. It is known as "The End of the Beginning" speech: "Now this is not the end. It is not even the beginning of the end. But it is, perhaps, the end of the beginning." An oft-quoted line from this speech, now tinged with irony, touches directly on the future of the British Empire: "I have not become the King's First Minister in order to preside over the liquidation of the British Empire." Less often quoted is this line: "I am proud to be a member of that vast commonwealth and society of nations and communities gathered in and around the ancient British monarch, without which the good cause might well have perished from the face of the earth. Here we are, and here we stand, a veritable rock of salvation in this drifting world."

That British imperial rock of salvation survived big and impressive for a brief moment after the Second World War—and then various nationalist, anti-colonialist forces took hammers and sickles and pangas to hack it to pieces. On 18 June 1940, after the fall of France to the Nazis, Churchill braced Britain for a battle that was, for the moment, to leave the British Empire fighting alone against National Socialist Germany, its then-ally Soviet Russia, Fascist Italy, and imperial Japan. He said, "Upon this battle depends the survival of Christian civilization. Upon it depends our own British life, and the long continuity of our institutions and our empire.... Let us therefore brace ourselves to our duties, and so bear ourselves that if the British Empire and its Commonwealth last for a thousand years, men will still say, 'This was their finest hour.'" It might very well have been Britain's finest hour, but the Empire, far from lasting a thousand years, began dissolving almost immediately after the war's end: the Commonwealth is largely inconsequential and Christian civilization is, to put it mildly, not what it once was.

Churchill's life was a thoroughly imperial one. As a young cavalry officer he served with the Malakand Field Force, fighting on the Northwest Frontier of India. He rode in what is often considered the last great cavalry charge of the British army, with the 21st Lancers at the Battle of Omdurman in the Sudan. In the Boer War in South Africa he fought, was captured by the enemy, and made a dramatic escape. He drafted strategies at the Admiralty and served in the trenches in World War I. He enlisted Lawrence of Arabia to help him design the post-Great War borders of the liberated territories of the Ottoman Empire. He fought to keep India within the Empire between the wars, was the rhetorical leader of the victorious Anglo-American alliance in World War II, and worked to consolidate the unity of the English-speaking peoples as a postwar power bloc. But for Churchill all these achievements rang hollow. Britain's imperial greatness, which had made all the rest possible, was gone: India given over to partition and slaughter, Suez transformed from a headquarters of British military might into a site of humiliation at the hands of a petty pan-Arabist dictator, Africa left prey to tribalism and corruption. Britain's imperial vigor was sapped, replaced by a sybaritic swinging London and a stultifying corporatist, "I'm all right, Jack," welfare state. Churchill was far from a Puritan killjoy (quite the reverse) and he had himself helped enact a limited welfare state (albeit in part for imperial purposes: "If the British people will have a great Empire… [it would not be] upon the shoulders of stunted millions crowded together in the slums of cities"[2]) but this was not the future he had fought for or envisioned for his country.

An Imperial Life

Winston Churchill (1874–1965) was the son of Lord Randolph Churchill and Jennie Jerome, a beautiful American heiress who always seemed to Churchill "a fairy princess,"[3] as indeed she seemed to a great many young Englishmen. Winston was, famously, not much of a student, and his father, despairing of his prospects, decided that a young man who liked nothing better than playing with toy soldiers was fit only for cannon fodder. Winston crammed his way into Sandhurst where he excelled, graduating eighth in his class and proving "that I could learn quickly enough the things that mattered"[4]—things like horsemanship, field fortifications, tactics, and military history.

As a young officer, he was given leave to cover the Cuban rebellion against Spain as a war correspondent, granted the leisure in India to educate himself (reading Gibbon and Macaulay and parliamentary speeches from his father's time in Parliament), and permitted to combine active service with journalistic dispatches, which he then turned into books. Churchill proved as unafraid to criticize his superiors in print as he was unafraid of the bullets, spears, and swords of the enemy in the field. As he noted in *The Story of the Malakand Field Force*, "Nothing in life is so exhilarating as to be shot at without result."[5]

It was a swashbuckling life, a "roving commission," as he called it, and it propelled him into Parliament at the age of twenty-five. Like his father, Churchill was a Tory, but a maverick one, and in 1904 he joined the Liberals over the issue of free trade (he was in favor of it and opposed to imperial tariffs). He was rewarded with ministerial office in 1905, declining a position at the Treasury in order to take a more junior position as Under Secretary of State for the Colonies. It was not dull numbers that motivated him but the vast questions of empire, including winning the Boers' happy consent to British rule by granting their republics their own constitutions and large dollops of self-government.

Like most British imperialists, his actions and beliefs were circumscribed by prudence and economy, but they were also guided by principles, which occasionally had to be modified and trimmed, but were constant. One of these was justice. For all his attachment to the superiority of the British race, he believed that superiority could only be justified by "bearing peace, civilization, and good government."[6] His attitude towards the non-white peoples of the Empire was generally paternal. Like most Englishmen he had an admiration for the fighting qualities of Muslims (though he saw their religion as ignorant and fanatical) and credited their loyalty in British India compared to the vexatious Hindus (whose religion he disparaged as decadent and immoral, with child weddings and widow-burnings and untouchables and whatnot).[7] He did not care much for the Chinese, but rather liked Africans (his first choice for a command in World War I was in East Africa), even if he regarded them (as many settlers did) as overgrown children, and was astonished, horrified, and saddened at the Mau-Mau rebellion among the Kikuyu in Kenya in the 1950s. If he uttered racist remarks about non-white peoples, he could be rather cutting about whites as well, including the Boers (though he learned to admire their courage and stubborn spirit of independence) and Germans ("the Hun is always either at your throat or at your feet"[8]), not to mention those who embraced the murderous doctrines of the Bolsheviks and the IRA.

In 1921, he returned to the Colonial Office as Secretary of State. In this position he is now notorious among his critics for advocating the use of gas against rebellious Iraqis. The sting of that charge is rather lessened, though, when one remembers that Churchill wanted Britain's boffins to develop a gas "which would inflict punishment on recalcitrant natives without inflicting grave injury upon them"[9]—in other words, a gas like tear gas, used to break up riots. Churchill lost his post simultaneously with losing his appendix in October 1922, and then lost his parliamentary seat to a candidate who favored prohibition (which Churchill of course did not).

By 1924 he was back with the Tories (as he said, anyone can rat, but it takes "a certain amount of ingenuity to re-rat"[10]) and received a surprise appointment as Chancellor of the Exchequer in the new Conservative government. On imperial matters, he became known as an ultra-imperialist on India, which he argued was held together only by Britain's humane and disinterested rule, without which Muslim and Hindu would butcher each other (as indeed happened at partition in 1947) and without which the rights of the "untouchables" could not be protected.

This put him at odds with his great World War II ally, President Franklin Roosevelt. Roosevelt was obsessed with promoting anti-colonialism, especially in India, which he thought should be reformed "somewhat on the Soviet line."[11] He told this to Stalin, with whom he

India Ain't What It's Cracked Up to Be

"It makes me sick when I hear the Secretary of State say of India, 'She will do this,' and 'She will do that.' India is an abstraction... India is no more a political personality than Europe. India is a geographical term. It is no more a united nation than the Equator."

Winston Churchill, 26 March 1931 at the Constitutional Club, London, quoted in Richard Langworth, ed., *Churchill By Himself: The Definitive List of Quotations* (Public Affairs, 2008), p. 163

was in alliance to foster an anti-colonialist future, because, as Roosevelt said, "Of one thing I am certain, Stalin is not an imperialist."[12] Stalin, of course, was a Communist, which to Roosevelt was a far lesser problem. As author Robert Nisbet noted, during the war, "second only to the defeat of Germany, the independence of India from the British Empire was Roosevelt's fondest aspiration. His ignorance of the real problems and issues in India was gargantuan."[13] Roosevelt told Churchill he had an "injection of a new thought" to offer on India, which was that the Indians were in the same position as the American colonists of 1776—a comparison that might elude most disinterested historians—and should be treated to a similar independence. To Roosevelt, the Soviet Union fit in well with the world's democratic future, but the British Empire did not.

Roosevelt, though he did not live to see it, had his way. After the war, Britain was broke and dependent on American aid. Churchill, whose wartime attitude had been "hands off the British Empire," was booted from

An Imperialist Stuck between a Communist and a Liberal

"There I sat with the great Russian bear on one side of me, with paws outstretched…and on the other side the great American buffalo, and between the two sat the poor British donkey, who was the only one of the three who knew the right way home."

Churchill on his experience at the 1943 Tehran Conference with Stalin and FDR, quoted in Richard Toye, *Churchill's Empire: The World that Made Him and the World He Made* (Macmillan, 2010), p. 246

office in 1945, even before the war was over. The new Labour government seemed only too eager to dispense with India and several other troublesome spots, including Palestine. In a speech before Parliament, on 6 March 1947 Churchill said, "It is with deep grief I watch the clattering down of the British Empire, with all its glories and all the services it has rendered to mankind.... We must face the evils that are coming upon us, and that we are powerless to avert. We must do our best in all these circumstances...to help mitigate the ruin and disaster that will follow the disappearance of Britain from the East." If ruin and disaster attended independent Burma (which never joined the Commonwealth) and India in the immediate aftermath of independence and partition, ruin and disaster were less in evidence in Malaya, where Churchill (prime minister again, from 1951 to 1955) ensured that the country defeated a Communist insurgency, or in Singapore, or in Hong Kong. Australia and New Zealand remain anchors of British values in the Far East, and India appears to have outgrown its anti-colonial reaction and to be benefiting from British ideas of parliamentary government and free markets.

In the Near East, Churchill approved a coup in Iran that kept that country pro-Western until the fall of the Shah in 1979. In the Middle East, Palestine was a hornets' nest, and if independent Israel is still bedeviled by enemies, it must nevertheless be considered the democratic and economic success story of the region. British influence has helped to keep the Gulf States, Saudi Arabia, and Jordan more pro-Western than they might

History Lesson

Franklin Roosevelt: "I do not mean to be unkind or rude to the British but in 1841, when you acquired Hong Kong, you did not acquire it by purchase."
British Colonial Secretary Oliver Stanley: "Let me see, Mr. President, that was about the time of the Mexican War."

Exchange cited in Richard Toye, *Churchill's Empire: The World that Made Him and the World He Made* (Macmillan, 2010), p. 246–67

otherwise have been. In Africa, the story is certainly mixed, but it is British institutions and ideals that provide the appropriate direction for reform where corruption and dictatorship have held sway. In the Americas it can hardly be said that the United States, which grew from the Empire's thirteen colonies, or Canada have been anything other than a rousing success; and the Falkland Islands still remain a jolly good place to raise sheep.

Churchill's Legacy

"He presided, in fact, over the inauguration of an American empire."

John Grigg, in an essay marking Churchill's death, published 25 January 1965 in *The Guardian*

If there was any consolation for Churchill in the retreat from empire, it was that Britain's global role had been transferred from one English-speaking, Anglo-Saxon people to another, his mother's people in fact. Churchill had long believed that "The British Empire will last so long and only so long as the British race is determined to maintain it."[14] More than anything else this was why Britain had to shear itself of empire: the burden had become too great. In many parts of the world, Britain made a gallant fighting retreat against evil forces that threatened to derail a peaceful transfer of power, but the transfer itself had become inevitable.[15]

To return to the question Churchill posed himself—was his life a failure, because he oversaw the demise of the British Empire? No, because the Empire was not a failure. And no man better represented that Empire than Sir Winston Churchill—its military adventures, its high ideals, its humane spirit, and its vision of the English-speaking peoples acting as an enduring global force for good.

NOTES

Chapter 1

1. Letter from John Adams to Nathan Webb, 12 October 1755.

2. Letter from Thomas Jefferson to James Madison, 27 April 1809.

3. John S. D. Eisenhower, *So Far from God: The U.S. War with Mexico, 1846–1848* (Random House, 1989), p. 367.

4. Worse if they are sentimental about, sympathetic to, or supportive of the murderers belonging to the Irish Republican Army.

5. Niall Ferguson, *Empire: The Rise and Demise of the British World Order and the Lessons for Global Power* (Basic Books, 2002), p. 113.

6. Robin Blackburn, *The Overthrow of Colonial Slavery: 1776–1848* (Verso, 2000), p. 472, n. 55.

7. Christopher Dawson, *Enquiries into Religion and Culture* (Catholic University of America Press, 2009), p. 17.

8. George Santayana, *Soliloquies in England and Later Soliloquies* (Barber Press, 2008), p. 32.

9. L. H. Gann and Peter Duignan, *The Rulers of British Africa, 1870–1914* (Croom Helm, the Hoover Institution, 1978), p. 202.

Chapter 3

1. The reference here is to British Foreign Secretary George Canning's famous affirmation of his de facto support for the Monroe Doctrine in a speech in the House of Commons on 12 December 1826: "I resolved that, if France had Spain, it should not be Spain with the Indies. I called the New World

into existence to redress the balance of the Old." Winston Churchill echoed the famous phrase in his "We Shall Fight on the Beaches" speech to Parliament on 4 June 1940: "we shall never surrender, and even if, which I do not for a moment believe, this island or a large part of it were subjected and starving, then our Empire beyond the seas, armed and guarded by the British fleet, would carry on the struggle, until in God's good time, the new world, with all its power and might, steps forth to the rescue of the old."

2. It really was an English empire at this point; the union with Scotland was in 1707, after which the Scots took a disproportionate role in the British Empire.

3. "The Struggle for Legitimacy and the Image of the Empire in the Atlantic," by Anthony Pagden in *The Oxford History of the British Empire, Volume I, The Origins of Empire*, ed. Nicholas Canny (Oxford University Press, 1998), p. 35.

4. Many half-educated people will protest here that Scotch is a drink and one should refer to the Scottish, but this is a myth propagated by chippy Scotchmen, as any reader of English literature can attest; see also Welch, as in the Royal Welch Fusiliers, rather than Welsh.

5. Except for galley slaves who were captured in wars against the Muslims.

6. Robert C. Davis, *Christian Slaves, Muslim Masters: White Slavery in the Mediterranean, the Barbary Coast, and Italy, 1500–1800* (Palgrave Macmillan, 2003), p. 23.

7. Paul Johnson, *A History of the American People* (HarperCollins, 1997), p. 124.

8. Imperial military service ran in the family. Washington's half-brother and unofficial guardian, Lawrence, from whom George inherited Mount Vernon, had served from 1740 to 1742 in a disastrous British campaign in the Caribbean that included an assault on Cartagena and a hostile landing at Guantanamo Bay, Cuba.

9. Walter O'Meara, *Guns at the Forks* (Prentice-Hall, 1965), p. 89.

10. Chris Wrigley, *Winston Churchill: A Biographical Companion* (ABC-CLIO, 2002), pp. 88–89.

11. Francis Parkman, *France and England in North America*, (The Library of America, 1983), vol. II, pp. 1325–56.

12. Geoffrey Treasure, *Who's Who in Early Hanoverian Britain* (Shepheard-Walwyn, 1992), pp. 228–89.

13. Geoffrey Regan, *The Guinness Book of Decisive Battles* (Canopy Books, 1992), p. 135.

14. Parkman, op. cit., p. 1400.

15. Major-General J. F. C. Fuller, *A Military History of the Western World* (Funk & Wagnalls, 1955), vol. II, p. 270n.

16. David Horowitz, *The First Frontier: The Indian Wars & America's Origins, 1607–1776* (Simon & Schuster, 1978), p. 206.

17. Ibid., pp. 203–04.

18. Dan Cook, *The Long Fuse: How England Lost the American Colonies, 1760–1785* (Atlantic Monthly Press, 1995), p. 123.

19. J. M. Roberts, *The Pelican History of the World* (Penguin, 1985), p. 693.

20. Victor Brooks and Robert Hohwald, *How America Fought Its Wars: Military Strategy from the American Revolution to the Civil War* (Combined Publishing, 1999), p. 162.

21. Edmund Burke's Speech on Conciliation with America, 22 March 1775.

22. *Taxation No Tyranny* was a pamphlet Dr. Samuel Johnson wrote in 1775 rebutting the charges of the American colonists against the British government.

23. Claire Berlinski, *There Is No Alternative: Why Margaret Thatcher Matters* (Basic Books, 2008), p. 173.

Chapter 4

1. Francis Drake at Nombre de Dios, 1572, quoted in Dudley Pope, *Harry Morgan's Way: The Biography of Sir Henry Morgan, 1635–1684* (House of Stratus, 2001), p. 34.

2. Harry Kelsey, *Sir Francis Drake: The Queen's Pirate* (Yale University Press, 1998), p. 109.

3. Stephen Coote, *Drake: The Life and Legend of an Elizabethan Hero* (Thomas Dunne Books/St. Martin's Press, 2003), p. 179.

4. Coote, op. cit., p. 233.

5. H. E. Marshall, *Our Island Story* (Yesterday's Classics, 2006), p. 428.

6. Both quotations are in John Cummins, *Francis Drake: The Lives of a Hero* (St. Martin's Press, 1995), p. 256. I have modernized the spelling.

7. Alfred Noyes, from his poem "Drake" in *Collected Poems* (Frederick A. Stokes Company, 1913), vol. I, pp. 366 and 369.

Chapter 5

1. Dudley Pope, *Harry Morgan's Way: The Biography of Sir Henry Morgan, 1635–1684* (House of Stratus, 2001), p. 70.

2. Pope, op. cit., pp. 96–97.

3. As per the Treaty of Tordesillas of 1494 in which the pope divided the western and eastern hemispheres between the then-dominant maritime powers of Spain and Portugal. In the sixteenth and seventeenth centuries an oft-invoked phrase was "no peace beyond the line" (or "lines")—roughly speaking, west of the Canary and Cape Verde Islands.

4. Edward Morgan arrived in Jamaica in mourning. His eldest daughter, held to be a beauty and of good character, had died during the voyage. The cause: "a malign distemper by reason of the nastiness of the passengers."

5. David F. Marley, *Pirates and Privateers of the Americas* (ABC-CLIO, 1994), p. 265.

6. Both letters quoted in Peter Earle, *The Sack of Panama: Captain Morgan and the Battle for the Caribbean* (Thomas Dunne Books/St. Martin's Press, 1981), pp. 110–11. Spelling and punctuation have been modernized.

7. Morgan had no children, but in his will stipulated that upon his wife's death his estate would pass to his nephew, Charles Byndloss, if he agreed to change his surname to Morgan.

Chapter 6

1. Franklin and Mary Wickwire, *Cornwallis: The Imperial Years* (University of North Carolina Press, 1980), p. 79.

2. Letter from the First Earl Cornwallis to the First Duke of Newcastle, 15 July 1758.

3. Letter from Charles to William Cornwallis, 21 October 1779.

4. Franklin and Mary Wickwire, *Cornwallis and the War of Independence* (History Book Club, London, in conjunction with Faber and Faber Ltd., 1970), p. 221.

5. Ibid., p. 171.

6. Adam Hochschild, *Bury the Chains: Prophets and Rebels in the Fight to Free an Empire's Slaves* (Houghton Mifflin, 2005), p. 184.

7. Though any enthusiasm for "Bloody Ban" must be tempered by the fact that he was a Whig rather than a Tory (indeed, his chief opponent in debating the slave trade was the Tory William Wilberforce) and as a Whig he had the temerity to criticize Arthur Wellesley's military operations in Portugal, to which criticism the Iron Duke had the perfect reply, saying that "he would much rather follow his [Tarleton's] example in the field than his advice in the senate." Quoted in Anthony J. Scotti, *Brutal Virtue: The Myth and Reality of Banastre Tarleton* (Heritage Books, 2007), p. 242.

8. His American opponent was wily old Daniel Morgan.

9. Letter from Cornwallis to Lord Rawdon, 21 January 1781.

10. Franklin and Mary Wickwire, *Cornwallis and the War of Independence*, p. 289.

11. Franklin and Mary Wickwire, *Cornwallis: The Imperial Years*, p. 77.

12. Ibid., p. 248.

13. Geoffrey Treasure, *Who's Who in Late Hanoverian Britain* (Shepheard-Walwyn, 1997), p. 184.

14. Ibid., pp. 182 and 185.

Chapter 7

1. Norman Lloyd Williams, *Sir Walter Raleigh* (Cassell Biographies, 1988), p. 20.

2. Kipling was not opposed to all things Irish. His son served in the Irish Guards and he wrote a history of the Irish Guards in World War I. He liked the Irishman's fighting virtues as long as they were not directed against England.

3. As for "the Irish saving civilization" during the Dark Ages, it would be more accurate to say that through Irish monks, the Catholic Church saved

civilization. A hat tip goes to the Irish, and they deserve to be bought a round at the pub, but a full genuflection belongs to the Church.

4. Paul Johnson, *Ireland: A Concise History from the Twelfth Century to the Present Day* (Academy Chicago Publishers, 1996), p. 34.

5. Peter Neville, *A Traveller's History of Ireland*, 4th ed. (Interlink Books, 2003), p. 93. Despite its title this is a rather well done, if brief (278 pages), history of Ireland.

6. The Treaty of Limerick (1691) allowed Irish Catholic soldiers and their families to exile themselves to France—the so-called "Flight of the Wild Geese"—the Wild Geese being the name given to Irish mercenaries who fought throughout Europe. It would take the lifting of penal laws against arming the Catholic Irish (in 1793, though the laws were ignored, when convenient, before that) for the British themselves to make use of these tremendous fighters.

7. Neville, op. cit., p. 114.

8. Thomas Babington Macaulay, *The History of England*, abridged and ed. Hugh Trevor-Roper (Penguin Classics, 1986), p. 146.

9. Ibid., p. 143.

10. In signing this measure into law, then-governor George Pataki discarded real history and replaced it with a paranoid, but politically popular, conspiracy theory, saying, "History teaches us the Great Irish Hunger was not the result of a massive failure of the Irish potato crop but rather was the result of a deliberate campaign by the British to deny the Irish people the food they needed to survive." Raymond Hernandez, "New Curriculum from Albany—The Irish Potato Famine, or One View of It," *The New York Times*, 1 December 1996.

11. Michael Partridge, *Gladstone* (Routledge, 2003), p. 109.

12. John O'Beirne Ranelagh, *A Short History of Ireland* (Cambridge University Press, 1995), p. 145.

13. Denis Gwynn, *The Life of John Redmond* (G. G. Harrap, 1932), p. 55.

14. John Ranelagh, *Ireland: An Illustrated History* (Oxford University Press, 1981), p. 211.

15. T. M. Kettle, *The Open Secret of Ireland* (General Books LLC, 2010), see the introduction by Redmond, p. 6.

16. This is a chapter title in Richard Bennett, *The Black and Tans: The British Special Police in Ireland* (Barnes & Noble Books, 1995), a useful, short (228 pages) history of this period, though the endless violence rather palls.

17. You can see an example of such men in the photo insert between pp. 96 and 97 of ibid.

Chapter 8

1. This was Raleigh's response when told he should show less courage, while awaiting execution, because his cool-headed fortitude might provoke his enemies. Robert Lacey, *Sir Walter Raleigh* (Atheneum, 1974) p. 375.

2. The Irish (and the then Spanish ambassador) claimed the Spaniards surrendered on a condition of amnesty; the English at the time denied this. The surrendering Spanish had made a point that they had not come on orders of the king of Spain, but as soldiers fighting for the pope—which might have only deepened the hostility of the English commander, Lord Grey, a Catholic-hating Puritan. "The faith of Grey" is an Irish byword for perfidy.

3. Norman Lloyd Williams, *Sir Walter Raleigh* (Cassell Biographies, 1988), p. 33.

4. Sir Robert Naunton, quoted in ibid., p. 49.

5. That biographer is Robert Lacey in *Sir Walter Ralegh* (op. cit.)—note the alternative spelling; Raleigh's name was spelled many ways in his lifetime—see p. 75.

6. The very fact that Indians were dying mysteriously through disease at the appearance of the white man might have given credence to the godly theory, if the rule between mortals and gods was *noli me tangere*.

7. Raleigh Trevelyan, *Sir Walter Raleigh* (Henry Holt, 2002), p. 280.

Chapter 9

1. Christopher Hibbert, *Wellington: A Personal History* (Addison Wesley, 1997), p. 3.

2. Elizabeth Longford in *Wellington: The Years of the Sword* (Harper and Row, 1969), p. 34, has him burning his violin, which is the usual account; Christopher Hibbert in op. cit., p. 11, has him giving it away.

3. Hibbert, op. cit., p. 30.

4. Ibid., p. 37.

5. "A disciplined infantry that keeps its order and reserves its fire has little to fear from cavalry." Quoted in Geoffrey Treasure, *Who's Who in Late Hanoverian Britain* (Shepheard-Walwyn, 1997), p. 245.

6. Longford, op. cit., p. 139.

7. Treasure, op. cit., p. 243.

8. One of his tasks was convincing France to follow Britain's example in abolishing the colonial slave trade. There was no anti-slavery sentiment in France, such as there was in England, but he did get the French king to at least consider abolishing the trade in five years. J. H. Stocqueller points out that William Wilberforce and other abolitionists wanted an immediate renunciation of the slave traffic; this Wellington could not deliver, and did not himself think reasonable given French public opinion, but he did procure a promise that France's Navy would join Britain's in patrolling the African coast against slavers. See J. H. Stocqueller, *The Life of Field Marshal the Duke of Wellington* (Ingram, Cooke, and Company, 1852), vol. I, pp. 355–57.

9. Robert Eccleshall and Graham Walker, *Biographical Dictionary of British Prime Ministers* (Routledge, 1998), p. 125.

10. Quoted in virtually every other Wellington biography, but see Gordon Corrigan, *Wellington: A Military Life* (Hambledon Continuum, 2001), p. 371, n. 11.

11. Neville Thompson, *Wellington After Waterloo* (Routledge & Kegan Paul, 1986), p. 80.

Chapter 10

1. Roger Ellis, *Who's Who in Victorian Britain* (Shepheard-Walwyn, 1997), p. 206.

2. Byron Farwell, *Eminent Victorian Soldiers: Seekers of Glory* (W. W. Norton & Company, 1988), pp. 77–78.

3. Colonel Sir William F. Butler, *Sir Charles Napier* (Cornell University Library Digital Collections, no date, reprint of Macmillan's 1894 edition, originally published 1890), p. 1.

4. It should be added that he disdained clerics.

5. Butler, op. cit., p. 215.

6. Farwell, op. cit., p. 70.

7. Lieutenant-General Sir William Napier, *The Life and Opinions of General Sir Charles James Napier, G.C.B.* (John Murray, 1857), vol. II, p. 153.

8. Farwell, op. cit., p. 81.

9. Butler, op. cit., p. 113.

10. Napier, op. cit., vol. II, p. 356.

11. Butler, op. cit., p. 147.

12. Napier, op. cit., vol. IV, p. 343.

13. Farwell, op. cit., p. 94.

14. Butler, op. cit., p. 174.

15. Ibid., p. 186.

16. Ibid., p. 199.

Chapter 11

1. Speech delivered in the House of Commons, 10 July 1833.

2. Some modern historians have made unconvincing attempts to debunk the first-hand testimony of one of the survivors, John Zephaniah Holwell, an upright surgeon, civil servant, and occasional military officer of the East India Company who wrote a thoroughly believable and meticulous account of the incident (including the names of the dead).

3. Napoleon's invasion of Egypt (1798–1801), was, in part, an attempt to establish a route to supply anti-British Indian rulers.

4. Lawrence James, *Raj: The Making and Unmaking of British India* (St. Martin's Press, 1997), p. 98.

5. Francis Yeats-Brown, *The Lives of a Bengal Lancer* (Blue Ribbon Books, 1933), pp. 34–35.

6. The other ranks were a different and more brutish story entirely, of course.

7. James, op. cit., p. 415.

8. Andrew Roberts, *A History of the English-Speaking Peoples Since 1900* (HarperCollins, 2007), p. 150. His is the best, short summary of the events at Amritsar; for a detailed examination of Amritsar, the most authoritative

recent book is Nigel Collett's *The Butcher of Amritsar: General Reginald Dyer* (Hambledon Continuum, 2006).

9. Nigel Collett, *The Butcher of Amritsar: General Reginald Dyer* (Hambledon Continuum, 2006), p. 424.

10. Speech at Winchester House, 23 February 1931.

Chapter 12

1. Thomas Babington Macaulay, *Essay on Clive* (Longmans' English Classics, Longmans, Green and Co., 1928), p. 5.

2. Mark Bence-Jones, *Clive of India* (Book Club Associates, London, 1974), p. 3.

3. Robert Harvey, *Clive: The Life and Death of a British Emperor* (Hodder & Stoughton, 1998), p. 43.

4. The Mahrattas fed their horses opium, giving new meaning to the expression, "get off your high horse."

5. Once, during the final campaign against Chanda Sahib, Clive stumbled behind enemy lines into a gang of six armed Frenchmen, but managed to convince them they were surrounded: three surrendered and three fled. Clive led a charmed life on the battlefield.

6. Macaulay, op. cit., p. 43.

7. Harvey, op. cit., p. 346.

8. Bence-Jones, op. cit., p. 287.

Chapter 13

1. Byron Farwell, *Armies of the Raj: From the Great Indian Mutiny to Independence: 1858–1947* (W. W. Norton & Company, 1989) p. 205.

2. This had originally been remarked of another parliamentarian and then adopted to describe Curzon, which it did most perfectly.

3. David Gilmour, *Curzon: Imperial Statesman* (Farrar, Straus and Giroux, 2003), p. 5.

4. Ibid., p. 45.

5. James Morris, *Farewell the Trumpets: An Imperial Retreat* (The Folio Society, 1992), p. 79.

6. Gilmour, op. cit., p. 36. Curzon remarried, but never gained the male heir for which he hoped and never regained the happiness his first wife had given him.

7. Ibid., p. 432.

8. He wanted to decline, but his wife prevailed upon him to accept.

9. Chris Wrigley, *Winston Churchill: A Biographical Companion* (ABC-CLIO, Inc., 2002), p. 150.

Chapter 14

1. Philip Warner, *Auchinleck: The Lonely Soldier* (Cassell & Co., 1981), pp. 211–12.

2. He made a few himself, including an arrow-flight sound simulator to accompany a shipboard showing of the Douglas Fairbanks version of *Robin Hood*.

3. Philip Ziegler, *Mountbatten: The Official Biography* (Collins, 1985), p. 104.

4. Unlike the American government, Mountbatten defended French imperialism as well, thinking the French necessary and rightful allies in the fight to get the Japanese out of Indochina.

5. Ziegler, op. cit., p. 328. Mountbatten had supported Aung San.

6. What is astonishing is that the slaughter caught Labour and Indian politicians by surprise. British imperial die-hards, who accurately predicted what would happen, had been dismissed as reactionaries.

7. Martin Gilbert, *Winston S. Churchill: Never Despair, 1945–1965* (Houghton Mifflin Company, 1988), p. 354.

8. The agreement on India's and Pakistan's Commonwealth status helped Churchill give his reluctant consent to their independence.

Chapter 15

1. G. A. Henty, *The March to Coomassie* (Tinsley Brothers, London, 1874), p. 385.

2. Field Marshal Viscount Wolseley, *The Story of a Soldier's Life* (Archibald Constable, & Company, 1903), vol. II, p. 370.

3. Thomas Pakenham, *The Scramble for Africa: The White Man's Conquest of the Dark Continent from 1876 to 1912* (Random House, 1991), p. 459.

4. Ibid., p. 669.

5. James Morris, *Heaven's Command: An Imperial Progress* (The Folio Society, 1992), p. 443.

6. James Morris, *Farewell the Trumpets: An Imperial Retreat* (The Folio Society, 1992), pp. 323–24.

7. This is the estimate of Donald R. Morris in his classic study of the Zulu, *The Washing of the Spears: The Rise and Fall of the Zulu Nation* (Touchstone, 1965), p. 26: "When Van Reibeck landed at the Cape in 1652, the nearest Bantu were 500 miles to the north and 1,000 miles to the west...."

8. Morris, *Heaven's Command*, pp. 361–62.

9. Alistair Horne, *Macmillan, 1957–1986*, Volume II of the Official Biography (Macmillan, 1989), pp. 195–96.

Chapter 16

1. Field Marshal Viscount Wolseley, *The American Civil War: An English View, The Writings of Field Marshal Viscount Wolseley*, introduced and ed. James A. Rawley (Stackpole Books, 2002), p. 69.

2. In this, the witty Strachey, a homosexualist (and sado-masochistic) subversive, did what all liberals do: make virtue look like hypocrisy in order to make one's own vices appear morally acceptable. Interestingly, Strachey's father, a general, embodied to some degree the ideal Strachey pilloried. Strachey's mother was a leader of the women's suffrage movement, which is perhaps where the rot set in.

3. Gordon's family had been devoted Bible readers but he had not been noticeably devout until some epiphany struck him in Pembroke.

4. John Pollock, *Gordon of Khartoum: An Extraordinary Soldier* (Christian Focus, 2005; originally published as *Gordon: The Man Behind the Legend*, Constable & Company, 1993), p. 51.

5. Ibid., p. 79. Roy MacGregor-Hastie notes in *Never to Be Taken Alive: A Biography of General Gordon* (Sidgwick & Jackson, 1985), p. 63, that though "Lytton Strachey is bitter about 'the destruction of the Summer Palace at Peking—the act by which Lord Elgin, in the name of European civilization,

took vengeance on the barbarism of the East,' everything that could be saved had been saved. Elgin had given orders to this effect and what was eventually blown up was the seat of government, as a warning to the Emperor not to misbehave again.... The lesson was salutary."

6. Charles Chenevix Trench, *The Road to Khartoum: A Life of General Charles Gordon* (Dorset Press, 1987), p. 28.

7. Pollock, op. cit., p. 139.

8. Gordon was remarkably ecumenical (and idiosyncratic) in his views. He was a friend equally to evangelicals and Catholics; the former claimed him, and Frank Power, *The Times* correspondent in Khartoum, and a Catholic, thought Gordon was a near-Catholic.

9. Robert Wilkinson-Latham, *The Sudan Campaigns, 1881–1898* (Osprey, 1996), p. 24. It is striking that the Sudanese Muslims respected Gordon for his Christian piety.

10. British troops were in the Sudan at Suakin, but their task was to keep Mahdist forces from threatening the Red Sea coast. After defeating the dervishes at the Battle of Tamai on 13 March 1884, the British troops were withdrawn.

11. Lytton Strachey, *Eminent Victorians: Cardinal Manning, Florence Nightingale, Dr. Arnold, General Gordon* (A Harvest/Harcourt Brace Jovanovich Book, no date), p. 344.

12. Such was his faith in the power of redcoats.

13. Trench, op. cit., p. 282.

14. Strachey, op. cit., p. 347. As Strachey notes, this is one of several versions of Gordon's death.

15. Byron Farwell, *Eminent Victorian Soldiers: Seekers of Glory* (W. W. Norton & Company, 1988), p. 146.

Chapter 17

1. Byron Farwell, *Eminent Victorian Soldiers: Seekers of Glory* (W. W. Norton & Company, 1988), p. 347.

2. His given name was Horatio Herbert Kitchener. His father was Henry Horatio Kitchener. Both Horatios were respectful nods in the direction of Lord Nelson.

3. Philip Warner, *Kitchener: The Man Behind the Legend* (Atheneum, 1986), p. 20.

4. Gordon sometimes had a high opinion of Kitchener, seeing him as his eventual successor as governor-general of the Sudan, and Kitchener venerated Gordon; during the siege of Khartoum, however, Gordon criticized Kitchener in his diary.

5. Valentine Baker (1827–87) had been a general in Ottoman service before accepting an appointment to the Egyptian police, where Baker's role was as much military as constabulary as he fought in the dervish wars. He had been cashiered from the British army, in which he reached the rank of colonel, after allegedly assaulting a woman in a railway carriage. As a soldier, he was immensely talented and brave, and Kitchener, a man of strong, Christian moral views, seems to have had no qualms about his character. Baker's brother was the celebrated explorer Samuel Baker.

6. Warner, op. cit., p. 89.

7. Much is sometimes made of the fact that Kitchener insisted on single men as his staff officers and personally interviewed and selected only single men for the Egyptian campaign. Kitchener justified such discrimination on the grounds that it saved the taxpayers money, because such officers were not entitled (obviously) to marriage allowances, and that single men could give themselves fully to the job at hand. But if the implication is that Kitchener was assembling a collection of toy boys, it should be noted that all but one of his staff officers eventually married and that there was never a recorded instance of scandal between Kitchener and his "cubs" (as his young staff officers were known).

8. Lord Cromer averred that Kitchener lost interest in the college, and his opinion has generally been taken as accurate, but one of Kitchener's most thorough biographers, John Pollock, says Kitchener remained deeply interested in the college's development and success; see John Pollock, *Kitchener: Architect of Victory, Artisan of Peace* (Carroll & Graf, 2001), p. 165.

9. Pollock, op. cit., p. 209.

10. There were several variations on this theme.

11. David Fromkin, *A Peace to End All Peace: The Fall of the Ottoman Empire and the Creation of the Modern Middle East* (Avon Books, 1989), p. 126.

Chapter 18

1. Peter Godwin and Ian Hancock, *'Rhodesians Never Die': The Impact of War and Political Change on White Rhodesia, c. 1970–1980* (Baobab Books, 1999; originally published by Oxford University Press, 1993), p. 67.
2. Smith included in this list cultural facilities, and for all the stereotype of the white Rhodesian being a boozy, outdoorsy philistine, Peter Godwin and Ian Hancock estimate that "probably no other transplanted English-speakers had done more—with similar resources—to reproduce and practise the parent culture." See Godwin and Hancock's excellent, comprehensive study, op. cit., p. 38.
3. Robert Edgerton quotes this line and says that "surely Smith knew better"—but it makes more sense of Smith's character and actions that he did not. See Robert B. Edgerton, *Africa's Armies: From Honor to Infamy, A History from 1791 to the Present* (Basic Books, 2004), p. 91.
4. The British were, however, indirect abettors of violence. For instance, the British government subsidized Radio Zambia, which in its propaganda broadcasts urged black Rhodesians to join the terrorist campaign against white rule.
5. Peter Godwin, *Mukiwa: A White Boy in Africa* (Atlantic Monthly Press, 1996), p. 358.

Chapter 19

1. James Morris, *Farewell the Trumpets: An Imperial Retreat* (The Folio Society, 1992), p. 201.
2. For readers interested in this aspect there is, among other books, James C. Simmons, *Passionate Pilgrims: English Travelers to the World of the Desert Arabs* (William Morrow and Company, 1987).
3. Byron Farwell, *Queen Victoria's Little Wars* (W. W. Norton & Company, 1985), p. 254.
4. The 1936 Anglo-Egyptian treaty.

5. William J. Durch, ed., *The Evolution of UN Peacekeeping: Case Studies and Comparative Analysis* (St. Martin's Press, 1993), p. 108.

6. Karl E. Meyer and Shareen Blair Brysac, *Kingmakers: The Invention of the Modern Middle East* (W. W. Norton & Company, 2009), p. 312.

7. Ibid., p. 338.

8. Perhaps the most famously heinous attack was the Irgun's bombing of the King David Hotel in Jerusalem on 22 July 1946, which killed ninety-one people.

9. The British mandate over Palestine was acquired in 1920 and relinquished on 15 May 1948.

10. This was the phrase Mitchell used to describe his methods; it is quoted in *The Daily Record* (of Scotland), 23 August 2008.

11. Mitchell's obituary in *The Daily Telegraph*, 24 July 1996.

Chapter 20

1. Fawn Brodie, *The Devil Drives: A Life of Sir Richard Francis Burton* (W. W. Norton, 1984), p. 15.

2. Ibid.

3. Byron Farwell, *Burton: A Biography of Sir Richard Francis Burton* (Penguin Books, 1990), p. 32.

4. Ibid., p. 113.

5. Ibid., p. 178.

6. Edward Rice, *Captain Sir Richard Francis Burton: The Secret Agent Who Made the Pilgrimage to Mecca, Discovered the* Kama Sutra, *and Brought the* Arabian Nights *to the West* (Scribners, 1990), p. 280.

7. Brodie, op. cit., p. 225.

8. Rice, op. cit., p. 350.

9. This was a moniker of the British East India Company.

10. Rice, op. cit., p. 357.

11. Ibid., p. 392.

Chapter 21

1. Harold Orlans, *T. E. Lawrence: Biography of a Broken Hero* (McFarland & Company, 2002), p. 29.

2. Though Lawrence quickly lost his faith, he was well-read in the Bible.

3. Some have tried to claim that Lawrence was homosexual, in part because of his tolerance for the practice among the Arabs. He publicized this tolerance in his memoir of the war, *Seven Pillars of Wisdom*, which made his own sexuality a subject of public rumor, innuendo, and conjecture, especially as he asserts that he was homosexually raped by a Turk. But the weight of the evidence is that Lawrence—who had earlier in his life suddenly proposed marriage to a girl and been embarrassingly rejected—regarded all sexuality as unclean, and forcibly repressed it in himself. Probably the best and most thorough discussion of this matter, for those who wish to pursue it, is to be found in John E. Mack's Pulitzer Prize-winning biography, *A Prince of Our Disorder: The Life of T. E. Lawrence* (Little, Brown and Company, 1976). Mack, who died in 2004, was a psychiatrist and a professor at the Harvard Medical School.

4. Apart from occasional breaks in England, Egypt (archaeological work), and Palestine (survey work).

5. T. E. Lawrence, *Seven Pillars of Wisdom* (Penguin Modern Classics, 1983), p. 24.

6. Isaiah Friedman, *Palestine, A Twice-Promised Land?: The British, the Arabs & Zionism, 1915–1920* (Transaction, 2000), vol. I, p. 29.

7. Lawrence, op. cit., p. 92.

8. Letter from T. E. Lawrence to Colonel C. E. Wilson, quoted in Michael Yardley, *T. E. Lawrence: A Biography* (Stein & Day, 1987), p. 92.

9. That biographer is Lawrence James in *The Golden Warrior: The Life and Legend of Lawrence of Arabia* (Abacus/Little Brown, 1995); see, for instance, p. 394.

10. From the dedication to Lawrence, *Seven Pillars of Wisdom*, op. cit.

11. Yardley, op. cit., p. 140.

12. Though fluent in French, Lawrence was a dedicated Francophobe.

13. "Declaration to the Seven," 16 June 1918.

14. Yardley, op. cit., p. 163.

15. Mack, op. cit., p. 314.

16. B. H. Liddell Hart, *Lawrence of Arabia* (Da Capo, 1989), pp. 336–67.

17. Mack, op. cit., p. 314.

18. Karl E. Meyer and Shareen Blair Brysac, *Kingmakers: The Invention of the Modern Middle East* (W. W. Norton & Company, 2008), p. 197.

19. Lawrence, *Seven Pillars of Wisdom*, op. cit., p. 92.

Chapter 22

1. Larry Collins and Dominique Lapierre, *O Jerusalem!* (Simon and Schuster, 2007), p. 197.
2. John Glubb, *Into Battle: A Soldier's Diary of the Great War* (Cassell, 1978), p. 186.
3. Lieutenant-General Sir John Bagot Glubb, *War in the Desert: An RAF Frontier Campaign* (Hodder & Stoughton, 1960), p. 94.
4. Trevor Royle, *Glubb Pasha: The Life and Times of Sir John Bagot Glubb, Commander of the Arab Legion* (Little, Brown and Company, 1992), p. 137.
5. Ibid., pp. 213–14.
6. Ibid., p. 209.
7. Ibid., pp. 201–02.
8. Ibid., p. 271.
9. Ibid., p. 268.
10. Collins and Lapierre, op. cit., p. 197.
11. Sir John Bagot Glubb, *A Soldier with the Arabs* (Hodder & Stoughton, 1957), p. 5.

Chapter 23

1. The Dutch East India Company and the Swedes had also shown some interest in Australia, but the former thought it likely to be unprofitable and the latter's plans never left the drawing board.
2. Marjorie Barnard, *A History of Australia* (Frederick A. Praeger, 1966), p. 69.
3. Voting rights for Aborigines similarly varied by colony.
4. New Zealand was not far behind with a casualty rate of 59 percent, compared to 51 percent for Britain and 50 percent for Canada. These figures come from Frank G. Clarke, *The History of Australia* (Greenwood Press, 2002), p. 109.
5. Barnard, op. cit., p. 510.
6. Clifford Kinvig, *Scapegoat: General Percival of Singapore* (Brassey's, 1996), p. 2.

7. Technically the *Repulse* was a battlecruiser and the *Prince of Wales* a battleship.

8. Jeremy Black, *A Military History of Britain: From 1775 to the Present* (Praeger Security International, 2006), p. 137.

9. John H. Chambers, *A Traveller's History of New Zealand and the South Pacific Islands* (Interlink Books, 2004), p. 227, an excellent book for students who would like to learn more about the area.

10. Robert Andre LeFleur, *China* (ABC-CLIO, 2010), p. 354.

11. James Morris, *Farewell the Trumpets: An Imperial Retreat* (The Folio Society, 1992), p. 114.

12. Ibid.

13. Noel Barber, *The War of the Running Dogs: How Malaya Defeated the Communist Guerrillas, 1948–1960* (Cassell Military Paperbacks, 2004), p. 323.

Chapter 24

1. G. M. Trevelyan, *British History in the Nineteenth Century* (Forgotten Books, 2010), pp. 139–40.

2. Maurice Collins, *Raffles* (John Day Company, 1968), p. 45.

3. Ibid., p. 125.

4. Lady Raffles, *Memoir of the Life and Public Service of Sir Thomas Stamford Raffles* (James Duncan, London, 1835), vol. II, p. 54.

5. Geoffrey Treasure, *Who's Who in Late Hanoverian Britain* (Shepheard-Walwyn, 1997), p. 196.

6. A shipwreck, among other hindrances, got in the way.

7. Steven Runciman, *The White Rajahs: A History of Sarawak from 1841 to 1946* (Cambridge University Press, 2009), p. 51.

8. Nigel Barley, *White Rajah: A Biography of Sir James Brooke* (Abacus, 2009), p. 32.

9. Ibid., p. 59.

10. Brunei became a formal British protectorate in 1888; it achieved full independence in 1984. Labuan became a Crown Colony in 1848 and became part of Malaysia in 1963.

Chapter 25

1. From Blamey's remarks accepting the surrender of the Japanese 2nd Army at Morotai, Indonesia, 9 September 1945.
2. Australia had only recently formed a national army; previously each Australian state had its own defense forces.
3. D. M. Horner, "Blamey and MacArthur: The Problem of Coalition Warfare," in William M. Leary, ed., *We Shall Return!: MacArthur's Commanders and the Defeat of Japan* (The University of Kentucky Press, 2004), p. 24.
4. Ibid.
5. John Heatherington, *Blamey: The Biography of Field Marshal Sir Thomas Blamey* (F. W. Cheshire, Melbourne, 1954), p. 88.
6. Ibid., p. 143.
7. Robert Leckie, *Delivered from Evil: The Saga of World War II* (Perennial Library, 1988), p. 462.
8. Excerpted from Blamey's speech accepting the surrender of the Japanese 2nd Army at Morotai, Indonesia, 9 September 1945.
9. Heatherington, op. cit., p. 233.

Chapter 26

1. Margaret Shennan, *Out in the Midday Sun: The British in Malaya, 1880–1960* (John Murray, 2000), p. 319.
2. John Cloake, *Templer: Tiger of Malaya* (Harrap, 1985), p. 15.
3. Ibid., p. 29.
4. Max Hastings, *Winston's War: Churchill, 1940–45* (Knopf, 2010), p. 364.
5. Cloake, op. cit., p. 167.
6. Shennan, op. cit., p. 321.
7. Templer organized the Ibans into the Sarawak Rangers. See Cloake, op. cit., p. 247.
8. Harry Miller, *Menace in Malaya* (Harrap, 1954), pp. 208–09.
9. Noel Barber, *The War of the Running Dogs: How Malaya Defeated the Communist Guerrillas, 1948–1960* (Cassell Military Paperbacks, 2004), p. 244.

Chapter 27

1. See Anthony Montague Brown, *Long Sunset: Memoirs of Winston Churchill's Last Private Secretary* (Indigo, 1996), pp. 302–03.

2. Richard Toye, *Churchill's Empire: The World that Made Him and the World He Made* (Macmillan, 2010), p. 120.

3. Winston S. Churchill, *My Early Life: A Roving Commission* (Fontana, 1985), p. 12.

4. Ibid., pp. 66–67.

5. Winston S. Churchill, *The Story of the Malakand Field Force: An Episode of Frontier War* (Seven Treasures Publications, 2009), p. 95.

6. Churchill used this phrase in a speech in 1897. Toye, op. cit., p. 5.

7. It was seditious Hindus he had in mind when he once burst out, "I hate Indians. They are a beastly people with a beastly religion." Quoted in Barnes, John and Nicholson, David, eds., *Empire at Bay: The Leo Amery Diaries 1929-1945* (Hutchinson, 1988), p. 832. Outbursts like this have been used to make the case that Churchill was somehow culpable for the Bengali Famine of 1943. But while Churchill might at first have been dismissive of reports of famine in Bengal—blaming it on Indian incompetence—and annoyed by requests for the diversion of wartime resources to deal with the disaster, it is clear that Churchill himself eventually realized that strong action had to be taken to mitigate a famine of catastrophic scale, which the British were already trying to alleviate. The cause of the famine was not Churchill or the British Raj, of course, but a combination of natural disaster and the Japanese occupation of Burma, from which Bengal previously received much of its rice.

8. Richard Langworth, ed., *Churchill by Himself: The Definitive List of Quotations* (Public Affairs, 2008), p. 143.

9. Toye, op. cit., p. 145.

10. Norman Rose, *Churchill: The Unruly Giant* (The Free Press, 1994), p. 208; Churchill insisted he was "what I always have been—a Tory Democrat," or someone "conservative in principle but liberal in sympathy."

11. Robert Nisbet, *Roosevelt and Stalin: The Failed Courtship* (Regnery, 1988), p. 48.

12. Sir Arthur Bryant, *Triumph in the West: Based on the Diaries of Lord Alan-brooke* (Collins, 1959), p. 304.
13. See Nisbet, op. cit., pp. 100–01.
14. Toye, op. cit., p. 192.
15. An excellent book on this is Robin Neillands, *A Fighting Retreat: The British Empire, 1947–97* (Coronet Books, 1997).

INDEX